THE RMS
TITANIC

MISCELLANY

By

John D.T. White

IRISH ACADEMIC PRESS
DUBLIN • PORTLAND, OR

First published in paperback in 2012 by Irish Academic Press

2 Brookside,	920 NE 58th Avenue, Suite 300
Dundrum Road,	Portland, Oregon,
Dublin 14, Ireland	97213-3786, USA

© 2011 John D.T. White
First published in hardback in 2011

www.iap.ie

British Library Cataloguing in Publication Data
White, John (John David Thomas)
The RMS Titanic Miscellany.
1. Titanic (Steamship)-Miscellanea.
I. Title
623.8'2432'dc22

978 0 7165 3086 2 (cloth)
978 0 7165 3156 2 (paper)

Library of Congress Cataloging-in-Publication Data
An entry can be found on request

Typeset by FiSH Books, Enfield, Middx.
Printed in China through Printworks Int. Ltd

FOREWORD

I was absolutely delighted when John asked me to write the Foreword to this, his *RMS Titanic Miscellany*. I know John extremely well through his involvement with The George Best Carryduff Manchester United Supporters Club, a club I am proud to be the President of. Like John, I too grew up in Belfast and some of my earliest memories from my schooldays are about *Titanic*. I was totally amazed to discover that the world's biggest, most luxurious and most famous ocean liner was built in the City where I was born. There is simply no escaping the impact that *Titanic* has had, and continues to have, on the people of Belfast. Quite rightly Belfast is extremely proud to be the birthplace of *Titanic* and you only have to be in and around Belfast's Titanic Quarter on any day of the week to see the countless number of tourists who are keen to have their photograph taken at one of the many sites in the city which are associated with the ship.

The *Titanic*, escorted by a group of tugs, proceeds up the Victoria Channel en route to Belfast Lough for her sea trials (Jonathan Smith postcard collection)

The Queen of the Ocean, The New Wonder of the World, The Unsinkable Ship are just a few of the descriptions given to the ship when *Titanic* is discussed. However, the people of Belfast, and in particular those families whose forefathers helped build *Titanic*, still mourn the loss of so many lives when the cruel and unforgiving icy waters of the North Atlantic took this great ship to her Ocean bed in the early hours of Monday 15th April 1912. It is almost 100 years since this disaster occurred but let's also remember that at 12.15pm on 31st May 1911, the hull of *Titanic* was successfully launched at Belfast's famous Harland & Wolff Shipyard with 100,000 people in attendance, at the time the largest man-made object ever moved. John grew up in the Short Strand area of East Belfast under the shadows of Harland & Wolff's famous cranes, Sampson and Goliath, while his father worked all of his life in the shipyard.

And so to John's book. Just open it at any page and he manages to take you on a magical journey back in time. With meticulous detail, John has managed to capture within the pages of his book just why the world has become so fixated with *Titanic*. There are many wonderful, interesting and quirky facts sprinkled throughout the book, stories of lucky escapes, biographies of passengers and crew members and the odd spooky tale or two. It is simply jam-packed with all you ever wanted to know about this most famous of ships. Indeed, I dare you to open it and then put it down without reading it from first page to last. And to add to your reading pleasure the book contains some magnificent photographs.

I am pleased that a Belfast man has written this book and as it has been said all too often:

'The world can mourn for *Titanic* but only Belfast can celebrate her'.

Eamonn Holmes

INTRODUCTION

I started to compile my *Titanic Miscellany* on 31st March 2009, 100 years to the very day that *Titanic's* keel was laid down at the world-famous Harland & Wolff Shipyard, Belfast under Yard No. 401. I was visiting my mother, Rosaleen Doherty White, at the family home in the Short Strand (*Ballymacarrett* – from the Irish: '*Baile Mhic Gearóid*' meaning '*MacGearóid's town land*') area of East Belfast and not for the first time I saw two Belfast landmarks which towered upwards into the early evening sky, Samson & Goliath. I used to think that these two cranes touched the clouds until one day my Dad took me on a tour of the Harland & Wolff Shipyard where I stood beneath these steel giants. I will always cherish the times my father, John McDermott White, walked down our street after a hard day's work as a fitter, and later as a welder, at the world's most famous shipyard. My Dad, who I still miss so very much, worked all of his life at Harland & Wolff. He was a quiet but hugely respected Belfast man and often spoke of the *Titanic* with his barrelled chest bursting with pride, pride in the knowledge that the men who worked in the shipyard many years before him, his place of work, built the most famous ocean liner in the world. Consequently, from an early age I knew all about the *Titanic* and this magnificent vessel's connection with my place of birth, Belfast.

During this particular visit to my Mum's, my mind took me back to my childhood and the many happy days I enjoyed kicking a football in Harper Street along with my mates. Innocent but terribly dark and frightening days as the spectre of 'The Troubles' was hanging over me and my family, a daily nightmare which lasted for almost 30 years. However, this is not a book about my childhood growing up during the conflict in Northern Ireland; it is a book about the most famous ship in the world, *Titanic*, a White Star Line passenger ocean liner built by men from the place of my birth. It was only when I started to research the *Titanic* that I truly realised the importance this magnificent vessel has in history and how much it means to the people of Belfast. No matter where you go in the world today everyone has heard about the *Titanic*; James Cameron's 1997 Hollywood blockbuster of the same name propelled her on to the world stage some 85 years after she made her final journey to rest at the bottom of the North Atlantic Ocean.

There are just so many interesting stories about the *Titanic*; from her designers, to her owners, to the men from Belfast who built her, to the passengers and the crew who sailed on her. It is difficult to decide just what to leave in and what to omit. So I quickly decided that I wanted everything I learned about this magnificent vessel to be included in my book. However, I have to say that the one entry which I spent the most time on and which caused me the most concern is perhaps the most important entry in my book: the number of people who lost their lives when this leviathan sank to the bottom of the North Atlantic Ocean at 2:20 am on Monday 15th April 1912. My extensive research which comprises books, reports, contact with webmasters of numerous *Titanic* websites and members of various *Titanic* Societies around the world, still did not uncover a definitive figure for the number of lives lost in what is agreed to be one of the world's worst maritime disasters. According to the National Archive's website, when the *Titanic* collided with an iceberg at 11:40 pm on Sunday 14th April 1912, a total of 1,316 passengers and 885 crew members (2,201 people) were onboard with only 711 survivors. *Shipbuilders To The World: 125 Years of Harland & Wolff, Belfast 1861–1986,* by Michael Moss and John R. Hume, states that the *Titanic* was carrying a total of 2,224 passengers and crew when she left Queenstown on 11th April 1912. Hence my dilemma.

Therefore, with the utmost respect to those poor souls who set sail on *Titanic's* doomed maiden voyage from Southampton to New York on Wednesday 10th April 1912, including those who embarked the ship at Cherbourg (France) and Queenstown (now Cobh), Ireland for many unaware that they would never reach their final destination, I have decided to use the figure of 1,523 victims who lost their lives and the figure of 705 for her survivors. However, if you disagree with these figures then I respectfully ask for your forgiveness and hope you appreciate just how difficult it is, bearing in mind there is no list of stowaways (a common occurrence when ships set sail from port in the early 20th century), to arrive at a definitive figure for either.

As you travel through my book I hope it brings you as much pleasure reading it as it brought me writing it. I have tried to make the book as interesting as possible and therefore opted to make it a cornucopia of all things *Titanica.* My book is neither a fact book, nor a history book, nor a statistics book, nor a trivia book; it is more a sprinkling of all four coupled with an insight to what life would have been like onboard this 'Queen of the Ocean.' I have also compiled numerous biographies detailing the lives of many people associated with *Titanic,* including the ship's designer (Thomas Andrews), the White Star Line Chairman and Managing Director (J. Bruce Ismay), many of her passengers (including Millvina Dean) and her captain (Captain Edward John Smith).

So in closing, I hope you enjoy my book and if you are a *Titanic* enthusiast and you come across one entry in my book which leaves you scratching your head saying: 'I didn't know that,' then all of the hours, days and months I have spent researching the ship's history will have been worthwhile. I can't end without expressing my utmost gratitude to my Mum and Dad, brother (David) and sisters (Donna, Michelle and Danielle) and the people of the Short Strand for enabling me to have such a wonderful childhood. Finally, special thanks to my wife, Janice, and our two sons, Marc and Paul, who gave me so much support to see this project through and who were always there for me to drive me on when I needed a little bit of encouragement.

John White *A Belfast Boy*

SPECIAL THANKS

In compiling my *Titanic Miscellany*, I wish to thank the following people for all of their advice, help and support in ensuring that I kept my entries as accurate as I possibly could. In the event that anyone notices any error(s) in the book, please feel free to notify me through the Irish Academic Press and accept my unequivocal apology should I have erred in any way.

I wish to express my utmost thanks to Bruce Beveridge, Scott Andrews, Steve Hall, Daniel Klistorner and Art Braunschweiger, authors and editor of *TITANIC: The Ship Magnificent*, for sharing their considerable expertise and reviewing the technical, interior and photographic information presented herein, and to Art for proofreading the completed manuscript.

My editor and publisher, Lisa Hyde and the Irish Academic Press, for having the faith in me to compile the book.

Wolfgang Abratis for his kind permission to reproduce *Titanic's* Cargo List from his website – http://www.abratis.de

The Addergoole Titanic Society, The Dispensary, Lahardane, Ballina, Co Mayo – *www.mayo-titanic.com* for their help and advice.

Andrew A. Aldridge BA Hons, FAV MRICS, Chartered Valuation Surveyor, Henry Aldridge and Son, Unit 1 Bath Road Business Centre, Bath Road, Devizes, Wiltshire, England SN10 1XA for his kind offer to reproduce some material from the website.

Charles Anesi for for his kind permission to reproduce *Titanic's* casualty figures from his website – http://www.anesi.com/titanic.htm

Art Braunschweiger from the Titanic Research and Modeling Association for kindly allowing me to use some of his material on flags, rigging and paint colours from the TRMA website – http://www.titanic-model.com

Mark Chirnside, author of: *The Olympic-Class Ships: Olympic, Titanic, Britannic,* for kindly reviewing my entries on RMS *Olympic.*

Andrew Clarkson for providing such a wonderful *Titanic* forum on his website – http://www.titanic-titanic.com/forum/index.php

Cyril Codus for colouring a black and white postcard used on the cover of my book.

Dan Conlin, Curator of Marine History, Nova Scotia Museum Collections Unit Maritime Museum of the Atlantic, 1675 Lower Water Street, Halifax, Nova Scotia B3J 1S3, Canada for very kindly permitting me to reproduce the Museum's lists of *Titanic* victims.

Glenn Dunstan, for his kind permission to reproduce *Titanic's* Radio Messages Page from his website – http://www.hf.ro/

Sir Alex Ferguson CBE for his supportive quote for my book and to all those people who kindly gave supportive quotes.

Becky Grice, Editor of the *East Cork Journal* for her guidance.

Eamonn Holmes for such a wonderful Foreword to my book.

Jason, Josh and Kim and their superb website dedicated to *Titanic* – http://library.thinkquest.org/18626/index.html

Karen Kamuda, Vice President, Titanic Historical Society Incorporated and Titanic Museum, PO Box 51053, 208 Main Street, Indian Orchard, MA, USA 01151-0053 for kindly giving permission to use several entries from their website.

Chantal Keogh and her fellow Irish Titanic Historical Society members for their help in proofreading my material.

David McVeigh, Sales and Marketing Manager, Harland and Wolff Heavy Industries Limited, Queen's Island, Belfast BT3 9DU for helping with the many enquiries I had about *Titanic* and the men who built her.

The Nova Scotia Government for kindly permitting me to reproduce the list of *Titanic* victims recovered from the disaster by the ships: *CS Mackay-Bennett, CS Minia, CGS Montmagny* and *SS Algerine* – http://www.gov.ns.ca/nsarm/virtual/ titanic/deaths.asp

J. David Rogers, Ph.D., P.E., R.G., C.E.G., C.HG., Karl F. Hasselmann Chair in Geological Engineering, Department of Geological Sciences & Engineering, Missouri University of Science & Technology, USA for allowing me to use his lecture notes on the *Titanic*.

Jonathan Smith from the *Titanic Research and Modeling Association* for kindly allowing me to use some of his amazing images, material on *Titanic's* anchors plus his valued assistance with several other entries.

Errol Somay, Director at the Library of Virginia, Richmond, Virginia, USA for his kind permission to reproduce both crew and passengers lists from *Titanic's* maiden voyage.

Jim Wallace and Alan Ward at Stena Line Ferries.

And last, but certainly not least, to my wife, Janice, and our two sons, Marc and Paul, for all of their encouragement and the countless cups of tea and sandwiches. I could not have done it without the three of you.

I thank you one and all.
John

DEDICATION

I wish to dedicate my book to my father, John McDermott White, and to my mother, Rosaleen Elizabeth Doherty White.

Mum – you and Dad you did more for me than I could ever manage to repay and for that I am eternally grateful.

Dad – we all miss you. Please continue to watch over me and your family; Mum, my brother, David, my sisters Donna, Michelle & Danielle, your daughter-in-law Janice and Frankie and Gerard. And not forgetting your grandchildren: Marc John David, Shasta Naomi, Paul Robert Michael, Amy-Jo, Aisling, John Preston, David, Paul, Paris and Shéa.

Your Proud Son,
John

1911 advertisement postcard for *Olympic* and *Titanic* (Jonathan Smith collection)

THE BEGINNING OF A JOURNEY

History has it that the *Titanic*, the world's single most celebrated ship, was conceived at a meeting following dinner between Lord William James Pirrie of the Harland & Wolff Shipyard, Belfast and J. Bruce Ismay, Chairman and Managing Director, of the White Star Line at Lord Pirrie's London home on 30th April 1907. After a 3-year construction period (*Titanic's* keel was laid down at Harland & Wolff under Yard No. 401 on 31st March 1909), RMS *Titanic* set sail on her maiden voyage from Southampton to New York on Wednesday 10th April 1912, only for the world's most celebrated vessel never to reach her intended destination. *Titanic* was, at the time of her maiden voyage, the largest vessel afloat. However, as the world discovered in the early hours of Monday 15th April 1912, her fame came at a devastating price. 1,523 lives were lost after the White Star Line's most famous leviathan struck an iceberg in the North Atlantic at 11:40 pm on Sunday 14th April 1912 and sank at 02:20 am the following morning.

--- Did You Know That? ---

Titanic was built for the transatlantic passenger and mail service between Southampton and New York and caused shock waves around the world when the so called 'Unsinkable Ship' sank on her maiden voyage.

TITANIC'S CURSE

Shortly after *Titanic* sank on 15th April 1912, a New York journalist wrote a story for his newspaper claiming that the ship went down because it was cursed. The journalist reported that aboard the vessel was a sarcophagus containing the mummified body of an ancient Egyptian priestess of Amun-Ra, which was being sold by an unscrupulous art dealer to a museum in New York for $500,000. The story went on to claim that a crew member was paid to place the sarcophagus in one of the ship's lifeboats, that it was taken aboard one of the rescue vessels and arrived safely with the collector in New York. However, according to the story the mummy brought the collector a lot of bad luck and he sold it two years later to a collector in Europe and sent it to him aboard RMS *Empress of Ireland*, owned by the Canadian Pacific Steamship Company. On 29th May 1914, *Empress of Ireland* was struck amidships by the Norwegian coal ship SS *Storstad*, and sank claiming

1,012 lives. Her sinking remains the worst maritime disaster in Canadian history. But according to the reporter the sarcophagus was rescued and its new owner decided to return the unlucky mummy to Egypt on a third ship, RMS *Lusitania*, which was torpedoed and sunk by a German U-Boat on 7th May 1915, eight miles off the Old Head of Kinsale, Ireland resulting in the loss of 1,201 of the 1,962 people on board (127 of which were American citizens). The journalist ended his story by saying that the owner allowed his 'cursed' sarcophagus to lie at the bottom of the North Channel (Irish Channel). However, the story is completely untrue and the basis for the claim would appear to stem from a story about Amun-Ra which was told onboard *Titanic* by the famous spiritualist William T. Stead, during a dinner party.

Did You Know That?

The White Star Line-chartered CS *Mackay-Bennett* sailed from Halifax, Nova Scotia two days after *Titanic* sank and between Sunday 21st April 1912 and Friday 26th April 1912 the vessel retrieved bodies still floating at the wreck site.

THEY SHALL NEVER BE FORGOTTEN

A total of 1,523 passengers and crew died when *Titanic* sank, 815 passengers and 708 crew members (705 of the 2,228 on board her survived the disaster).

Port*	First class	Second class	Third class
Joined at Southampton	195	234	497
Joined at Cherbourg	142	30	102
Joined at Queenstown	0	7	113

* 34 passengers boarded *Titanic* at Southampton, England; 27 disembarked at Cherbourg, France and 7 disembarked at Queenstown, Ireland. One crew member also jumped ship at Queenstown.

People on board *Titanic* when she struck an iceberg at 11:40 pm on Sunday 14th April 1912 were:

- 337 First class
- 271 Second class
- 712 Third class
- 908 Crew
- Survived: 705
- Perished: 1,523
- Bodies recovered: 306

THE RATIO OF SURVIVORS

	Men	Women	Children
First class	33%	97%	100%
Second class	8%	86%	100%
Third class	16%	46%	34%
Crew	22%	87%	–

TITANIC'S FINAL RESTING PLACE

■ 1,000 miles due east of Boston, Massachusetts, USA and 375 miles southeast of St. John's, Newfoundland, Canada. Depth: 12,500 feet.

■ Stern Section: 41°43'35' N, 49°56'54' W.

■ Boilers: 41°43'32' N, 49°56'49' W.

■ Bow Section: 41°43'57' N, 49°56'49' W.

TITANIC'S CALL SIGN

RMS *Titanic* was assigned the call sign 'MUC' in January 1912. However, a few weeks later it was changed to 'MGY,' a call sign previously assigned to the American passenger vessel *Yale* of the Metropolitan Steamship Co. As Marconi was the world's leading marine radio company at the time *Titanic* set sail on her maiden voyage, the wireless company allocated their own call signs. Most of these began with the letter 'M,' thereby identifying a Marconi installation aboard the vessel regardless of its location or the country of registration of the vessel in which it was installed.

TITANIC NUMBERED

The Official Registration Number of the *Titanic* was 131428.

--- Did You Know That? ---

The skilled workers at Harland & Wolff Shipyard in Belfast who built *Titanic* were paid £2/$10 £32 today) per week and unskilled men were paid £1 or less per week. Therefore, despite having helped build the biggest and most luxurious ship in the world in 1912, a one-way trip on her in a first-class berth would have cost the Belfast yard's men 4 to 8 months wages.

TITANIC'S FINAL PORT OF CALL

Queenstown, now Cobh, a sheltered seaport town on the south coast of County Cork, Ireland, was *Titanic's* last port of call and the place where the majority of Irish passengers who were booked on her maiden voyage boarded her. *Titanic* arrived off Roches Point at 11.30am on Thursday 11th April 1912 and the passengers were ferried to the ship from Queenstown by two tenders, PS *America* and PS *Ireland*. A total of 123 passengers boarded the *Titanic* at Queenstown: 3 in first class, 7 in second class and 113 in third class. At 1.40pm on 11th April 1912, *Titanic* weighed anchor and set off for New York.

─────────────── Did You Know That? ───────────────

The dictionary's definition of 'titanic' is: (i) *Having great stature or enormous strength; huge or colossal* and (ii) *Of enormous scope, power, or influence.*

THE COST OF CONSTRUCTION

It cost £1.5 million ($7.5m) to build *Titanic*. It would cost $400 million to build the same ship today.

─────────────── Did You Know That? ───────────────

It cost in excess of $200 million to make James Cameron's movie *Titanic* (1997).

A COSTLY VOYAGE

The price of the most expensive one-way ticket on *Titanic's* doomed maiden voyage was:

- ■ First class (Parlour Suite)   £512/$2,560   (£8,192 today)
- ■ Second class   £13/$65   (£208 today)
- ■ Third class   £7 15s/$45   (£120 today)

Although we often see a figure of £870 as being the price for the most expensive suite booked on the *Titanic*, the highest amount paid for this suite was £512 by Mrs Charlotte Cardeza. The £512 included fares for her son and two servants, rail fares and excess luggage fees. The minimum first-class fare was £26 ($130). Prices for second-class berths varied between £12 ($60) and £13 ($65).

■ THE MOVIE TRIVIA ■■■■■■■■■■■■■■

The Studios wanted Brad Pitt to star in the movie but its director, James Cameron, insisted on Leonardo DiCaprio.

HORSE MOURNS HER OWNER

Onboard *Titanic* for her maiden voyage was Isidor Straus and his wife, Ida. Straus was co-owner of Macy's Department Store in New York with his brother, Nathan. Mr and Mrs Straus lost their lives on 15th April 1912 when *Titanic* sank, Mrs Straus refused to get in a lifeboat and remained aboard the doomed ship with her beloved husband. Isidor's body was recovered by the *Mackay-Bennett* and he was buried in Woodlawn Cemetery in the Bronx, New York while Ida's body was never recovered. By a strange twist of fate prior to sailing to Europe from the USA, Mr Straus sent his favourite horse, Bess, to a farm at the Montefiore Home, Bedford Hills, New York. Mr Straus thought that whilst he was away 6-year old Bess may as well rest. On the morning of Monday 15th April 1912, the same day *Titanic* claimed the lives of Mr and Mrs Straus, Bess was found dead in her stable. The vet who inspected her could not offer an explanation for her demise.

A COSTLY LECTURE

Titanic survivor Stuart Collet lodged a claim against the White Star Line for the sum of $50 in respect of damaged handwritten college-lecture notes.

KEEPING IN TOUCH

It cost 12 shillings and sixpence/$3.12 ($50 today) to send a wireless telegram (for the first 10 words, and 9d per word thereafter) onboard the *Titanic*.

——————— Did You Know That? ———————

In excess of 250 passenger telegrams were sent and received during *Titanic's* doomed maiden voyage.

BELFAST PROUD

'Titanic – the largest vessel in the world – floated proudly on the water, a monument to the enterprise of her owners and the ingenuity and skill of the eminent firm who built her.'

Belfast *News Letter*, 3rd April 1912

TITANIC CREW SALARIES

- Captain Edward John Smith: £105 a month
- Chief Radio Operator, Jack Phillips: £6 a month
- Look-Out, G.A. Hogg: £5 and 5 shillings a month
- Seaman, Edward Buley: £5 a month
- Steward, Sidney Daniels: £3 and 15 shillings a month
- Stewardess Annie Robinson: £3 and 10 shillings a month

TITANIC'S CAR

One car, a Renault 35, went down with *Titanic* when she sank. It was owned by Mr William Ernest Carter who boarded the *Titanic* at Southampton as a first-class passenger (Ticket No. 113760, £120, Cabins B-96 and B-98) along with his wife, Lucile, and their two children, William Jnr. and Lucile. Mr Carter's manservant Alexander Cairns, his chauffeur, Charles Aldworth, and Mrs Carter's maid, Auguste Serreplan, accompanied them. On the evening of Sunday 14th April 1912, Mr & Mrs Carter attended a dinner party hosted by Mr George Widener in the ship's Á la Carte Restaurant in honour of Captain Smith. Not long after the dinner party ended *Titanic* struck an iceberg at 11:40pm and when Captain Smith gave the order to lower the lifeboats, Mr Carter helped his wife and children into Lifeboat No.4. Mr Carter was able to get into Lifeboat Collapsible C which was the last one to be lowered from the *Titanic* and which was also occupied by J. Bruce Ismay. All four Carters were rescued by the *Carpathia* and safely taken to New York.

Did You Know That?

In addition to his car, Mr Carter also brought two dogs aboard *Titanic*. After the sinking he lodged a claim with the White Star Line for $5,000 for his car and $300 for the dogs who perished in the disaster.

AN ELECTRIC SHIP

The *Titanic* was equipped with four 400 kilowatt electrical generators, which were used to: power the electric heaters and lamps throughout the ship, the gymnasium equipment, the electric lifts which took passengers and crew between decks, cooking in the galley, the ventilation fans, releasing the lower watertight doors, operating the telephone system and the Marconi wireless equipment. The lower watertight doors were only released by an electric solenoid, after which they dropped under their own weight, with the speed of descent controlled by a

hydraulic system. Meanwhile, there were other watertight doors higher up in the ship that had to be cranked shut by hand. Interestingly, the refrigeration plant on *Titanic* was powered by steam, not by electricity.

Did You Know That?

All of *Titanic's* engineers lost their lives in the disaster, staying at their posts to man the pumps and those boilers which remained operable while the passengers evacuated the vessel.

TITANIC'S AUCTIONEERS

Twice a year, the auction firm of Henry Aldridge and Son, Unit 1 Bath Road Business Centre, Bath Road, Devizes, Wiltshire, conducts an auction of RMS *Titanic* and White Star Line memorabilia. They are the leading auctioneers of *Titanic* and White Star Line memorabilia in the world. On 18th April 2009, they held one of their *Titanic* auctions at their Devizes auction rooms. Barbara Dainton-West was only 10 months old when *Titanic* sank and was one of the last survivors of the disaster when she passed away in October 2007. Young Barbara set sail on *Titanic* from Southampton with her parents, Edwy Arthur and Ada, and her sister, Constance Joyce, on April 10th 1912. The West family were from Cornwall but living in Bournemouth, and they were travelling to New York to start a new life in the USA. Barbara's unique archive of letters had been kept in the family since 1912 and this was the first time their contents were being revealed to the world at large.

One of the most historically important documents within the collection was a narrative to the British Board of Trade giving an in-depth account of the sinking and Mrs West's (Barbara's mother) viewpoint on the crew's conduct. It also contains numerous anecdotes from their rescue and the aftermath: 'The noise they made drowned all the cries & we gradually drew away from the scene of the wreck & did not turn back until sometime after the Carpathia had appeared. I saw no signs of wreckage or bodies only icebergs – had no idea that the disaster had been so great. I might add that there were men in our boat who had concealed themselves under the ladies skirts & had to be asked to stop lighting cigarettes as there was a danger of the dresses becoming ignited.' The Barbara Dainton-West collection was sold for £69,000.

■ THE MOVIE TRIVIA ■■■■■■■■■■■■■■■■

Titanic was initially budgeted to cost $135,000,000, but after going two months over schedule James Cameron had to ask Paramount Pictures to contribute an additional $65,000,000 in exchange for USA distribution rights.

GOING FOR A SWIM

Titanic boasted a heated swimming pool which was actually large enough for the ship's passengers to both swim in and dive into. However, RMS *Adriatic* held the distinction of being the first liner to have a heated 'plunge bath', which although smaller than the pool on the *Titanic*, was nonetheless considered a swimming pool in White Star Line brochures. The *Titanic's* pool, like the *Adriatic's*, was filled with heated saltwater from the condensers. The six-feet-deep saltwater pool was reserved for first-class passengers and cost $1.00 to use. *Titanic's* older sister, the *Olympic*, also boasted a heated swimming pool. Interestingly, the *Adriatic* was launched on 20th September 1906, the same day the Cunard Line launched RMS *Mauretania*.

TITANIC BROUGHT BACK TO LIFE

The Titanic Historical Society, Inc. (THS) does not represent one nation but all countries and was the first to form for the purpose of preserving the history of RMS *Titanic* and the White Star Line. The society is one of several excellent authorities and sources for the *Titanic* and the White Star Line and for four decades has maintained that goal. Its main field of endeavor is *The Titanic Commutator*, the Society's official journal, insuring a permanent record of information. The THS Collection is a treasury of *Titanic* and White Star Line memorabilia at the Titanic Museum. The Society holds annual conventions at different locations with outstanding programmes that in the past have included *Titanic* survivors and travel experiences that bring the history of *Titanic* to life. The THS was founded on 7th July 1963 in Indian Orchard, Massachusetts at the home of Edward S. Kamuda with a handful of people, and has grown to become a worldwide organisation of several thousand members and is well known for its original research. The Society is non-profit and volunteer-supported by its officers and members who donate their time and talents as an avocation. Other *Titanic* organisations exist worldwide including: the Belfast Titanic Society, the Irish Titanic Historical Society, the Titanic International Society and the Titanic-Verein Schweiz (Swiss Titanic Society) to name just a few. Most have annual conventions and regular journals for their members. Meanwhile, there are also some truly outstanding online organisations, virtual though they may be, but comprised of very large memberships as well and which themselves are without peer in their collective knowledge. The Titanic Research and Modeling Association, for example, has no equal for technical information and Encyclopedia Titanica is unrivalled in passenger and crew information and research. The latter two organisations produce research articles and online reference information that stand up to the sternest of scrutiny in terms of accuracy and historical fact. The above are but several of many truly wonderful organisations whose existence ensures that the legacy which is *Titanic* lives on forever.

AND THE BAND PLAYED ON

The last tune the band aboard *Titanic* was playing before the ship sank is widely believed to be 'Autumn' by Louis Von Esch, a popular waltz at the time, and not, as legend would have it, 'Nearer My God to Thee'. The former belief is based on the reports of the surviving wireless operator Harold Bride while the author, Walter Lord, in his novel entitled 'The Night Lives On', (his sequel to his 'A Night to Remember'), states that Bride was actually speaking about 'Songe d'Automne', a popular ragtime number at the time. It is widely believed that had the band onboard *Titanic* actually played 'Nearer My God to Thee' it would have caused even more panic among the passengers as it would have given them the impression that they were about to die. The band was supplied by the Black Talent Agency, Liverpool; they signed on the ship for one shilling a month and were housed in both second-class and crew quarters.

Did You Know That?

None of the band members survived the disaster while, quite coldly, the Black Talent Agency sent the violinist's family a bill for the cost of the unpaid and unreturned uniform he was wearing when the ship went down.

THE 9-DAY SEARCH FOR LIFE

After the *Titanic* sank to the bottom of the Atlantic at 02:20 am on 15th April 1912, the search for survivors and bodies lasted 9 days.

HAND-ME-DOWNS

It is believed that *Titanic's* surviving lifeboats were auctioned off in New York and re-painted after being tied up in red tape for a period of time.

TITANIC'S MAN OF GOD

As the *Titanic* was slowly sinking it has been claimed that the Reverend John Harper gave away his life jacket telling people that: 'I am going up, not down!' Some survivors of the disaster said that he walked around near the lifeboats telling the men to let women and children and unsaved people on the life boats because the unsaved were unprepared to die and be ushered into eternity. Meanwhile other survivors stated that Rev. Harper stood on the deck and said the 'Sinners Prayer' for anyone that wanted to seek forgiveness from God. It is also claimed that a very close friend of Rev. Harper asked him to get off the *Titanic* when it was anchored just off Queenstown, Ireland because he felt there was something not quite right

with the vessel. His friend was booked on another liner which was due to set sail for New York sometime after *Titanic's* maiden voyage and the friend even offered to pay Rev. Harper's travel costs. Rev. Harper politely refused the kind offer of his friend informing him that he had God's work to do.

—————————— Did You Know That? ——————————

It has been suggested that Rev. Harper was the person who asked the band to play 'Nearer My God, To Thee' in an effort to bring about a level of calmness on the Boat Deck as the ship slowly began to sink.

A SHORTAGE OF BATHTUBS

Despite the grandeur of the *Titanic*, remarkably there were only 2 bathtubs aboard which were available for the approximate 700 passengers in third class. There were a number of public baths throughout first class and second class. However, only the two B Deck promenade suites in first class had exclusive private bath rooms whilst some staterooms throughout B and C Decks also shared a private bath en suite with the adjoining stateroom.

THE PATRIOTIC LINE

The third and last of the *Olympic* class trio of ships built for the White Star Line was originally named *Gigantic*, but was renamed *Britannic* after the *Titanic* sank. Many people at the time believed that the White Star Line was making some form of patriotic statement. Though it is unknown for certain why the name of the ship was changed, it is quite possible that *Britannic*, a reference to Great Britain, was used in response to the Hamburg-America Line's *Vaterland*, the term used by Germans to refer to the German homeland (fatherland). The *Vaterland* was completed in the spring of 1914 and at 54,282 gross tons she became the world's largest ship at the time. The *Britannic* met her doom very soon after striking a mine during World War I off the Greek island of Kea.

—————————— Did You Know That? ——————————

At the launching of the *Titanic* one worker from the Harland & Wolff Shipyard in Belfast was overheard saying: 'They just builds her and shoves her in!'

THE RUDDER

The rudder of the *Titanic* weighed a mammoth 100 tons.

—————— Did You Know That? ——————

The Parsons turbine onboard *Titanic* produced 16,000 hp (165 rpm).

THE PROPELLERS

The *Titanic* had 3 propellers – Centre turbine: 17 feet and Left/Right wings: 23 feet, 6 inches. Her propellers were capable of forcing *Titanic* through the water at a speed of 24 knots.

—————— Did You Know That? ——————

Titanic's displacement at load draft was 52,310 tons.

■ THE MOVIE TRIVIA ■ ■ ■ ■ ■ ■ ■ ■ ■ ■ ■ ■

**Leonardo DiCaprio's famous line from the movie:
'*I'm the king of the world,*' was voted as the No.100 movie quote
by the American Film Institute (out of 100).**

THE RAILWAY FUNNELS

Each one of *Titanic's* four funnels was large enough to drive two trains through side by side.

IT'S GOOD TO TALK

In addition to the guests being able to communicate with family and friends via the Marconi wireless system on *Titanic*, there was a telephone system for use of the crew only.

—————— Did You Know That? ——————

There was no telephone line connecting the Marconi operating room
and the navigating bridge.

POPE BLAMED FOR *TITANIC* SINKING

One urban legend places the blame for the sinking of the *Titanic* on sectarianism at the Harland & Wolff Shipyard in Belfast. The story went that when *Titanic* was being constructed at the Belfast shipyard it was given the British Board of Trade registration number 390904, which when read backwards reflected in the water spelt 'NO POPE'. The world-famous Harland & Wolff Shipyard is situated in Protestant east Belfast and had a predominantly Protestant workforce. It is claimed that very few Roman Catholics worked on the construction of *Titanic* as a direct result of not wishing to travel from other parts of the city into east Belfast. The 'No Pope' story is believed to have been concocted after dockworkers in Queenstown, Ireland (*Titanic's* last port of call before setting sail for New York) claimed that they found anti-Roman Catholic graffiti written on the ship's coal bunkers when they were loading coal on her. However, the story is a complete myth in that the *Titanic* had the British Board of Trade registration number 131428 (and the H&W yard No. 401) when it was being built and more than likely the story stems from a joke or two made in one of the Protestant pubs in and around the shipyard. Furthermore, Lord Pirrie, the Chairman of the Harland & Wolff Shipyard, was actually sympathetic to Home Rule and hired workers for their talents and abilities regardless of their religion.

■ THE MOVIE TRIVIA ■■■■■■■■■■■■■■■■

Titanic contains over 100 speaking parts and over 1,000 extras, all of whom needed to be dressed in authentic Edwardian period costume.

NOAH'S ARK AND THE *TITANIC*

Whereas it took some 37 months to construct *Titanic*, it is estimated that it took 1,200 months to construct Noah's Ark (100 years). When Noah is first mentioned in the Holy Bible (*Genesis* 5:32) he was 500 years old (when God commanded him to build the Ark). The Bible also tells us that Noah was 600-years old when the Ark was completed.

TITANIC'S GRAND STAIRCASE

The Forward Grand Staircase, one of the ship's outstanding features, connected 7 decks. Many movies about the sinking of the *Titanic* have nearly all depicted the Grand Staircase, some accurately and some not. It features in the video game entitled: 'Titanic: Adventure Out of Time'. The Forward Grand Staircase is depicted correctly, but in the After Grand Staircase there is no clock on the A Deck landing.

ISMAY TARGETED BY THE PRESS

J. Bruce Ismay, the Chairman and Managing Director of the White Star Line when the *Titanic* disaster occurred, was held to blame for the loss of the vessel by the American press and in particular by those newspapers owned by William Randolph Hearst. Hearst was a newspaper magnate and one of the richest and most powerful men in the USA at the beginning of the 20th century. There was no love lost between Ismay and Hearst who had met one another 20 years before *Titanic's* doomed maiden voyage when Ismay was the White Star Line's agent in New York. Ismay refused to co-operate with the press, which angered Hearst and many others in the newspaper industry. After the loss of so many lives in the North Atlantic on 15th April 1912, Hearst began his concerted campaign to ruin Ismay and printed a full-page cartoon image of Ismay in one of his newspapers that depicted the White Star Line boss in a lifeboat watching the sinking *Titanic* with the header: 'This is J. Brute Ismay' and 'We respectfully suggest that the emblem of the White Star be changed to that of a yellow liver.'

Did You Know That?

Numerous stories asserted that Ismay was guilty of pressurising *Titanic's* captain into pushing the ship faster than he wanted; of cowardice in taking the place of a passenger in one of the lifeboats; and of resigning from the company shortly after the disaster rather than face the public outcry. None of these allegations were true, but despite the facts, the image created by Hearst survives to this day.

A TASTE OF FRANCE

The Café Parisien, a sun-lit veranda, was situated outside the first-class Á la Carte Restaurant. It even had French waiters working in it to add to its appeal.

SLOWLY SINKING

It was originally estimated that it probably took *Titanic* around 15 minutes to sink to her final resting place on the ocean floor. Therefore, this equates to a sinking speed of 10 miles per hour (or 16 km per hour). However, Dr Robert Ballard, who discovered the wreck of the *Titanic*, later estimated that it probably took around 9 minutes for the stern section to submerge.

BLIND VISION

Although the *Titanic's* lookouts were provided with binoculars when she left Belfast for Southampton on Tuesday 2nd April 1912, no binoculars were provided to the lookouts when she set sail on her maiden voyage from Southampton to New York on Wednesday 10th April 1912. Frederick Fleet and Reginald Lee were the lookouts on duty in the crow's nest when *Titanic* struck an iceberg at 11:40 pm on Sunday 14th April 1912. However, research by Art Braunschweiger of the Titanic Research and Modelling Association shows that even if the lookouts had been in possession of binoculars they would have done little to aid them in spotting the iceberg on that cold dark fateful night. Meanwhile, by the time the officers on the bridge received the iceberg alert from the ship's lookouts they only had a mere 37 seconds to react before the moment of impact, an insufficient amount of notice as it tragically transpired.

--------- Did You Know That? ---------

The term 'iceberg' is believed to originate from the Dutch term *ijsberg* meaning 'ice hill'. In German, the word *berg* means 'mountain'.

IF ONLY, TRUE OR FALSE?

Titanic struck the iceberg on the starboard (right) bow. Some writers claim that had she struck the iceberg head-on *Titanic* would have suffered much less damage and many more lives would have been saved. However, this ignores the complete illogicality of a ship's officer knowingly steering his ship directly into an obstacle in her path. Many maritime experts have stated that no officer of a large passenger liner would have ever taken the decision to steer his ship directly into an iceberg. To do so would almost certainly result in catastrophic damage to the vessel as opposed to putting the helm over and most likely missing the iceberg, or at worse, risking a glancing blow. A head-on impact may well have confined the flooding to the one or two compartments furthest forward, thereby saving the ship from sinking, but would have resulted in horrific results elsewhere: hundreds of passengers and crew would have been injured and the majority of off-duty firemen, trimmers and greasers would almost certainly have suffered even more serious injuries or been killed outright, their quarters all being located in the bow area. This does not even take into consideration the damage that might have resulted to *Titanic's* engines from a head-on impact. Meanwhile, some writers have also claimed that *Titanic* may have avoided the iceberg completely if First Officer Murdoch had not issued orders for the engines to be reversed 'Full Astern' prior to steering the ship to the left, 'Hard-A-Starboard'. Some experts claim that this action would have decreased the forward momentum of the ship causing it to turn at a much slower rate. But while it is true to say that had the engines been reversed then this would have resulted in a slower rate of turn, the 'Full Astern' order has never been conclusively proven to have been given (there is contradicting testimony) and more importantly, *Titanic's* reciprocating engines could not be reversed instantly as a modern diesel-electric propulsion system can. Taking the latter further, the one indisputable fact from the *Titanic* disaster is that even if Murdoch had ordered 'Full Astern' at the precise moment the bridge received the iceberg alert from the ship's lookouts, it would not have not changed the outcome of the *Titanic* disaster whatsoever as a mere 37 seconds (as later estimated) elapsed between receipt of the notification and the tragic moment of impact.

Did You Know That?

Titanic is the largest passenger liner ever lost in regular service, while the former *Queen Elizabeth* burned in Hong Kong Victoria Harbour in January 1972 with no loss of life.

ICEBERGS

Size	Height (above water)	Length (or width)
GROWLER	less than 1 metre	less than 5 metres
BERGY BIT	1–4 metres	5–14 metres
SMALL	5–15 metres	15–60 metres
MEDIUM	16–45 metres	61–120 metres
LARGE	46–75 metres	121–200 metres
VERY LARGE	greater than 75 metres	greater than 200 metres

(*Source: International Ice Patrol*)

LOYAL TO HIS POST

When *Titanic* struck the iceberg the ship's Physical Education Instructor, Mr T. W. McCauley, remained at his post in the ship's first-class gymnasium and went down with the *Titanic*.

Did You Know That?

Icebergs are normally 20% to 30% longer under water than above and not quite as deep as they are long at the waterline.

SO NEAR, YET SO FAR AWAY

Captain Edward Smith ordered the first lifeboats lowered from *Titanic* to be rowed towards a ship visible several miles away. It appears that this ship (widely believed later to be the *Californian* under the command of Captain Stanley Lord), was close enough to row over to, drop passengers off, and then row back to pick up some more. The lights of the mystery ship were visible from *Titanic's* lifeboats throughout the night and one lifeboat is known to have rowed towards them, but never seemed to get any closer. Indeed, at the subsequent United States Senate Committee inquiry which commenced on 19th April 1912, the day the *Californian* arrived in Boston, Massachusetts survivors from the *Titanic* disaster recalled seeing the lights of another ship that was spotted after *Titanic* had hit the iceberg. However, at the US Senate Committee Inquiry it was discovered that Fourth Officer Boxhall of the *Titanic* attempted signalling the mystery ship with a Morse lamp, but received no response.

Did You Know That?

The MMSA (Mercantile Marine Service Association), a union to which Captain Lord belonged, presented petitions to the UK Government in 1965 and 1968 but failed to reverse the findings of the original British inquiry into the *Titanic* disaster which were critical of Lord's inaction after *Titanic* struck the iceberg.

THE DAMAGE

The *Titanic* struck an iceberg at 11:40 pm on 14th April 1912 while travelling at a speed of 22.5 knots. Less than 10 seconds after the impact her hull was opened below the waterline on the starboard side, causing intermittent damage that extended approximately 300 feet aft from the bow. Within 10 minutes *Titanic's* five forward compartments were flooded to a height of 14 feet above the keel. A sixth compartment was then flooded and the ship sank at 2.20 am on 15th April 1912 when the weight of the water in the flooded compartments pulled the ship's head down faster than the pumps could cope.

A COSTLY LESSON LEARNED

The *Titanic's* 20 lifeboats were in excess of British Board of Trade requirements at the time which were based on tonnage, as opposed to the number of passengers aboard, and only required her to carry 16 lifeboats. When Sir Alfred Chambers of the British Board of Trade was asked at the British Inquiry following the disaster why regulations governing the number of lifeboats required on passenger ships had not been updated since 1896, he informed the panel members that he felt there were too many lifeboats on passenger ships. Sir Alfred said that if there had been fewer lifeboats then there would have been more of a rush to fill them and so they would have left full, thereby saving more lives. *Titanic's* 20 lifeboats were situated on the uppermost deck and could accommodate 1,178 people whereas the existing British Board of Trade Regulations only required a passenger ship of her size to provide lifeboat capacity for 1,060 people. A plan had been submitted for the ship to carry 32 lifeboats but this number was reduced to 20 because open deck space was a selling point for passenger steamers. *Titanic* would have needed a total of 63 Class A lifeboats to accommodate all of her passengers and crew when she left Southampton. Some White Star Line officials were also of the opinion that a large number of lifeboats affected the overall beauty of *Titanic*, a vain and costly error as it later proved. Furthermore, when the Cunard Line's and White Star Line's leviathans were built in the early part of the 20th century, a large number of lifeboats onboard passengers liners was felt to be unnecessary given the fact that they were more intended for use in ferrying passengers to another vessel nearby, not as a refuge for the entire complement of passengers and crew. Indeed, *Titanic* was actually exempt from carrying more than the minimum number of lifeboats because she was in compliance with the watertight bulkhead standards prescribed by the British Board of Trade (Rule 12). Many passengers also refused to get into *Titanic's* lifeboats believing that the risk in the sea was greater than staying on board. Quite ironically just as *Titanic* was preparing for her maiden voyage, the British Board of Trade was in the process of attempting to update their Rules and in particular, the rule governing the minimum number of lifeboats a ship had to carry in proportion to the number of passengers and crew. Following the British Inquiry into the disaster, the British Board of Trade introduced new requirements for passenger vessels which included having a sufficient number of lifeboats aboard to accommodate all passengers and crew. The Board's Advisory Committee sent their letter of recommendation to the Marine Department of the British Board of Trade on 16th April 1912, the day after *Titanic* sank to the bottom of the North Atlantic.

—————————— Did You Know That? ——————————

If *Titanic* had left Southampton with 63 lifeboats, but inadequate watertight sub-divisions, she would have sunk much quicker than she actually did, and most of the lifeboats would have gone down with her.

A MARK OF RESPECT

As a mark of respect to those who lost their lives when *Titanic* sank, the Harland & Wolff Shipyard, Belfast closed for one day on Saturday 20th April 1912. The workforce was collectively shaken by the death of Thomas Andrews, one of her designers, and of the yard's Guarantee Group which sailed onboard the *Titanic*.

PRACTICALLY UNSINKABLE

Both the *Olympic* and her younger sister, *Titanic*, were constructed at the Harland & Wolff Shipyard in Belfast with a double-bottom and 16 watertight compartments which were formed by 15 bulkheads running across the ship. Each one of the watertight doors in the bulkheads could be closed off immediately by means of an electric switch on the bridge. Indeed, so sophisticated was the new system at the time that if any two of the largest watertight compartments became flooded, the vessel could remain afloat for an indefinite period. Consequently the combination of 16 divided watertight compartments coupled with the double-bottom led 'The Shipbuilder' magazine to state that the *Olympic* and the *Titanic* were 'practically unsinkable'. Many articles were written about the *Titanic* when she was being constructed, mainly appearing in the 'Belfast Morning News', the 'Irish News' and 'The Shipbuilder' magazine. In one such article the following sentence appeared: 'The Captain may, by simply moving an electric switch, instantly close the doors throughout and make the vessel practically unsinkable.' Other ships with comparable watertight door systems were similarly described whilst in the 1908 Souvenir edition of 'The Shipbuilder', RMS *Mauretania* was described as being: 'Practically unsinkable owing to the Watertight Bulkhead Doors being hydraulically controlled by the Stone-Lloyd System.' (The Stone-Lloyd system was not used aboard the *Titanic*.)

—————————— Did You Know That? ——————————

The term 'Unsinkable Ships' first appeared as an advertising headline on the front page of a catalogue issued by Stone-Lloyd, an English company which specialised in making watertight doors. However, the inside of the catalogue refers to 'Ships Practically Unsinkable'.

THE FIRST MESSAGE

The first message sent by a passenger after the *Titanic* sank is believed to have been sent by Major Arthur Peuchen to his family after he was rescued by RMS *Carpathia* and it simply read: 'Safe.'

THE LAST MESSAGE

The last message sent from the *Titanic* was sent at 1.50 am to the *Frankfurt* and read: 'YOU FOOL, STDBI AND KEEP OUT.' The last transmission from *Titanic* that could be understood was the partial transmission 'CQ'.

THE WARNINGS

On the day *Titanic* hit the iceberg, the ship received 6 ice warnings.

──────────── Did You Know That? ────────────

During World War I, RMS *Olympic* was converted to a transport ship, becoming HMT (His Majesty's Transport) *Olympic*. She is believed to have travelled nearly 185,000 miles burning almost 350,000 tons of coal.

A SIGN OF THINGS TO COME

Seven months before *Titanic* sank, her older sister, *Olympic*, having left Southampton on her fifth voyage, collided with the British cruiser HMS *Hawke* (under the command of Commander W.F. Blunt) on 20th September 1911 in the Spithead Channel. The ships were sailing parallel through the channel when *Hawke* veered into the starboard side of *Olympic* which was travelling at a speed of 19 knots. The collision destroyed the *Hawke's* bow and resulted in two large holes in *Olympic*, one above the waterline and another below it. Fortunately, no one was killed and the two ships were able to make it back to port under their own steam. At the subsequent Admiralty Court investigation into the collision *Hawke* and her crew were exonerated from blame while it was thought that the large amount of water displaced by *Olympic* had generated a suction that had drawn *Hawke* off her course thereby causing her to veer into *Titanic's* elder sister.

──────────── Did You Know That? ────────────

HMS *Hawke*, launched in 1891, was the sixth British warship to be named *Hawke*. On 5th October 1914 a German U-boat torpedoed *Hawke*, causing her to sink with the loss of her Captain, 26 officers and 500 men (just over 60 survived).

TITANIC'S ROMANTIC COUPLE

One known romance was brought about as a result of the *Titanic* disaster. Robert Daniel and Mary Eloise Smith, both travelling in first class, survived the sinking of the great ocean liner but Mrs Smith's husband, Lucien, died. Mary met Robert aboard the ship which rescued the pair of them, RMS *Carpathia*. The newly acquainted couple became very good friends and married within two years.

Did You Know That?

HMS *Hawke*, launched in 1891, was the sixth British warship to be named *Hawke*. On 15th October 1914, a German U-Boat torpedoed the *Hawke* causing her to sink with the loss of her captain, 26 officers and 500 men (just over 60 men survived).

TITANIC'S SPEED

The speed of *Titanic* when she struck the iceberg was 22.5 knots.

Did You Know That?

The speed of *Carpathia* as it raced to rescue *Titanic* survivors was 9 knots.

MORE PASSENGERS COULD HAVE BEEN SAVED

Following the sinking of *Titanic*, it emerged that the number of lifeboat seats not used amounted to 472.

THE ANGELS IN HEAVEN

Only one child out of the seven travelling in first class on the *Titanic* died when the ship sank while all of the children in second class were saved. However, 49 children from third class perished in the disaster.

Did You Know That?

Nearly every first-class woman survived, in comparison to 86% of those in second class and less than 50% of those in third class. Meanwhile, only 20% of the men survived compared to almost 75% of the women. First-class men were four times more likely to survive than second-class men, and twice as likely to survive as third-class men.

WHAT REALLY SANK THE *TITANIC*?

In 1994 a group of metallurgists at the National Institute of Standards and Technology (NIST) were presented with various pieces of the *Titanic's* hull which were retrieved from the wreck site. Up until then, scientists had speculated that if the Harland & Wolff Shipyard had carried out extensive tests for embrittlement on the steel used in the construction of the hull, as opposed to concentrating on the tensile strength, they concluded that when *Titanic* struck the iceberg the ship's hull would have been better placed to absorb more shock than it did.

In his 'inter-agency' report Timothy Foecke, a metallurgist at the NIST, supported the view that the 'poor' quality of the rivets used in *Titanic's* hull contributed to the ship's inability to stay afloat. In April 2008, Foecke and his colleague, Jennifer Hooper McCarty, had a book published entitled *What Really Sank the Titanic?* which outlines the full account of their investigation. However, it is important to bear in mind that the steel plates and the 3 million iron and steel rivets used to build *Titanic* were made to the standard quality of the day and were considered the best available. Perhaps then it may be true to say that if *Titanic's* builders had access to the type of steel and iron produced today, then maybe the damage caused by the iceberg would not have been quite as catastrophic. However, both of *Titanic's* sister ships, the *Olympic* and the *Britannic*, were built from the very same quality of steel plates and rivets used to build *Titanic*. Neither of these vessels ever displayed any signs of weakness in their hulls, with *Olympic* logging 24 years of both civilian and military service and earning the nickname 'Old Reliable'.

--------- Did You Know That? ---------

Titanic was so well constructed that she could have lost her bow and still stayed afloat and would have been able to slowly steam backwards to a nearby port for temporary repairs.

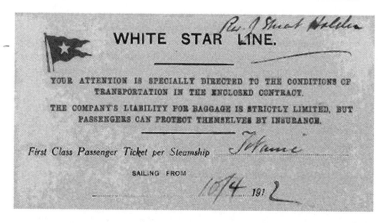

WHITE STAR LINE.

YOUR ATTENTION IS SPECIALLY DIRECTED TO THE CONDITIONS OF TRANSPORTATION IN THE ENCLOSED CONTRACT.

THE COMPANY'S LIABILITY FOR BAGGAGE IS STRICTLY LIMITED, BUT PASSENGERS CAN PROTECT THEMSELVES BY INSURANCE.

First Class Passenger Ticket per Steamship

SAILING FROM

191

Did You Know That?

At the United States Senate Committee Inquiry into the disaster, Second Officer Charles Lightoller stated in his testimony that he thought the last water temperature taken by *Titanic's* Quartermaster prior to the collision was around 33 or 34 degrees below zero. For high-quality steel to shatter the water temperature must reach 130 degrees below zero.

BOX OFFICE APPEAL

Titanic, the 1997 movie directed by James Cameron, was the No.1 box office movie in the USA from 14th December 1997 to 29th March 1998. It was also the No.1 movie in the United Kingdom from 25th January 1998 to 15th April 1998 (exactly 86 years after the great ship sank).

TITANIC'S LADIES

Out of the *Titanic's* total crew of 908 when she set sail from Queenstown for New York on Thursday 11th April 1912, only 23 were female. These comprised a Turkish bath attendant, 2 cashiers (from the Á la Carte Restaurant), a masseuse, the third-class matron and 18 stewardesses. Three of the women lost their lives: Lucy Violet Snape (stewardess), Katherine Walsh (stewardess) and Catherine Jane Wallis (third-class matron).

THE RUBAIYAT OF OMAR KHAYYAM

Aboard *Titanic* on her ill-fated maiden voyage was a very rare copy of *The Rubaiyat of Omar Khayyam* which was bought at auction for £405 by an American bidder in March 1912. The book contained 1,000 poems whilst the binding of its peacock-design gold cover contained many precious stones. Omar Khayyam (1048–1122) was a Persian astronomer, mathematician and philosopher. The original book's binding took two years to complete and was encrusted with 1,500 precious stones. The price paid for this copy was the equivalent of 15 years pay for a junior crew member onboard *Titanic*.

Did You Know That?

In the computer game *Titanic: Adventure Out of Time,* the object is to save three important items from the sinking ship: one of Adolf Hitler's paintings, a notebook that proved German leaders were attempting to gain geo-political advantage by instigating a communist revolution and *The Rubaiyat of Omar Khayyam.*

A ROOM WITH A VIEW

Titanic had 1,116 sidelights (portholes) and 419 windows in her hull and various deck houses throughout the ship. Additionally, there were also a number of deadlights (non-opening glass fitted to circular openings in doors and numerous other areas).

ONBOARD FACILITIES

Titanic had a number of facilities designed to make her first-class passengers' journey across the Atlantic as comfortable as possible:

- smoking rooms in first class and second class (for the men).
- 2 barber shops (one each for first-class and second-class passengers).
- 4 electric lifts complete with lift operators. (3 in first class; 1 in second class).
- a heated swimming pool.
- a Turkish bath.
- a gymnasium complete with 2 electric horses, 1 electric camel, 1 electric back rubbing machine and 1 electric vibration machine.
- a squash court on G deck with an observation gallery on F Deck.
- reading and writing room.
- a second class library which doubled as a reading and writing room. In the first-class section of the ship there was no separate library; books were stored in a locked bookcase in the first-class lounge and were lent to passengers by a steward.
- 10,488 square-foot first-class dining saloon with a seating capacity of 554.
- authentic Parisian Café with French waiters.
- a Veranda Café with real palm trees.
- electric lighting in every berth/room.
- electric heating in every first-class stateroom.
- a consultation room/surgery.
- a 5kW Marconi wireless transmitting apparatus and receiving instruments.
- a 50 phone switchboard complete with operator for intra-ship calls between various departments of *Titanic* (but not for public use). Although the 'Shipbuilder' magazine stated that private phones were fitted for passengers, this was not the case.
- two parlour suites each with a 48 feet private promenade.

Captain Edward Smith and Chief Purser Hugh McElroy outside the Officers' Quarters at the forward end of *Titanic's* Boat Deck (Jonathan Smith collection)

ISMAY'S FAVOURED TRIO

During his entire business life, J. Bruce Ismay, the Chairman and Managing Director of the famous White Star Line, surprisingly only went on three maiden voyages of his company's vessels: RMS *Adriatic* in May 1907, RMS *Olympic* in June 1911 and RMS *Titanic* in April 1912.

MAKING SURE SHE WAS GOING IN THE RIGHT DIRECTION

After *Titanic* left Belfast Lough on 2nd April 1912 her steering compasses on the Navigating Bridge and Docking Bridge and the standard compass on the Boat Deck were calibrated out at sea. This was done to avoid any land-based magnetic interference.

A SHAGGY DOG'S STORY

Only three of the nine dogs aboard survived the sinking of *Titanic*: Henry Sleeper Harper's Pekinese (Lifeboat No.3), Margaret Hay's Pomeranian (Lifeboat No.7) and Elizabeth Rothchild's dog (Lifeboat No.6). It is rumoured that a passenger (some believe it was the millionaire US businessman John Jacob Astor IV) freed the dogs from the kennels when all hope of the vessel staying afloat was gone.

WHEN THE BAND PLAYED THE LAST POST AND CHORUS

No member of RMS *Titanic's* band survived the sinking of the ship.

THE GOOD LUCK CHARM

Aboard the *Titanic* was a fashion journalist named Edith Russell. Ms Russell brought her good luck charm, a toy pig which played 'Maxixe' when its tail was wound, with her on the great ship's maiden voyage. When *Titanic* struck an iceberg, Ms Russell was placed in a lifeboat along with her good luck charm. Sometime later she gave the toy pig to the author Walter Lord who wrote *A Night To Remember*.

Did You Know That?

The actual toy pig owned by Edith Russell
was used in the 1958 movie *A Night To Remember*.

WHAT WAS ONBOARD FOR THE PASSENGERS

- Fresh meat 75,000 lbs
- Fresh fish 11,000 lbs
- Salt & dried fish 4,000 lbs
- Bacon and ham 7,500 lbs
- Poultry and game 25,000 lbs
- Fresh eggs 40,000
- Sausages 2,500 lbs
- Potatoes 40 tons
- Onions 3,500 lbs
- Tomatoes 3,500 lbs
- Fresh asparagus 800 bundles
- Fresh green peas 2,500 lbs
- Lettuce 7,000 heads
- Sweetbreads 1,000
- Ice cream 1,750 lbs
- Coffee 2,200 lbs
- Tea 800 lbs
- Rice, dried beans etc.10,000 lbs
- Sugar 10,000lbs
- Flour 250 barrels
- Cereals 10,000 lbs
- Apples 36,000
- Oranges 36,000
- Lemons 16,000
- Grapes 1,000lbs
- Grapefruit 13,000
- Jams and marmalade 1,120 lbs
- Fresh milk 1,500 gal
- Fresh cream 1,200 qts
- Condensed milk 600 gals
- Fresh butter 6,000lbs
- Ales and stout 15,000 bottles
- Wines 1,000 bottles
- Spirits 850 bottles

- Minerals 1,200 bottles
- Cigars 8,000
- 57,600 items of crockery
- 29,000 pieces of glassware
- 44,000 pieces of cutlery

Among these:
- Tea cups: 3,000
- Dinner plates: 12,000
- Ice cream plates: 5,500
- Soufflé dishes: 1,500
- Wine glasses: 2,000
- Salt shakers: 2,000
- Pudding dishes: 1,200
- Finger bowls: 1,000
- Oyster forks: 1,000
- Nut crackers: 300
- Egg spoons: 2,000
- Grape scissors: 1,500
- Asparagus tongs: 400

Linens
- Aprons: 4,000
- Blankets: 7,500
- Table cloths: 6,000
- Bed covers: 3,600
- Eiderdown quilts: 800
- Single sheets: 15,000
- Table napkins: 45,000
- Bath towels: 7,500
- Fine towels: 25,000
- Roller towels: 3,500
- Double sheets: 3,000
- Pillow-slips: 15,000

LORD VILIFIED BY THE PRESS

Captain James Henry Moore was Master of the Canadian Pacific vessel SS *Mount Temple*, who learned of *Titanic*'s emergency messages for help and reached what he believed was the scene of the disaster around 04.30am on 15th April 1912. Moore was one of many witnesses called before the US Senate Committee Inquiry and the subsequent British Inquiry held following the sinking of *Titanic*. According to Moore's original testimony the *Mount Temple* found herself on the western side of a great ice barrier, and concluded that *Titanic* had collided with the iceberg on the eastern side, perhaps as many as eight miles further east. Moore then claimed that it was a few hours later before he saw any ship and that ship was SS *Californian* under the command of Captain Stanley Lord. At the British Inquiry Lord was asked at what time he passed *Mount Temple*. Lord replied to Question 7,260 as follows: 'I passed her somewhere about half-past seven — somewhere in the vicinity of half-past seven.' Both vessels were in close proximity to the exact area from which *Titanic* sent her SOS but could find nothing there (the wreckage of *Titanic* was found in 1985 in excess of 13 nautical miles to the east and a little to the south of the ship's distress co-ordinates). Lord said that his vessel was 19½ miles from the SOS position when he ordered her engines to be stopped for the night, while the ship commenced her engines again at 06:00 am. As the *Californian* had a top speed of 13 knots (nautical miles per hour) then his claim that he passed *Mount Temple* 'somewhere about half-past seven' was consistent given the 19½ miles Lord claimed he was away from *Titanic* coupled with overnight drift, *Californian* starting her engines again at 06:00 am and her speed.

However, there were claims that the *Mount Temple* could be seen by the *Californian* as early as 06:00 am on 15th April 1912 which cast serious doubt over Lord's testimony. But, Moore did not categorically inform the US Inquiry that he could see *Californian* at 06:00 am, he said: 'I suppose about 6 o'clock in the morning… I sighted the (Cunarder) *Carpathia* on the other side of this great ice pack, and there is where I understand she picked up the boats. So this great pack of ice was between us and the *Titanic*'s position.' He then went on to add: 'I saw the *Californian* myself cruising around there, sir. She was there shortly after me.' Senator Smith then asked Moore: 'On which side of the ice pack was the *Californian*?' Moore responded: 'The *Californian* was to the north, sir. She was to the north of the *Carpathia* and steaming to the westward, because, after I had come away and after giving up my attempt to get through that pack, I came back again and steered back, thinking I might pick up some soft place to the north. As I was going to the north the *Californian* was passing from east to west.' Despite Moore not once actually confirming that he positively saw the *Californian*, Senator Smith continued: 'And you were also cut off from the *Carpathia* by this ice pack?' In reply Moore said: 'Yes, sir; by this ice pack. She (*Californian*) was then north of the *Carpathia*, and she must have been, I suppose, about the same distance to the north of the *Carpathia* as I was to the westward of her.' Yet again Moore appeared to be merely making guesses as to the location of the *Californian*. However, a somewhat different account of events emerged when Moore faced the British Inquiry. Question 9,244: 'And I think shortly before 08:00 am you came in sight of the *Carpathia* and the *Californian*?' Moore replied: 'Yes.' Therefore, the assumption that the *Californian* was visible to *Mount Temple* at 06:00 am remains unsubstantiated and purely based on assumptions. However, it was Captain Stanley Lord who was vilified by the press and public alike for not responding to *Titanic's* distress signals, a serious lack of prudent judgment given the fact that *Titanic* fired 8 distress rockets, all of which were seen by the *Californian*.

Cyril Evans, the radio operator onboard the *Californian*, was asked to give evidence to the US Senate Inquiry. Evans said that on the evening of Sunday 14th April 1912 (around 9:00pm New York time) Captain Lord informed him that he was stopping the ship for the night because there was just too much ice in close proximity to them. Evans said that Lord asked him if he was aware of any other ships close by and when Evans said that *Titanic* was not far away from their position, Lord instructed him to inform *Titanic* that *Californian* was surrounded by ice and stopped for the night. Evans immediately returned to his station and at 9:05pm (New York time) and he called Jack Phillips, *Titanic's* senior wireless operator, and said: 'Say, old man, we are stopped and surrounded by ice.' When asked what Phillips reply was, Evans said: 'Shut up, shut up, I am busy; I am working Cape Race.' Upon receiving this somewhat terse reply, Evans said he decided to retire and switched his radio off for the night.

By way of a footnote it is worth remembering that although shipboard wireless operators carried junior officer rank, this was a nominal title only and they drew their principal pay from the Marconi Company. As such they were not required to give any priority to messages to the Bridge, nor had any regulations been put in place up to that point to require them to do so. Therefore, it is true to say that 'the system' was just as much at fault here as Lord or Phillips. Indeed, in the famous photograph of Jack Phillips which appears in many books about *Titanic*, his cap badge is that of the Marconi Company, and not the badge of the White Star Line.

--------------------- Did You Know That? ---------------------

The *Mount Temple* was used in November 1901 as a Boer War transport ship and saw action in the First World War when she had a 75 mm gun mounted on her stern.

THE SERVANTS

Approximately 40 maids and manservants accompanied the 190 first-class families aboard RMS *Titanic*.

A SPOOKY MIRROR IMAGE

In 1898 Morgan Robertson wrote a novel entitled *Futility,* a story about the largest ship in the world ever built and her collision with an iceberg in the Atlantic Ocean on a cold April night. Robertson called his ship *Titan* while both *Titan* and *Titanic* had been labelled as being unsinkable. There were certain similarities between the two ships: both sailed on their maiden voyage in April; *Titan* was 800 feet long while *Titanic* was 882 feet, 9 inches long; there were 24 lifeboats on *Titan* compared to *Titanic's* 20; *Titan* struck an iceberg at midnight whereas *Titanic* struck an iceberg at 11:40 pm and both ships sank in the North Atlantic. However, many experts are of the opinion that Robertson's book was not some form of psychic warning, rather an adaptation of something he may have read about the White Star Line's plans to build a fleet of large ocean liners to ferry passengers across the Atlantic. Six years before Robertson's book was published the White Star Line issued a press statement in which it said that Harland & Wolff Shipyard in Belfast had been commissioned to build several large passenger liners with the *New York Times* informing its readers about plans to build a ship named *Gigantic,* including its' specifications, on 17th September 1892. Shortly after *Titanic* sank, the publishers of *Futility* decided to reprint the book under a new title, *The Wreck of the Titan.*

■ THE MOVIE TRIVIA ■ ■ ■ ■ ■ ■ ■ ■ ■ ■ ■ ■ ■ ■

The engine room scenes were partially filmed aboard the World War II Liberty ship, *Jeremiah O'Brien.* The crew working on the movie made the ship's railings smaller and installed catwalks to make the engines appear much bigger than they actually were.

THE LUCKY DISGUISE

Daniel Buckley, aged 21, from Kingwilliamstown (now Ballydesmond), Co. Cork, Ireland boarded the *Titanic* as a third-class passenger at Queenstown, Ireland on Thursday 11th April 1912. Realising that the ship was going to sink Buckley jumped into Lifeboat No.13 with several other men. However, when the men loading the lifeboat saw this they dragged all of the men out of the lifeboat except Buckley. One of the women in the lifeboat placed a shawl around his head to conceal his identity and no doubt, saved his life. He died in 1918 during the conflict of World War I.

THE ICE-MAN

Titanic's chief baker, Charles Joughin, who reportedly had been drinking heavily on the evening the *Titanic* struck the iceberg, was one of only a few people who survived from being in the water in the freezing cold Atlantic conditions. At the subsequent British Inquiry into the *Titanic* disaster Joughin recalled just how lucky he was to survive the sinking of the ship. He said that he made his way to the starboard side of the poop deck and soon found himself in the freezing cold waters. Joughin then noticed what he thought was a piece of wreckage floating in the water and swam towards it. However, it was in fact a collapsible lifeboat with about 25 other men on it including Second Officer Charles Lightoller. Joughin said when he tried to get on the boat he was pushed off it and then decided to make his way to the opposite side of the boat where the entree cook, John Maynard, helped him by holding on to him until the *Carpathia* arrived to rescue them.

ADVERTISING TITANIC

First-class Parlour Suite, Titanic

'It is impossible to adequately describe the decorations in the passenger accommodation... They are on a scale of unprecedented magnificence. Nothing like them has ever appeared before on the ocean.'

White Star Line, Belfast March 1912

THE LIFEBOATS

RMS *Titanic* had 20 lifeboats:

- 14 wooden lifeboats measuring 30 feet long with a capacity of 65 persons each.
- 2 wood cutters measuring 25 feet, 2 inches with a capacity of 40 persons each.
- 4 Engelhardt collapsible boats (wooden bottoms with canvas sides) measuring 27 feet, 5 inches long with a capacity of 47 persons each.

BELFAST PROUD

'When the tugs were left behind the compasses were adjusted, after which a satisfactory speed run took place, and the latest triumph of the shipbuilder's art then left for Southampton, carrying with her the best wishes of the citizens of Belfast.'

Belfast *News Letter*, 3rd April 1912

NOT FIT TO LEAD?

None of the officers who survived the sinking of the *Titanic* went on to be given their own commands by the White Star Line. However, Second Officer Charles Lightoller attained command of a Royal Navy vessel during World War I.

TAKING HER TIME

Contrary to popular belief, and mainly due to misrepresented stories at the time, J. Bruce Ismay, the Chairman and Managing Director of the famous White Star Line, did not order or put pressure on Captain Smith to make a record passage to New York for *Titanic's* maiden voyage. Indeed, on the North Atlantic there were defined shipping lanes which all passenger and cargo liners followed. The northern track, used during August to December, was approximately 200 miles shorter than the southern track (used from January to July). *Titanic* was sailing on the southern track, just as *Olympic*, her sister ship, had done on her maiden voyage in June 1911. When the *Titanic* left Southampton on 10th April 1912, Britain was gripped by a National Coal Strike and therefore rather than Ismay worrying about capturing the coveted Blue Riband for making the fastest ever Atlantic crossing by sea, he was more concerned about fuel supply. Indeed, several of the ship's boilers were not lit in an effort to preserve the fuel supply onboard and so economy was paramount for *Titanic's* maiden voyage. It was also felt that attempting to plough through the North Atlantic at full speed could potentially cause some damage to *Titanic's* engines.

─────────────── Did You Know That? ───────────────

In the early 20th century large passenger ocean liners were discouraged from arriving at their port of destination ahead of schedule. The reason for the latter being the fact that fresh provisions for the ship's return voyage were ordered to be delivered to the port for the scheduled arrival date and time and the fact that passengers had made confirmed hotel bookings based on the scheduled arrival. If the ship was late and arrived in New York after 8:00 pm, passengers had the option of remaining onboard overnight and landing after breakfast the following morning. Consequently, feeding and tending to passengers over and above what was generally accounted for in an average crossing was not cost effective for the company.

TITANIC'S CAPACITY

Titanic's total capacity was 3,547 passengers and crew, fully loaded.

THE EXPENSIVE LIFEJACKET

A lifejacket from a *Titanic* victim was sold to a collector from Ireland for £55,000 at an auction held by Henry Aldridge and Son on 18th April 2009.

A HERO REMEMBERED

Harland & Wolff's Design Department Manager Thomas Andrews' body was never found following the sinking of *Titanic*, but within one year his heroic efforts to save women and children were deemed worthy of being memorialised. At the request of Sir Horace Plunkett, MP, a short biography of Andrews was written by Shan Bullock.

Did You Know That?

Eight other brave men from Harland & Wolff lost their lives along with Andrews: William Campbell, Apprentice Joiner; Roderick Chisholm, Ships' Draughtsman; Alfred Fleming Cunningham, Apprentice Fitter; Anthony W. Frost, Outside Foreman Engineer; Robert Knight, Leading Hand Engineer; Frank Parkes, Apprentice Plumber; William Henry Marsh Parr, Assistant Manager Electrical Department and Ennis Hastings Watson, Apprentice Electrician. These men were part of Harland and Wolff's Guarantee Group and were aboard to assist with any problems or adjustments that might arise with various machinery and equipment.

ROYAL PROTECTION

RMS *Titanic*, like all ships at the time bearing the *RMS* designation, was protected by the British Crown and consequently any attack on one of them constituted an attack on the Crown and an act of war.

THE FINAL INSPECTION

Lord Pirrie, Chairman of Harland & Wolff, and J. Bruce Ismay, Chairman and Managing Director of the White Star Line, were photographed making a final inspection of the *Titanic* on the slipway about half an hour prior her launch in Belfast on 31st May 1911. Unlike other vessels launched at Harland & Wolff there was no ceremonial breaking of a bottle of champagne on *Titanic's* bows when the ship slid down the slipways and into the waters of Belfast harbour. The White Star Line did not believe in formal christenings prior to the launch of their ships.

TITANIC IS LAUNCHED

Titanic's movement down the greased slipways into the water began at 12:15pm on 31st May 1911. The hydraulic launching rams were located at the head of the slipway, directly below the bows of *Titanic* and a pressure gauge controlled the hydraulic launching triggers which held the vessel while the timber shores and blocks were removed. It took 1 minute, 2 seconds for *Titanic's* mammoth 882 feet, 9 inches-long hull to slide from her building berth into the waters of Belfast harbour.

Did You Know That?

Only the propellers of the *Titanic* were fitted in dry dock. Her engines, boilers, machinery, funnels, furnishings and fittings etc, were put aboard at the Fitting-Out Wharf.

TITANIC'S MUSCLE

Titanic's two massive reciprocating engines which drove the two wing propellers, and the turbine engine, which drove the centre propeller, were first assembled in the Engine Work's Erecting Shop at Harland & Wolff Shipyard. All three were then dismantled and taken to the Fitting-Out Wharf for re-assembly in *Titanic's* engine rooms.

Did You Know That?

Titanic's combination of two reciprocating steam engines and a low-pressure steam turbine made the most efficient use of coal because the low-pressure turbine used residual steam whose remaining energy potential would have otherwise been wasted.

TITANIC NOT READY

When *Titanic* set sail, it was only after her construction and fitting-out had been delayed several times. Among other things there had been a delay in getting the propeller boss castings from Darlington Forge and on two occasions work had to be partly suspended on the *Titanic* in favour of emergency repairs to the *Olympic*. When the first passengers boarded *Titanic* some of the paintwork onboard was still wet whilst her painters were still touching up the paint on her port side up until the day before she set sail. Interestingly, had there been no delays to the construction of the *Titanic*, she would have set sail on her second voyage from Southampton to New York on the very same date she made her maiden voyage.

TWO SISTERS SAY FAREWELL

On 1st March 1912, RMS *Olympic* returned back to Belfast for replacement of a dropped port-side propeller blade which had fallen off during an eastbound crossing on 24th February 1912. *Olympic's* scheduled arrival time back at Belfast missed that evening's high tide, resulting in the *Titanic* remaining in the dry dock until the following morning with *Olympic* being moored at the nearby Fitting-Out Wharf. That same day Harland & Wolff's contracted photographer, Robert J. Welch, captured several images of the *Titanic* being manoeuvred out of the dry dock and over to the Fitting-Out Wharf, and *Olympic* being manoeuvred in. A well-known photograph of both ships in echelon prior to the move, often cited as being taken on 6th March 1912, was in fact taken by Welch on the 1st March. The *Olympic's* new blade was fitted by late afternoon of 3rd March 1912 and she was removed from the dock the following morning. The *Belfast Telegraph* later reported that while turning for departure on 4th March 1912, the *Olympic* grounded and was required to re-enter the dock for inspection. Apart from this lone newspaper report, no further documentation exists of this event. There is one further photograph (a lantern slide) of the ships in echelon which does show *Olympic* in dry dock and *Titanic* at the Outfitting Wharf, and this relatively unknown image could possibly have been taken on 6th March 1912. This could, in part, explain this often-misidentified photograph as the last taken of the two sisters together.

——————————— Did You Know That? ———————————

Titanic wasn't officially titled RMS *Titanic* until she actually carried Royal Mail; it was SS (Steamship or Screw Steamer) or, as her builder designated her, TSS (Triple Screw Steamer) *Titanic*, up until then.

TITANIC'S DECKS

Titanic had a total of 11 decks: in order from top to bottom, the Boat Deck, the Promenade (A) Deck, B, C, D, E, F, G, Orlop, Lower Orlop Deck and the Tank Top. The boiler rooms spanned a number of these decks.

——————————— Did You Know That? ———————————

Whereas it took some 3,000 men to build the *Titanic*, the Bible tells us that only 4 men built Noah's Ark.

A THIRSTY SHIP

Titanic's water consumption amounted to some 14,000 gallons of fresh water per day.

THE RADIO ACT OF 1912

Shortly after *Titanic* sank on 15th April 1912, the United States Congress enacted the Radio Act of 1912, a US Federal Law that required all seafaring vessels to maintain 24-hour radio watch and keep in contact with nearby ships and coastal radio stations.

BIG GIRLS

The White Star Line's three big sisters, the *Olympic*, the *Titanic* and the *Britannic* were very similar in size, each measuring 882 feet, 9 inches long. *Olympic* and *Titanic* were 92 feet, 6 inches wide extreme, while *Britannic* was 94 feet at her extreme breadth. This was done to increase stability and compensate for heavier displacement that was brought about by the additional weight on her topsides. At the time they were the largest vessels ever constructed. Of the three, the youngest, *Britannic*, displaced 48,158 gross registered tons while the *Titanic* displaced 46,328 gross registered tons and the *Olympic* displaced 45,323 gross registered tons. When all three ships were designed *Titanic* was to have the largest GRT but after she sank modifications were made to the *Britannic* resulting in her GRT being increased. All three leviathans were originally intended as running mates to allow the White Star Line to maintain a continuous weekly transatlantic service in both directions.

—————— Did You Know That? ——————

Queen Mary measured 1,019 feet long, *Queen Elizabeth* measured 1,031 feet long and the now retired *Queen Elizabeth II* measured 963 feet long.

THE STATEROOMS

Titanic had a total of 835 Staterooms made up as follows:

First class	416
Second class	162
Third class	257

WAS THE WAIT WORTH IT?

The construction and fitting out of *Titanic* took 3 years.

A LOT OF RIVETS

Some 3 million rivets were embedded in the hull of *Titanic*.

THE ENGINE ROOM

Titanic's propulsion was provided by two 4-cylinders, triple expansion, direct-acting, inverted reciprocating steam engines of 30,000 hp at 77 rpm and 1 low pressure Parsons Turbine at 16,000 hp 165 rpm. *Titanic* had a total of 29 boilers (24 double-ended boilers and 5 single-ended boilers) with a total of 159 furnaces providing a total heating surface of 144,142 sq. feet. This gave *Titanic* a top speed of 24 knots in calm seas.

——————— Did You Know That? ———————

The designed working pressure of *Titanic's* boilers was 215psi.

■ THE MOVIE TRIVIA ■ ■ ■ ■ ■ ■ ■ ■ ■ ■ ■ ■ ■ ■ ■

Titanic was the first movie to have a budget in excess of $200,000,000.

TITANIC – THE MYSTERY SHIP DISAPPEARS

During the United States Senate Committee Inquiry into the *Titanic* disaster which began on 19th April 1912, Captain Stanley Lord, the captain of the *Californian* (widely believed to be the closest ship to *Titanic* when she struck an iceberg) testified that he did not believe the ship that he had seen on the horizon could have been *Titanic*. Lord claimed that the ship he saw was too small to be *Titanic*, and that the two ships were too far apart to be visible to each other. However, not all of the testimonies given at the US Inquiry by the crew from the *Californian* matched. Most damningly of all, Captain Lord said he was not told that the mystery ship (*Titanic*) had disappeared but this contradicted testimony from James Gibson, an apprentice on the *Californian*, who said he reported to Lord that the ship had disappeared and that Lord had acknowledged him.

——————— Did You Know That? ———————

The American and British inquires held after *Titanic's* sinking found that the *Californian* must have been closer than 19½ miles (31 km) to *Titanic* and that both ships were visible from each other. Both inquiries concluded that Captain Lord failed to provide proper assistance to *Titanic* and the British Inquiry further concluded that had the *Californian* responded to *Titanic's* rockets and gone to her assistance, that it 'might have saved many if not all of the lives that were lost'.

ADVERTISING TITANIC

First-class Suites, Titanic

'The Staterooms in their situation, spaciousness and appointments will be perfect havens of retreat where many pleasant hours are spent, and where the time given to slumber and rest will be free from noise or other disturbance.'

White Star Line, Belfast March 1912

PERSONAL FLOTATION DEVICES

There were 3,560 lifejackets and 49 lifebuoys aboard *Titanic*.

CARGO REPORTED AS LOST

- Nearly 3,400 bags of mail and some 700–800 parcels.
- 1 Renault 35 hp automobile owned by passenger William Carter.
- 1 Marmalade Machine owned by passenger Edwina Trout.
- An oil painting by Blondel, '*La Circasienne Au Bain*', owned by Hokan Björnström-Steffanson.
- 7 parcels of parchment of the *Torah Scrolls* owned by Hersh L. Siebald.
- 3 crates of ancient models for the Denver Museum.
- 1 case of toothpaste shipped by Park & Tilford.
- 11 bales of rubber for the National City Bank of New York.
- 2 cases of tennis balls (96 in total) shipped by R.F. Downey & Co.
- A cask of china headed for Tiffany's.
- 34 cases of golf clubs and tennis rackets shipped by A.G. Spalding.
- A jewelled copy of *The Rubaiyat of Omar Khayyam*, with illustrations by Eliku Vedder that sold for £405 at auction in March of 1912 to an American bidder.
- Four cases of opium.

A GIANT IN THE WATER

RMS *Titanic* measured a mammoth 60.5 feet from the waterline to the boat deck and 175 feet from the keel to the top of the funnels. The vessel had a draft of 34 feet, 6 inches in forward and 34 feet, 7 inches in aft. She was 882 feet, 9 inches long; 92 feet, 6 inches at her extreme breadth; and her beam measured 92 feet, 6 inches (28 metres).

Did You Know That?

To this day, *Titanic's* lost mail remains the property of Her Majesty's Royal Mail Service.

A CASE OF BAD LUCK

Many of the passengers on *Titanic* were not originally supposed to be travelling on her doomed maiden voyage. However, as a result of a strike in early 1912 coal was in short supply and this forced the White Star Line to cancel transatlantic crossings on the *Adriatic* and *Oceanic* and transfer their passengers and coal stocks to the *Titanic*.

Did You Know That?

Titanic's coal consumption was estimated by her owners to be 850 tons per 24 hours at 22½ knots (a figure supplied by Harold Sanderson at the British Board of Trade Inquiry into the *Titanic* disaster). However, coal consumption varied enormously depending on the current, wind and sea conditions.

THE UNLUCKY 13

When *Titanic* left Queenstown, Ireland for New York on 11th April 1912, there were 13 couples on board celebrating their honeymoon. Of the honeymooning couples aboard, only three, Mr and Mrs George Harder, Mr and Mrs John Snyder and Mr and Mrs Dickson Bishop, survived the disaster to enjoy their marriage. The other 10 men drowned leaving their brides grieving widows.

Did You Know That?

Whereas *Titanic's* maiden voyage lasted just 4½ days, the Holy Bible tells us that the maiden voyage of Noah's Ark lasted approximately 370 days and nights.

BELFAST PROUD

First-class Swimming Bath

'Then the morning plunge in the great swimming bath where the ceaseless ripple of the tepid sea water was almost the only indication that somewhere in the distance 72,000 horses in the guise of steam engines fretted and strained under the skillful guidance of the engineers.'

Belfast Evening Telegraph

HARLAND & WOLFF SHIPYARD, BELFAST

The Harland & Wolff Shipyard in Belfast was founded in 1862 by Edward James Harland and Gustav Wilhelm Wolff. At its height, Harland & Wolff was one of the biggest shipbuilders in the world. Between 1900 and 1930, Harland & Wolff was Belfast's biggest employer with many thousands of men working in the famous Belfast shipyard at a time when demand for ocean liners was insatiable. Harland & Wolff constructed over 70 ships for the White Star Line, the most famous of which was the *Titanic*. When people speak about the famous Belfast shipyard the first thought that comes to mind is *Titanic*. However, today the shipyard which no longer makes ships is perhaps just as famous for its two cranes, *Goliath*, which was built in 1969 and *Samson*, which was built in 1974. These two cranes still dominate Belfast's skyline.

——————— Did You Know That? ———————

The Harland & Wolff Shipyard in Belfast has the world's largest dry dock.

ADVERTISING TITANIC

'On the boat deck, accommodation is provided for the captain and officers, containing smoke-room and mess-room. Rooms for the Marconi installation are also arranged in the same house, with the wheelhouse and navigating bridge adjoining at the fore-end.'

White Star Line, Belfast March 1912

SS *NOMADIC* AND SS *TRAFFIC*

In 1911, the White Star Line had two vessels, SS *Nomadic* and SS *Traffic*, purpose-built to ferry passengers from Cherbourg harbour out to RMS *Titanic* when she was anchored a mile offshore from France on 10th April 1912. Cherbourg's pier was not large enough to accommodate an Olympic class liner.

TITANIC CREW DISCHARGED
AS THE SHIP GOES DOWN

In July 2008, a letter outlining that the crew of the *Titanic* were discharged from their duties when news of its sinking reached Britain was valued at £1 million. The letter, never seen in public before, was sent by the White Star Line to steward Alexander Littlejohn. It has been claimed that the crew were discharged from their duties onboard *Titanic* to save the White Star Line from having to pay out thousands of pounds in wages to the survivors. However, this was not the case; it was just how things were done at the time and was even recorded in the crew account paperwork that was submitted to the British Board of Trade Inquiry which was held after the sinking of the *Titanic* and the subject of public record. The letter says survivor Alexander Littlejohn 'disembarked on the high seas' on 15th April 1912, the day *Titanic* struck an iceberg and sank. The valuable document was passed to the Titanic Foundation by Alexander's grandson Phillip, from Maidenhead, Berkshire, England.

SOME OF *TITANIC*'S LAST PHOTOGRAPHS

In 1985, a collection of some 42,000 photographs, including the photographs Father Browne snapped of *Titanic*, were found in the basement of a house in Dublin. Father Browne had started taking photographs in 1895 and continued to do so up until his death in 1960. In early 1912, his Uncle Robert (the Bishop of Cloyne) sent him a ticket for the first leg of *Titanic's* maiden voyage, taking in the sailing from Southampton to Cherbourg and then on to Queenstown (Cobh), County Cork, Ireland. Whilst on the luxury liner he befriended an American millionaire couple who offered to pay for Father Browne to continue on *Titanic's* maiden voyage to New York. When Father Browne's Jesuit superior received his request for permission to travel on to New York he was furious and immediately cabled Queenstown with the following message: 'GET OFF THAT SHIP. PROVINCIAL.' So Father Browne disembarked *Titanic* at Queenstown but before doing so he took several of the last known photographs of *Titanic* and the only photograph taken in the ship's Marconi room. After the sinking of the *Titanic*, Father Browne's photographs of the vessel appeared on the front pages of newspapers around the world. Shortly after the disaster Father Browne wrote a poem in memory of those who lost their lives entitled '*In Memoriam, 15th April*

1912.' On 31st July 1915, the 35-year old Father Browne was ordained as a Roman Catholic priest and moved to Europe where he joined the Irish Guards as a chaplain. He served at the Battle of the Somme in 1916 and was injured several times during World War I. He was awarded the Military Cross and Bar for his bravery in combat. It would be 73 years before the public saw new photographs of the *Titanic* when her wreckage was discovered in 1985.

Did You Know That?

Another series of photographs were snapped by a *Titanic* passenger, a member of the Odell family, believed to be Kate Odell, who was travelling with Jack Odell, her son, who was on holiday at the time with his family. The Odells boarded *Titanic* in Southampton and disembarked at Queenstown, Ireland, *Titanic's* last port of call. Kate took a photograph of *Titanic* while they were on the tender boat heading back to Queenstown.

SOS

It is often claimed by historians that the *Titanic* was the first ship to issue an 'SOS' call. However, this is incorrect. In the late 19th and early 20th centuries SOS did not exist while 'CQD' was the recognised call sign for a ship in distress. The CQD signal had been devised by the Marconi Company and was supposed to mean 'All Stations – Urgent', but many shipping companies re-translated its meaning to 'Come Quick – Danger' or 'Come Quickly Down'. On 3rd November 1906, the SOS signal was agreed upon as the international call sign for ships in distress at the second International Radiotelegraphic Convention, which took place in Berlin, Germany. However, it was not to be formally introduced until 1st July 1908 and on 10th June 1909, it was transmitted for the first time when the *Slavonia*, a Cunard Line vessel, was wrecked off the Azores. Two steamers close by the *Slavonia* received her signals and went to the rescue, nearly three years before *Titanic's* SOS message. At 12:15 am on Monday 15th April 1912, 35 minutes after she struck the iceberg, *Titanic* sent her first distress signal – CQD (6 times), MGY (6 times) and position 41.44 N. 50.24 W. *La Provence* and *Frankfurt* were the first ships to receive *Titanic's* distress signals. *Titanic* then sent her position to *Frankfurt* and *Frankfurt* replied: 'OK: stand by.' The message 'CQD' was a general call to all vessels letting recipient ships know that the issuing vessel was in distress and required immediate assistance. At the time of the *Titanic* disaster, the Marconi Company's 'CQD' was still in common use although it had been officially replaced by 'SOS'. However, as Marconi dominated the infant marine radio industry in the early 1900s, many shipping companies still used CQD, rather than SOS. Indeed, when Jack Phillips sent *Titanic's* first and last distress calls he stuck to the company's CQD signal. The SOS signal, contrary to popular belief, does not stand for 'Save Our Souls' or 'Save

Our Ship'. SOS was chosen specifically to be easily and instantly recognisable in Morse code *dit dit dit, dah dah dah, dit dit dit*. SOS remained the maritime radio distress signal for 90 years until it was replaced by the Global Maritime Distress Safety System in 1999 although it is still recognised as a visual distress signal.

--------------------- Did You Know That? ---------------------

The first radio distress signal was sent by the *East Goodwin Sands* lightship on 17th March 1899 when the *Elbe*, a merchant vessel, ran aground on the Goodwin Sands. The message was received by the radio operator on duty at the South Foreland lighthouse, who was able to contact the Ramsgate lifeboat and ask it to go to *Elbe's* aid. By a strange twist of fate, on 30th April 1899, Goodwin Sands featured in another 'maritime first' when the *East Goodwin Sands* lightship was rammed by SS *R. F. Matthews* and was forced to send a distress message calling for help.

AN EARLY RETIREMENT

Captain Smith was planning to retire after *Titanic's* maiden voyage. However, he went down with his command.

--------------------- Did You Know That? ---------------------

Captain Smith was 59 years old when *Titanic* made its maiden voyage while the Bible tells us that Noah entered the Ark in the 600th year of his life, on the 17th day of the second month (*Genesis:* 6:14–21).

A NOISY SHIP

When *Titanic* was constructed in 1912, the ship's triple-chime whistles, like those of her older sister, the *Olympic*, were at the time the largest ever made. Indeed, *Titanic's* whistles could be heard from a distance of 11 miles.

A SLOW STOP

Prior to the launch of the *Titanic* on 31st May 1911, a test was carried out on the White Star Line leviathan to determine her stopping distance. *Titanic* was run at 20 knots and then the engines were run full astern. It was almost half a mile from the point at which the engines were reversed before the ship finally came to a stop.

—————————— Did You Know That? ——————————

Titanic carried over 2,500 tons of cargo and over 19,500 cubic feet of baggage. Baggage was measured by cubic feet, not weight, and third-class baggage was mixed with cargo so it is impossible to give definitive figures for each.

VERY LITTLE PROTECTION OR JUST THE RIGHT AMOUNT?

The *Titanic* carried 20 lifeboats and 3,560 lifejackets. The lifejackets were made of canvas and cork. Of the 20 lifeboats, 14 were Class A wood boats with a capacity of 65 persons each, 2 were wood cutters with a capacity of 40 persons each and 4 were collapsible (wood bottoms with canvas sides) with a capacity of 47 persons each. A plan was drawn up showing *Titanic* carrying a total of 32 lifeboats, but the White Star Line felt that more lifeboats were unnecessary and would detract from the beauty of the vessel. Alexander Carlisle, *Titanic's* designer, and the Welin Davit Company, supplier of the davits, attempted to persuade the White Star Line to install more lifeboats but their request fell on deaf ears. Deck cups were fitted in the deck planking inboard of the existing lifeboats for extra chocks, however. This possibly was in anticipation of updated lifeboat regulations which were well under discussion by the end of 1911. In the early 20th century a large number of lifeboats on a passenger liner were deemed to be unnecessary, given the one-in-a-million chance of a collision with an iceberg and the fact that the sea lanes across the Atlantic Ocean were very busy back then. No one seriously considered the possibility that anything would happen that would require everyone to take to the lifeboats all at once. It is also important to note that it took right up until the time the ship foundered to launch all of the 18 'decked' lifeboats; the remaining two collapsibles haphazardly floated off as the ship sank beneath them. 'Boats for all' may have sounded comforting to those crossing the Atlantic in the years following, but the fact remains that even though the *Titanic* sank slowly, and the crew maintained order until the very end, the ship would have likely gone down with as many as half her boats still onboard had she been equipped with twice the number of boats.

—————————— Did You Know That? ——————————

The wooden lifeboats were numbered from forward to aft, with even numbers to port and odd to starboard. The first two boats on either side (Nos. 1 and 2) were the emergency cutters, and while at sea were kept swung out and ready for immediate lowering in case someone fell overboard.

Artist's impression of *Titanic* sinking. It is now known that *Titanic* broke apart
at the surface just before her final plunge, a fact that was hotly disputed in 1912.
(*The Sphere*/Jonathan Smith collection)

LAUNCHING THE LIFEBOATS

The following table charts the launching of *Titanic's* lifeboats on Monday 15th April 1912:

Boat 1	Boat 2	Boat 3	Boat 4	Boat 5
Starboard side	Port side	Starboard side	Port side	Starboard side
Capacity: 40	Capacity: 40	Capacity: 65	Capacity: 65	Capacity: 65
Time: 1:10am	Time: 1:45am	Time: 1:00am	Time: 1:55am	Time: 12:55am
5 First-class	8 First-class	25 First-class	23 First-class	31 First-class
7 Crew	10 Third-class	15 Crew	1 Servant	7 Crew
	3 Crew	1 dog	6 Third-class	
	4 others		12 Crew	

Boat 6	Boat 7	Boat 8	Boat 9	Boat 10
Port side	Starboard side	Port side	Starboard side	Port side
Capacity: 65	Capacity: 65	Capacity: 65	Capacity: 65	Capacity: 65
Time: 12:55am	Time: 12:45am	Time: 1:10am	Time: 1:20am	Time: 1:20am
20 First-class	22 First-class	26 First-class	6 First-class	9 First-class
2 Crew	3 Crew	4 Crew	17 Second-class	17 Second-class
6 Others	3 Others	2 Others	3 Third-class	6 Third-class
1 dog	1 dog		15 Crew	4 Crew

Boat 11	Boat 12	Boat 13	Boat 14	Boat 15
Starboard side	Port side	Starboard side	Port side	Starboard side
Capacity: 65	Capacity: 65	Capacity: 65	Capacity: 65	Capacity: 65
Time: 1:25am	Time: 1:25am	Time: 1:35am	Time: 1:30am	Time: 1:35am
5 First-class	15 Second-class	1 First-class	4 First-class	1 First-class
14 Second-class	1 Third-class	13 Second-class	24 Second-class	1 Second-class
6 Third-class	4 Crew	27 Third-class	4 Third-class	38 Third-class
24 Crew		24 Crew	15 Crew	25 Crew

Boat 16	Collapsible A*	Collapsible B*	Collapsible C	Collapsible D
Port side	Starboard side	Port side	Starboard side	Port side
Capacity: 65	Capacity: 47	Capacity: 47	Capacity: 47	Capacity: 47
Time: 1:35am	3 First-class	3 First-class	Time: 1:40am	Time: 2:05am
3 Second-class	8 Third-class	1 Second-class	2 First-class	7 First-class
23 Third-class	5 Crew	5 Third-class	36 Third-class	2 Second-class
11 Crew		18 Crew	6 Crew	9 Third-class
				7 Crew

* Collapsible lifeboats A and B floated off when *Titanic* sank and were used as rafts by survivors.

THE MEN WHO BUILT *TITANIC*

When the keel of *Titanic* was laid on 31st March 1909 at the Harland & Wolff Shipyard in Belfast the workers worked from 7:30 am to 5:30 pm five days a week, plus a half-day on Saturdays. All workers were given two unpaid days off per year: at Easter and Christmas, and one week unpaid holidays in July. The average wage at the time was about £2 ($10) a week.

A SLIPPY ENTRANCE

When the *Titanic* was launched on 31st May 1911, 22 tons of grease (tallow, soap, and train oil) were used to help slide the vessel down the slipway.

ALEXANDER'S RAGTIME BAND

'Alexander's Ragtime Band' was a music record made in 1911 by the Victor Military Band and is a song that many survivors of the sinking of RMS *Titanic* recall being played on the night she struck the iceberg.

BELFAST PROUD

First-class Bathroom In Parlour Suite

'The Titanic also contains special suites of rooms, consisting of bedrooms, sitting room, bathroom and servants' room, and these will have their own private promenade, shut off from the rest of the ship, and not overlooked by other passengers.'

Belfast News Letter, 1912

THE LOST CHORD

Enrico Caruso, the legendary tenor, was born in Naples, Italy on 25th February 1873. On Monday 29th April 1912, two weeks after *Titanic* sank, Caruso recorded his version of 'The Lost Chord' and that evening he would sing it again, in the Metropolitan Opera House at a benefit concert for the families of the victims of the *Titanic* disaster.

ADVERTISING TITANIC

First-class main staircase

'In the middle of the hall rises a gracefully curving staircase, its balustrade supported by light scroll-work of iron with occasional touches of bronze, in the form of flowers and foliage... The staircase is one of the principal features of the ship, and will be greatly admired as being without doubt the finest piece of workmanship of its kind afloat.'

White Star Line, Belfast March 1912

THE RELIEF FUNDS

'Stand To Your Post' by Bennett Scott and 'Be British' by Lawrence Wright and Paul Pelham were written and recorded within weeks of the *Titanic* sinking. Ernest Gray recorded 'Stand To Your Post' on the Winner Label in remembrance of those who lost their lives on the *Titanic*. The proceeds from sales of both records helped support the relief funds set up to help the victims' families. The lyrics of 'Be British' included these immortal lines:

All went well, and the laugh and jest
And the dance went gaily on,
Till they met the ice, and a rasp and a jar,
Told there was something wrong.

─── Did You Know That? ───

Illustrative coloured lantern slides could be bought or hired
from the publisher of the sheet music for 'Be British'.

TITANICA

For almost a century, *Titanic* has placed a captivating hold on the imagination of people all over the world. Indeed, the sinking of *Titanic* is the most iconic image when most people are asked to recollect a famous disaster in history. Titanicism is an international phenomenon and one of the great metaphors of our time. Meanwhile, items of Titanica include: bars of soap, wall plaques, salt and pepper shakers (a half of the broken ship was used for the salt and the other broken half for the pepper), ales and beers, mugs, keyrings, paintings, teapots and even a motorised inflatable model of *Titanic* which included an inflatable iceberg.

TITANIC'S SHARKS

When *Titanic* left Southampton harbour on 10th April 1912 she had on board her several professional gamblers. However, in an attempt to outwit the ship's passengers, the card sharks travelled under assumed names.

■ THE MOVIE TRIVIA ■ ■ ■ ■ ■ ■ ■ ■ ■ ■ ■ ■ ■ ■ ■

When director James Cameron decided to include real footage of the *Titanic's* remains lying on the seabed, he did not want to shoot the footage from inside a submersible. Therefore, to allow filming from outside the submersible, his brother, Mike, and Panavision developed a deep-sea camera system which was capable of withstanding the 400 atmospheres of pressure at the seabed's depth.

SLEEP LIKE A BABY

Amazingly, after the *Titanic* struck the iceberg, an Armenian passenger was roused from her cabin in third class by a steward and got into a lifeboat where she slept throughout the sinking. When her lifeboat was rescued by RMS *Carpathia* the woman, who had never travelled by sea before, simply thought that it was normal practice to change ships in the middle of the ocean, just as she had previously changed trains on land.

THE 747s OF THE WATER

Titanic, and her older sister, *Olympic*, could best be described as being the 747s of their day. Both leviathans were enormous people carriers which travelled at a moderate speed and had huge space for large cargoes. These White Star Line vessels were specifically built to compete with the Cunard Line's RMS *Lusitania* and RMS *Mauretania* which entered service in 1907 and ruled the North Atlantic passenger route until the arrival of the *Olympic* and *Titanic*.

————————— Did You Know That? —————————

The giant shipping line, Cunard, introduced the inaugural transatlantic passenger service in 1840 and over the following 50 years the population of the USA quadrupled.

FOUR-FUNNELLED GIANTS OF THE SEAS

Titanic was one of just fourteen famous four-funnelled ocean liners ever built. The first was the SS *Kaiser Wilhem de Grosse* which was launched on 4th May 1897, some 39 years after the SS *Great Eastern* which actually had five funnels when it was launched, the only ship ever to sport more than four funnels, but one was later removed. The last four-funnelled liner to be built was SS *Windsor Castle* (later remodelled and turned into a two-stacker) which was launched on 9th March 1921. Four of the 14 were sunk during the World Wars and all except the *Titanic* were scrapped. RMS *Aquitania* (a Cunard Line vessel nicknamed the 'Ship Beautiful') was the largest of all the four-funnelled liners and the only one to survive through both World Wars. However, although the *Aquitania* was longer than the *Olympic*, as a direct result of the difference in the gross registered tonnage for each vessel, the *Olympic* was actually considered larger. Indeed, throughout the 1920s the *Olympic* was always advertised as the largest British-built steamship.

ADVERTISING TITANIC

First-class Elevators

'We may be spared the labour of mounting or descending stairs by entering one of the smoothly-gliding elevators which bear us quickly to any other of the numerous floors of the ship we may wish to visit.'

White Star Line, Belfast March 1912

IN MEMORY OF *TITANIC*

The *Britannic*, owned by the White Star Line, was originally to be called *Gigantic* but was renamed after *Titanic* sank. The *Britannic* was launched on 26th February 1914.

Did You Know That?

HMHS stands for His/Her Majesty's Hospital Ship.

TITANIC IN BLACK AND WHITE

From her keel to the base of her funnels *Titanic* stood nearly 11 storeys high. Her hull was painted with a black gloss paint, while the entire superstructure was painted white.

List of Four-Funnelled Ships in Chronological Order

Ship	Owner	Launched	Fate
SS *Kaiser Wilhelm der Grosse*	North German Lloyd Line	4th May 1897	Sank on 6th August 1914
SS *Deutschland*	Hamburg-Amerika Line	1900	Scrapped in 1925
SS *Kronprinz Wilhelm*	North German Lloyd Line	30th March 1901	Scrapped in 1923
SS *Kaiser Wilhelm II*	North German Lloyd Line	12th August 1902	Scrapped in 1940
RMS *Lusitania*	Cunard Line	7th June 1906	Sank on 7th May 1915
RMS *Mauretania*	Cunard Line	20th September 1906	Scrapped in 1935
SS *Kronprinzessin Cecilie*	North German Lloyd Line	1st December 1906	Scrapped in 1940
SS *France*	Compagnie Générale Transatlantique	10th September 1910	Scrapped in 1936
RMS *Olympic*	White Star Line	20th October 1910	Scrapped in 1935
RMS *Titanic*	White Star Line	31st May 1911	Sank on 15th April 1912
RMS *Aquitania*	Cunard Line	21st April 1913	Scrapped in 1950
HMHS *Britannic*	White Star Line	26th February 1914	Sank on 21st November 1916
SS *Arundel Castle*	Union-Castle Line	11th September 1919	Scrapped in 1959
SS *Windsor Castle*	Union-Castle Line	9th March 1921	Sank on 23rd March 1943

Did You Know That?

The first SS *Windsor Castle* and her older sister, SS *Arundel Castle*, were the only four-stacked ocean liners built for a route other than the transatlantic (they plied their trade between England and South Africa).

NO CHAMPAGNE FOR *TITANIC* OR HER SISTERS

None of the White Star Line's famous trio of ocean liners, *Olympic*, *Titanic* and *Britannic*, were actually christened. *Titanic* hit an iceberg on the evening of 14th April 1912 and sank early the next morning. *Britannic* hit a mine on 21st November 1916 and sank with the loss of 30 lives. However, *Olympic* enjoyed a long and illustrious career (1911 to 1935) and was commonly referred to as 'Old Reliable' before she was scrapped. Indeed, *Olympic* made 514 peacetime Atlantic crossings covering some 1½ million miles and also crossed the Atlantic numerous times as a troop transport ship.

ONCE, TWICE, THREE TIMES A SURVIVOR

Violet Jessop was a first-class stewardess on RMS *Titanic* when it sank but survived the disaster. The previous year Jessop had been a stewardess on *Titanic's* sister ship, RMS *Olympic*, when the *Olympic* collided with HMS *Hawke*. Four years later, while working as a nurse, Jessop survived the sinking of HMHS *Britannic* after it struck a mine in the Aegean Sea at 8:12 am on 21st November 1916.

A HERO TO THE VERY END

Thomas Andrews, the man who supervised the design and construction of the *Titanic* at the Harland & Wolff Shipyard in Belfast, stayed aboard the sinking ship to the very end helping passengers put on their lifebelts and urging them to go up on deck and await a seat in one of the lifeboats. John Stewart, a steward onboard *Titanic*, said he last saw Andrews staring at a painting, 'Plymouth Harbour', above the fireplace in the smoking room in first class. The painting depicted the entrance to Plymouth Sound, which ironically *Titanic* was due to pass on her return voyage. Meanwhile, a stewardess whom Andrews helped place in one of the lifeboats, Mary Sloan, subsequently wrote in a letter: 'Mr. Andrews met his fate like a true hero, realising the great danger, and gave up his life to save the women and children of the Titanic. They will find it hard to replace him.'

————————— Did You Know That? —————————

In various movies about *Titanic*, the painting 'Plymouth Harbour',
is often incorrectly shown as depicting the entrance to
New York Harbour.

TITANIC'S VERY OWN MOVIE STAR

In August 1996, Eleanor Ilene Johnson Schuman joined fellow *Titanic* survivors
Edith Brown Haisman and Michel Marcel Navratil on an expedition cruise to the
site of the famous ship's wreck at the bottom of the Atlantic Ocean. Eleanor
remained active in *Titanic*-related activities well into her eighties. She was the only
survivor that James Cameron, director of the movie 'Titanic' in 1997, met while
filming and Cameron gave Eleanor the royal treatment. Indeed, she saw Cameron's
movie three times including a special screening with movie critics Roger Ebert and
Gene Siskel. After the movie's release and 11 Academy Award wins Eleanor herself
became a popular attraction. Indeed, such was her popularity that she had to
change her telephone number to an unlisted one after receiving numerous
telephone calls every day from people hoping to speak with her.

————————— Did You Know That? —————————

When Mrs Schuman died in 1998, only five remaining survivors
of the *Titanic* disaster were still living.

LES ENFANTS DU *TITANIC*

The daughter of *Titanic* survivor Michel Marcel Navratil, Élisabeth, who was
employed as an opera director, wrote a book entitled 'Les enfants du Titanic' ('The
Children of the Titanic') about the experiences of her father, her grandfather Michel
Snr. (who lost his life in the disaster), and her uncle Edmond (who was saved with
Michel Jnr.). Michel Navratil Snr.'s body was recovered by the rescue ship, CS
Mackay-Bennett, and as a result of his assumed Jewish surname he was buried in the
Baron de Hirsch Cemetery, a Jewish cemetery, in Halifax, Nova Scotia, Canada.

————————— Did You Know That? —————————

Michel Marcel Navratil was the last male survivor of the *Titanic*.
He died on 30th January 2001.

FATHER AND DAUGHTER TIMELY REUNITED

Edith Eileen Brown was just 15-years old when she boarded *Titanic* with her parents, Thomas and Elizabeth, at Southampton on 10th April 1912. The Browns travelled as second-class passengers. Thomas was a successful hotelier who owned a hotel in Cape Town, South Africa where Edith was born. Indeed, the reason for the family's journey to the USA was because Thomas was about to open a hotel in Seattle, Washington. The *Titanic's* hold contained furnishings for this hotel. In 1993, Edith Eileen Haisman (née Brown) took part in a ceremony in Southampton, England at which she was presented with a gold watch. The watch was believed to be her father's, recovered from a 1987 expedition to the wreckage of the great ship. RMS Titanic Incorporated held the rights at the time to the wreckage and had the watch placed on a silver sterling plate inscribed with the words: 'What better use for scientific technology than to reunite a father with his child.' Her father died in the sinking of the *Titanic* and his body, if ever recovered, was never identified. Her mother, Elizabeth, survived the disaster. In August 1996, Edith, aged 99, joined two fellow survivors, Michel Marcel Navratil and Eleanor Schuman, on a cruise to the location of the ship's wreckage. Before leaving the location, Edith tossed a single red rose into the Atlantic Ocean where she lost her father over 84 years earlier. Edith died in her Southampton nursing home aged 100 on 20th January 1997 and at her bedside stood a black and white photograph of her father wearing a straw boater, stiff collar and a bow-tie.

Did You Know That?

Edith was the last survivor of the *Titanic* disaster who was born in the 19th century (27th October 1896).

ADVERTISING TITANIC

First-class Dining Saloon

'This immense room has been decorated in a style peculiarly English – that, in fact, which was evolved by the eminent architects of early Jacobean times (early 1600s) . . . The furniture of oak is designed to harmonise with its surroundings.'

White Star Line, Belfast March 1912

Titanic anchored off Roaches Point, Queenstown (now Cobh) on 11 April 1912
(Father Browne collection/Jonathan Smith collection)

TITANIC'S ROCKETS

According to information entered into the record at the British Board of Trade Inquiry following the sinking of RMS *Titanic*, the ship carried 36 'socket signals in lieu of guns' and 12 'ordinary rockets'. This gave *Titanic* the capability of distress signalling either by day or night. The 1912 'Rules of the Road at Sea', Article 31, Distress Signals, states in part that when a vessel requires assistance it may use, in the daytime, 'a gun or other explosive signal to be fired at one minute intervals'. This requirement could be met by a type of gun (actually a small cannon) that fired a charge producing a loud report, or in *Titanic's* case, by socket signals. These were signal rockets that produced a loud report when they exploded at altitude, and which took their name from the method of firing from a tube (socket) mounted on the Bridge wing. For distress signalling at night, Article 31 specified, among other methods, 'rockets or shells, throwing stars of any colour or description, fired one at a time, at short intervals'. This requirement was met by the 'ordinary rockets' *Titanic* carried (and fired on the night of April 14th/15th). These exploded at altitude – several hundred feet above the ship – and threw out a cascade of white stars. *Titanic's* distress rockets were different from previous designs as they carried an explosive device that emitted a loud report in addition to throwing stars, but the loud report was simply an attention-getting device – the stars themselves were the distress signal. Because both types of rockets emitted a loud report, the ones fired from *Titanic* that night are frequently confused with the socket signals whose characteristics were different. Unfortunately for *Titanic*, the captain of the nearby *Californian* did not recognise *Titanic's* rockets as distress signals, perhaps believing

that they were 'company signals' – pyrotechnics used for signalling between two ships of the same company. But although company signals took many different forms, none included rockets throwing stars or sound-producing rockets fired at regular intervals.

Did You Know That?

Fourth Officer Boxhall gave the order to fire the first rocket from *Titanic* at 12:45 am. During the next hour or so an additional seven rockets were released into the cold night air. Therefore, a total of 8 rockets were discharged in 60 minutes or at intervals of approximately 7½ minutes each.

ADVERTISING TITANIC

First-class Turkish Baths Cooling Rooms

'One of the most interesting and striking rooms on the ship. The port-holes are concealed by an elaborately-carved Cairo curtain, through which the light fitfully reveals "something of the grandeur of the mysterious East."'

White Star Line, Belfast March 1912

THE WRONG PHOTOGRAPHS

In the mayhem to inform the public of news after *Titanic* struck an iceberg at 11:40 pm on 14th April 1912, many newspapers around the world carried their stories under a photograph of *Titanic's* sister ship, *Olympic*. It is true to say that most reporters at the time would not have known the difference between the two leviathans; they were practically identical from the exterior with the exception of *Titanic's* partial enclosure of the Promenade Deck for first-class passengers which had only been completed a few weeks prior to her maiden voyage. Whereas there were literally hundreds of photographs of the *Olympic*, launched one year before her sister amid a flurry of advertising publicity by the White Star Line, there were very few photographs taken of *Titanic* in comparison.

--------------------------------- Did You Know That? ---------------------------------

The word 'leviathan' is a Hebrew word denoting a sea creature
referred to in the Old Testament (Psalm 74:13–14; Psalm 104:26;
Job 41; *Isaiah* 27:1). The word has become synonymous
with any large sea monster or creature.

A FAMOUS DRESS

It is widely reported that the white silk evening dress which the American actress Dorothy Gibson wore in the 1912 movie 'Saved From The Titanic', was the actual dress she was wearing when rescued from the *Titanic*. Dorothy Gibson also co-wrote the movie.

ADVERTISING TITANIC

First-class Squash Racquet Court

'The court is situated on the lower deck and extends two decks high for a length of 30 feet. A spectator gallery is placed on the after end of the court on the middle deck level.'

White Star Line, Belfast March 1912

THE GHOST SHIPS

Apart from the *Californian*, which was close to the *Titanic* when she struck an iceberg, and *Samson*, the Norwegian seal hunter that its crew member, Hendrik Bergethon Naess, stated in a diary was within close proximity to *Titanic* on that fateful evening, the names of numerous other ships are very often mentioned as being near the ocean liner before she sank including: the *Dorothy Baird*, the *Frankfurt*, the *Saturnia* and the *Plymouth*. However, some of these reports are doubtful at best. The *Samson*, for example, had left port in Iceland only shortly before *Titanic's* sinking making her presence nearby impossible

TITANIC'S ACHILLES HEEL?

Popular belief holds that *Titanic's* rudder was too small and prevented her from turning in time to avoid the iceberg, thereby sealing her doom. However, this is nothing more than a myth as the rudder on *Titanic*, as on other large passenger liners of her era, was never designed for quick maneuverability. Tight maneuvering was normally done only in pilotage waters when the ship had to stay on course within the confines of a narrow, curving channel, such as was found between Southampton Water and the English Channel. In such situations the ship's speed was much lower and engines were used in addition to the rudder; going slow or half ahead on one engine only (thereby only turning the propeller on one side or the other) or even running one engine astern briefly while the ship maintained steerageway ahead. *Titanic* would never have been found running with all engines at Full Ahead anywhere other than in the open sea, where it was expected that any object large enough to present a hazard would be seen in enough time to avoid it – flawed thinking, as the events of 14th April 1912 proved, but the accepted belief up to that point nonetheless. And while *Titanic's* rudder blade presented slightly less surface area in relation to the vessel's overall length than would be required as a minimum today, the response time and turning circle data obtained from her sister ship *Olympic* showed these ships to be well within what is still considered acceptable today for ships of their size having a single rudder and one or more fixed-position propellers (as opposed to azipod propulsion). Only in warship construction, where the ability to carry out extreme evasive maneuvers was part of the design criteria, were rudders normally fitted that could give more rapid turning capabilities. Interestingly, at full speed, *Titanic* turned a full circle of 3,850 feet in diameter at 20.5 knots during her sea trials off Belfast Lough.

Did You Know That?

Achilles' heel is of mythological origin and refers to a fatal weakness in spite of overall strength, actually or potentially leading to eventual downfall.

THE TUGS

Titanic's sea trials were originally scheduled for 1st April 1912 and to facilitate the trials, several tugs owned by the Alexandra Towing Company were sent from Liverpool to Belfast on 31st March 1912. However, owing to poor weather the trials were put back 24 hours to avoid any damage to the ship's hull. As a result of the unexpected delay *Titanic's* engineers and officers spent the day examining the ship. On 2nd April 1912, the tugs *Hercules, Herculaneum, Herald, Hornby* and *Huskisson* safely negotiated *Titanic* down the Victoria Channel and Belfast Lough and out to the Irish Sea. The *Herald* was at her port bow lines, *Huskisson* and *Herculaneum* were at her port and starboard lines whilst *Herald, Hercules* and *Hornby* were at her bows. Some of the tugs which escorted *Titanic's* older sister, *Olympic*, when she left Belfast harbour on 29th May 1911 were also used to escort *Titanic*.

TITANIC HITS BROADWAY

Mrs Margaret Tobin Brown, aka 'Molly' Brown, a survivor from the *Titanic* disaster, had a Broadway musical named in her honour, *The Unsinkable Molly Brown*, in 1960 written by Richard Morris with music and lyrics by Meredith Wilson. The musical tells the fictionalised story of her life including her trip on *Titanic's* doomed maiden voyage. The musical's title got its name from Molly's alleged quote after she was rescued from the sinking *Titanic* when she told reporters: 'I'm a Brown. We're unsinkable.' The quote in fact comes entirely from the Broadway play and its namesake movie. The movie version of the musical was released in 1964 starring Harve Presnell and Debbie Reynolds who played the part of Molly Brown. It was the press that made reference to *The Unsinkable Mrs Brown*, it was not a moniker she chose for herself.

-------------------- Did You Know That? --------------------

Margaret Brown was never known as 'Molly' during her lifetime.
The name was entirely a Hollywood fabrication dating from the
late 1930s.

THE MISSING KEY

Over 400 lots of *Titanic* memorabilia from the ill-fated liner and her owners, the White Star Line, were put under the hammer at an auction conducted by Henry Aldridge and Son on 22nd September 2008. The star of the show was a small key that belonged to David Blair who was the original Second Officer on the *Titanic*, and which most likely was one of the keys that opened the telephone box in the crow's nest. He sailed with the ship from Belfast to Southampton and was due to carry out his duties as a Senior Officer on board until a last-minute change in personnel was decided by the management of the White Star Line. Henry Tingle Wilde was the First Officer of *Titanic's* older sister, *Olympic*, who was due for his own command and who was also a close friend of Captain Edward J. Smith. Consequently, as a result of Wilde's experience with an Olympic Class liner it was deemed a good idea to bring him over to the *Titanic* as her First Officer for her maiden voyage. Wilde signed on to join the ship on the 9th April 1912, the day before she set sail on her doomed maiden voyage. Blair's command as Second Officer then went to Charles Lightoller. However, in Blair's rush to leave the *Titanic*, he carried this key off the ship with him in his pocket and only found it after *Titanic* had left Southampton. Not being able to return the key to Captain Smith or Wilde, Blair kept it as a memento and treasured it throughout his life and passing it on to his daughter Nancy, who later gifted the Blair collection to the British International Sailors Society. Due to an apocryphal story about the lookouts' missing binoculars, it was believed by some that this key might have been to a cabinet that held the Second Officer's binoculars which, because they could not be found when *Titanic* sailed, were unavailable to the lookouts. (However, when the key reached auction, it carried a tag – most likely added by someone at a later date – identifying it as being for the crow's nest telephone.) Perhaps because of this story competition at auction for this key was fierce. It eventually came down to two bidders, one of whom owns one of the largest and most important collections of *Titanic* memorabilia in the world and the other a diamond company from China. The latter was successful, paying £90,000 for the privilege of owning this coveted piece of *Titanic* history. Blair also sent a postcard to his sister-in-law from the *Titanic*, written on 4th April 1912, after his arrival in Southampton. He wrote about his disappointment at leaving the ship but said that he hoped to serve on her one day. This postcard was sold to a telephone bidder from the USA for £11,000. Also offered up for auction were David Blair's medals which included the George V medal for gallantry at sea; these sold for £4,700.

■ THE MOVIE TRIVIA ■ ■ ■ ■ ■ ■ ■ ■ ■ ■ ■ ■ ■ ■

The name of the fictional character 'Caledon "Cal" Nathan Hockley', played in the movie by Billy Zane, derives from two small towns (Caledon and Hockley) near Orangeville, Ontario, Canada, where James Cameron's aunt and uncle live.

THE HEART OF THE OCEAN

The *Heart of the Ocean* (the *Cœur de la Mer* in French) appeared in James Cameron's 1997 blockbuster *Titanic* but no such item of jewellery was aboard the ship. However, another diamond exists and shares the same name, but it is not in the shape of a heart.

CAPTAIN SMITH TAKES CHARGE

When the *Titanic* left Belfast Lough on 2nd April 1912 to commence her sea trials, Captain Edward Smith was in charge of the vessel. However, Captain Smith was not the *Titanic's* first captain. Captain Herbert James Haddock took command of her in Belfast prior to her delivery to the White Star Line by the Harland & Wolff Shipyard, Belfast as Smith was captain of *Titanic's* older sister, *Olympic*, at the time. On 1st April 1912, Captain Smith relinquished command of the *Olympic* to Captain Haddock and a short time later took up his new post in command of the *Titanic*. Captain Haddock testified at both the United States Senate Committee Inquiry and the British Board of Trade Inquiry into the *Titanic* disaster.

ADVERTISING TITANIC

First-class Gymnasium

'Passengers can indulge in the action of horse riding, cycling, boat rowing etc, and obtain beneficial exercise, besides endless amusement.'

White Star Line, Belfast March 1912

Did You Know That?

The paintings of Monet and Picasso that were depicted in Cameron's *Titanic* were not actually on the real *Titanic*.

Titanic's First-Class Gymnasium
(Ulster Folk and Transport Museum/Jonathan Smith collection)

THE LUCKY FIREMAN

John Coffey, a 23-year-old fireman on *Titanic*, deserted the ship when it arrived at Queenstown, Ireland, her final stop before sailing to New York. Coffey jumped ship by stowing away on one of the tenders which was ferrying passengers from Queenstown to the *Titanic* as the waters at Queenstown harbour were too shallow to accommodate *Titanic's* size. Coffey hid amongst mailbags headed for Queenstown and after the *Titanic* sank he said that he jumped ship because he was superstitious about sailing and felt there was something not quite right with the ship.

Did You Know That?

John Coffey went on to work onboard RMS *Mauretania.*

TITANIC'S FINAL MESSAGE

The *Titanic's* last distress message, sent in International Morse Code, was:

CQD CQD SOS SOS CQD DE MGY MGY

Did You Know That?

The message was sent by Jack Phillips.

TITANIC'S OPERATING ROOM

The Marconi wireless system used on *Titanic* was at the time the most powerful and sophisticated type in the world. The principal transmitter was of a rotary spark design, powered by a 5Kw motor alternator which received its electricity supply from *Titanic's* lighting circuit. Two masts stretching 250 feet each above sea level supported the wireless system's 4-wire antenna. The Marconi wireless system occupied two rooms aboard the ship, the 'Marconi Operating Room' where her two operators, Jack Phillips and his assistant Harold Bride, sent and received messages and the adjacent 'Silent Room', which housed the actual transmitting equipment. The wireless system's guaranteed working range was 250 miles, but communications could be maintained for up to 500 miles during the day and up to 2,000 miles during the night.

―――――――――――― Did You Know That? ――――――――――――

The 'Silent Room' was so named because it was specially insulated to reduce the noise which was produced by the system's disc discharger when firing off. Essentially, the room was a large heavily sound-insulated closet containing all of the noisy components of the Marconi apparatus. This was necessary not only to allow the operators to hear the signals generated in their headphones, but also to contain the terrific noise so that it wouldn't disturb both passengers and ship's officers in the neighbouring accommodations.

―――――――――――― Antiques Roadshow ――――――――――――

Memorabilia connected to *Titanic's* launch in Belfast on 31st May 1911, are amongst the rarest and most sought-after from the ship. During a routine antiques valuation roadshow in Belfast, a ticket to the launch of the great liner was brought in for appraisal. Although these items are widely reproduced, this particular example was genuine and caused great interest in the *Titanic* community. It sold at auction on 22nd September 2008 for £33,000 to a telephone bidder who had just finished a round of golf in Portugal.

ADVERTISING TITANIC

Second-class Boat Deck

'Nothing has been omitted in the determination to place the two new White Star leviathans beyond criticism as to the excellence of the accommodation both in the second and third classes …….. the spaces provided for Second-class promenades are unusually spacious……the boat deck is surmounted only by the open canopy of heaven.'

White Star Line, Belfast March 1912

TITANIC'S CRICKETER

John Borland Thayer, Jr. was a first-class cricketer who died shortly before his 50th birthday when *Titanic* sank on 15th April 1912. Thayer, an American, is the only known first-class cricketer to have died in the disaster. He was a member of the Philadelphian cricket side which toured England in 1884. He scored 817 runs with an average of 28 and took 22 wickets for 21 runs on the tour.

A RECORD-BREAKING TRIP

Since the sinking of *Titanic* many writers have pointed to speed being the main reason for her eventual disaster, claiming that the White Star Line wanted the *Titanic* to cross the Atlantic in a record time. At the time of *Titanic's* maiden voyage the Cunard Line's RMS *Mauretania* held the coveted *Blue Riband* for making the fastest Atlantic crossing for a passenger liner. (The *Blue Riband* is an unofficial award given to the passenger liner crossing the Atlantic in regular service with the record highest speed, the term originating from horse racing.) And before the *Mauretania* her sister ship, *Lusitania*, dominated the lucrative shipping route in terms of speed. However, contrary to popular belief the White Star Line was more concerned with passenger comfort than the speed of her two leviathans, the *Olympic* and the *Titanic*. In fact, *Titanic* could never have won the *Blue Riband* even if she tried. *Titanic's* maximum speed was 24 knots whilst the Cunard Line's leviathans could reach speeds in excess of 26 knots. Although *Titanic* was not attempting to win the *Blue Riband* there was an unconfirmed report from one first-class passenger of a conversation between Captain Smith and J. Bruce Ismay in which they discussed *Titanic* beating the time that her sister ship *Olympic* had made on her maiden voyage. And therein lies the myth that *Titanic* was ignoring considerations of safety while running at full speed through an area known for ice, more concerned with winning a 'trophy' than the safety of her passengers.

■ THE MOVIE TRIVIA ■■■■■■■■■■■■■

Jack's hairstyle was based upon the hairstyle that John Connor (played by Edward Furlong) had in *Terminator 2: Judgment Day* (1991), a movie directed by James Cameron.

TOO BIG FOR THE BIG APPLE

The White Star Line contacted the City of New York authorities and asked them to enlarge and extend the piers to accommodate their new Olympic Class passenger liners, the *Olympic* and the *Titanic*. However, their request was turned down with city officials stating that the proposed new longer piers would extend too far into the Hudson River and, therefore, become a hazard to navigation. However, the American tycoon and owner of the White Star Line, John Pierpont Morgan, exerted his influence and the piers were extended.

Sister ships *Olympic* (left) and *Titanic* (right) photographed at high tide outside the Thompson Graving Dock at Harland & Wolff in early 1912. This was one of only a few occasions when both ships would be seen together. (Jonathan Smith postcard collection)

TITANIC AND HER SISTERS

Titanic was the second ship of an intended trio of Olympic Class passenger liners ordered by the White Star Line for their North Atlantic service. Her sister ships, the *Olympic* (1911) and the *Britannic* (1914) were built to compete with Cunard's express turbine-powered sister ships, the *Mauretania* and the *Lusitania*, which were both launched in 1906. Cunard's two leviathans had both won the coveted *Blue Riband* for the fastest North Atlantic crossing. The *Lusitania* had set four consecutive new speed records between October 1907 and August 1909 whilst the *Mauretania* held the *Blue Riband* from September 1909 until the *Bremen* set a new record twenty years later. The new White Star Line's ships were designed to be the largest and most luxurious ocean liners in the world but were not built to surpass the speed of the Cunard liners.

--------- Did You Know That? ---------

The *Lusitania* was sunk by a German U-boat on 7th May 1915 eight miles (15 km) off the coast of southern Ireland. The great vessel sank in just 18 minutes, resulting in the loss of 1,201 of the 1,961 people aboard.

ADVERTISING TITANIC

Second-class Two-Berth Stateroom

'It would have been difficult a few years ago to conceive such sumptuous appointments in the Second-class ...... natural light to each cabin; the rooms are finished enamel white and have mahogany furniture covered with moquette and linoleum tiles on the floor.'

White Star Line, Belfast March 1912

THE MOVIE TRIVIA

James Cameron was concerned that the davits might not be strong enough to lower the boats into the water when they were fully loaded. The davits used in the movie were fine and were actually made by the same company as the ones used on *Titanic* in 1912.

THE WORLD'S LARGEST SHIP

With a Gross Registered Tonnage (GRT) of 46,328 tons, *Titanic* was the world's largest ship in 1912. The *Olympic*, built before the *Titanic*, was used as the model for making *Titanic* bigger, better and much more luxurious. As a direct result of experiences during the first year of *Olympic's* service, several modifications were brought about by the White Star Line in conjunction with the Harland & Wolff Shipyard that improved *Titanic* by way of accommodation and comfort. Whilst the White Star Line's third ship in their trio of Olympic Class passenger liners, *Britannic*, was being fitted out at the Harland & Wolff Shipyard in Belfast, the First World War broke out in August 1914. *Britannic* was completed as a hospital ship, HMHS *Britannic*, and was sunk after striking a mine in 1916 and consequently never entered commercial service.

Did You Know That?

When the White Star Line's RMS *Celtic* was launched on 4th April 1901 at the Harland & Wolff Shipyard in Belfast, it was the largest ship in the world at the time (with a GRT of 20,904 tons).

HARLAND & WOLFF'S SLIPWAYS

In 1908, a mammoth steel gantry, designed and constructed for the Harland & Wolff Shipyard in Belfast by Sir William Arrol & Co. of Glasgow, weighing almost 6,000 tons with a height of 228 feet to the top of the upper crane, was erected over Slipways Nos. 2 and 3 at the Belfast yard for the construction of *Olympic* and *Titanic*. In 1911, Harland & Wolff had 9 slipways for the construction of ships of varying sizes. Slipways Nos. 2 and 3 were specifically built to accommodate the *Olympic* and the *Titanic* and replaced three smaller slips.

─────────── Did You Know That? ───────────

Prior to the outbreak of the First World War in August 1914, all of the White Star Line's ships, with the exception of one, were built in Belfast.

TITANIC'S DUMMY FOURTH FUNNEL

RMS *Titanic*'s 'dummy' fourth funnel was not connected to her 29 coal-fired boilers. It was positioned above the turbine engine room with the intention of giving the vessel a more powerful look as many people equated the number of funnels a ship had with the ship's power. However, the dummy funnel did actually provide ventilation for *Titanic*'s turbine engine room, the reciprocating engine room, the galleys, the first-class and second-class hospital and the coal-burning fireplace in the first-class smoking room.

─────────── Did You Know That? ───────────

In May 1911, some 15,000 men worked at the Harland & Wolff Shipyard in Belfast with 3,000 (20% of the workforce) working on the construction of *Titanic* alone. When the two ships were completed they were the largest moving objects in the world.

ADVERTISING TITANIC

Second-class Single-Berth Stateroom

'The White Star Line has done much to increase the attractions of second-class accommodation during recent years, having made a special feature of this in a number of their vessels; and in the Olympic and Titanic it will be found that this class of passenger has been generously provided for.'

White Star Line, Belfast March 1912

H&W'S DRAWING ROOM

Naval architects and draughtsmen designed *Olympic* and *Titanic* in Harland & Wolff's enormous drawing room. The spacious room had a high barrel ceiling and its large number of windows made maximum use of natural light.

──────────────── Did You Know That? ────────────────

The original drawing room and an adjacent drawing room have survived to the present day and can be found at Queen's Island, now incorporating *Titanic Quarter.*

OLYMPIC AND *TITANIC* NUMBERED

Harland & Wolff's 'Dimensions Book' recorded technical descriptions and particulars of all ships built at Queen's Island by the Belfast Shipyard. Every ship was identified by an individual Yard Number which was allocated in chronological order of the company receiving the order to build it. RMS *Olympic* was Yard No. 400 and RMS *Titanic* was Yard No. 401.

LOOKING GOOD

The shell plating of RMS *Titanic* was completed on 19th October 1910, the day before her sister ship, RMS *Olympic*, was launched in Belfast. Much publicity surrounded the two ocean liners at the time. The White Star Line wanted maximum public interest for the *Olympic* and the *Titanic* and ordered that the hull of the *Olympic* to be painted light grey so the ship would look outstanding when photographed at her launch. In contrast, the *Titanic* was not specially painted for her launch on 31st May 1911.

──────────────── Did You Know That? ────────────────

A special grandstand for spectators was built prior to the launch of the *Titanic*.

TITANIC – THE GAME

In 1998, *Titanic: The Board Game* became briefly available in Britain but has not been re-released since.

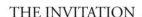

THE INVITATION

The White Star Line and Harland & Wolff Shipyard issued tickets to everyone connected with the construction of the *Titanic* to attend the official launch of the Olympic Class passenger liner in Belfast on 31st May 1911. The ticket read: *Launch of White Star Royal Mail Triple-Screw Steamer Titanic at Belfast, Wednesday 31st May 1911 at 12:15pm.*

THE LOST TREASURE

For many years after the *Titanic* sank on 15th April 1912, until the great ship was found lying on the floor of the Atlantic in September 1985, many people believed that a fortune in banknotes, jewels and gold bullion lay inside the ship's rusting hull. Numerous stories circulated after the sinking that her passengers were unable to retrieve their valuables because the Enquiry Office was not attended. Some survivors claimed that staff from the ship's Enquiry Office were too busy urging passengers to go back to their rooms to get dressed and put on lifebelts that they had no time to assist those passengers who were seeking to reclaim their possessions. However, to this day the wreck of RMS *Titanic* has never given up anything close to resembling a treasure of valuables.

WRONGLY ACCUSED

William Thompson Sloper, a stockbroker and estate manager, sailed on *Titanic's* maiden voyage on his way home to the USA after having spent three months in Europe on holiday. Sloper boarded *Titanic* in Southampton as a first-class passenger. When *Titanic* struck the iceberg, he was playing bridge with a friend, the actress Dorothy Gibson. Sloper watched Gibson get into Lifeboat No.7 and she urged him to join her. At first he refused informing her that the ship was 'unsinkable' before her pleas finally persuaded him to join her in the lifeboat. Lifeboat No.7 was picked up by the *Carpathia* and the *Titanic* survivors in it were taken to New York. As one of the few men rescued at the time, many of the local reporters in New York were clamouring for his story of events and pestered him at his room in the Waldorf-Astoria Hotel. However, one of Sloper's best friends was Jack Vance, the editor of his hometown paper, the *New Britain Herald*, and so Sloper decided that he was only prepared to relive his traumatic experience with Vance. The collective press in New York were angry with Sloper for spurning their advances and a journalist for the *New York Herald* printed a story on 19th April 1912 claiming that Sloper had dressed in women's clothes to escape the sinking ship. Sloper was enraged at being falsely accused of cowardice but on the advice of his father and family members he decided not to sue the paper or the reporter for defamation of character, believing that the furore would soon pass. However, he spent the rest of his life refuting the false accusation made

against him and died in May 1955. He was buried at Fairview Lawn Cemetery, New Britain, Connecticut. It is claimed that Sloper met Miss Alice Elizabeth Fortune on holiday in Europe in early 1912 and was so in love with her that he cancelled his trip home on the *Mauretania* in order to travel with Alice who was also booked on *Titanic's* maiden voyage to New York. Alice also survived the *Titanic* disaster and on 8th June 1912, she married her fiancé, Charles Holden Allen.

FIERCE COMPETITION

At the turn of the 20th century the White Star Line and a few other British shipping companies were owned by an American business conglomerate, the International Mercantile Marine Co. The White Star Line's main rival, the Cunard Line, did not have the finances available to construct new vessels without financial assistance. The British Government granted the Cunard Line a £2 million low interest loan repayable over 20 years with the caveat that the company remained in British hands. The injection of this fresh capital led to the construction of RMS *Lusitania* and RMS *Mauretania*.

◼ THE MOVIE TRIVIA ◼◼◼◼◼◼◼◼◼◼◼◼◼◼◼

Kate Winslet developed pneumonia while filming the water scenes.

—————— Did You Know That? ——————

In 1910, competition was so fierce for passengers on the transatlantic route that a person could book third class passage on a liner travelling from England to the USA for as little as £7.00 (about $35.00).

ON THE ROCKS

After *Titanic* struck the iceberg chunks of ice fell on to the forward Well Deck. In the 1958 movie *A Night To Remember*, passengers were shown picking up some of the small chunks of ice which fell on to the deck and dropping them in their drinks.

—————— Did You Know That? ——————

Icebergs smell of decaying sea life, not exactly something you would want to mix with your martini or whisky.

A FINAL MESSAGE

On 11th April 1912, Mr Robert Phillips, who was travelling on the *Titanic* in second class with his daughter, Alice, sent a postcard from the ship when it stopped at Queenstown, County Cork, Ireland. Queenstown was the ship's last port of call before sailing for New York. The postcard read:

Dear Bill,

Just a line to let you know we are all right up to now and having a jolly time. I wrote to Bill yesterday, if you call in he will tell what I have said. Kindest regards to you and the wife from one of the old school. Alice has made friends with a gentleman and wife and two daughters that sit at the same table.

R.Phillips

--- Did You Know That? ---

Mr Phillips lost his life in the *Titanic* disaster but Alice survived.

TO BOLDLY GO WHERE NO MAN HAS GONE BEFORE

Star Trek: Hidden Frontier was a *Star Trek* fan film project which featured 50 episodes between 2000 and 2007. In one of the episodes entitled 'Two Hours' we witness the sinking of the *Titanic* as a direct result of one of the characters in the episode tampering with a timeline.

ADVERTISING TITANIC

Second-class Dining Saloon

'The panelling of this room is carried out in oak … at the forward end a specially-designed sideboard, with a piano in the centre, is provided; the furniture is in mahogany, the upholstery of crimson leather and the floor has linoleum tiles of special design.'

White Star Line, Belfast March 1912

ITANIC

The *Intel*-manufactured Itanium microprocessor has often been jokingly referred to by the press as 'Itanic', because after its release the microprocessor's sales were spectacularly short of the company's expectations.

■ THE MOVIE TRIVIA ■■■■■■■■■■■■■■■

James Cameron was so overwhelmed following his first dive to explore *Titanic* he actually ended up spending more time with the ship than its living passengers did.

AN EXPENSIVE DINNER

At a *Titanic* memorabilia auction held by Henry Aldridge & Son at The British Titanic Society's annual convention in Southampton on 12th April 2002, a dinner menu from 10th April 1912 was placed up for auction. The menu had been sent by Charles Casswill, a Steward in *Titanic's* first-class section, to his wife Hilda. Although broken in two pieces, it realised a world record sum of £27,000. The menu showed that the first-class passengers onboard the *Titanic*, including John Jacob Astor IV (the richest man on the ship), J. Bruce Ismay (the Chairman and Managing Director of the White Star Line) and Captain Edward Smith would have dined upon such delights as turbot, whitebait, mutton, duckling and veal.

TITANIC GHOSTBUSTERS

In *Ghostbusters II,* the 1989 sequel to *Ghostbusters* (1984), a dock master at New York harbour calls the police and informs them that the *Titanic* had arrived in port. One of the dock workers turns to the other and says: 'Better late than never.'

THE DOROTHY BAIRD

It has sometimes been claimed that the *Dorothy Baird*, a three-masted schooner, was in close proximity to RMS *Titanic* after she struck an iceberg at 11:40pm on 14th April 1912. However, there is no documentary evidence to support this claim.

LADY PUNK OUT TO PROTECT *TITANIC*

Lady Punk, a popular Polish rock band which started in Warsaw in 1982, released more than 20 albums and over 200 songs. One of their songs, '*Zostawcie Titanica*', is an open plea by the band members for the wreck of the great ship not to be disturbed.

PUT TO THE SABRE

The Buffalo Sabres' 2006–07 season in the National Hockey League (NHL) saw the Sabres advance to the Eastern Conference Finals before losing in seven games to the Carolina Hurricanes (who went on to win the coveted Stanley Cup) is referred to as the *Titanic Season*.

THE *TITANIC* IN SPACE

Virgil Ivan 'Gus' Grissom, one of the original NASA Project Mercury astronauts and a United States Air Force pilot, whose *Liberty Bell 7 Mercury* spacecraft sank after its 1961 flight (the second American suborbital spaceflight), named his *Gemini 3* spacecraft *Molly Brown* as a reference to the famous 'Unsinkable Molly Brown' (a *Titanic* survivor) in the hope that his second craft would be unsinkable. After splashdown the craft's hatch blew off and the resulting flood of water into the small capsule caused her to sink, but Grissom managed to escape. He was killed along with fellow astronauts Ed White and Roger Chaffee during a training exercise and pre-launch test for the *Apollo 1* mission at the Kennedy Space Center, Florida, USA on 27th January 1967. Grissom was a recipient of the Distinguished Flying Cross and was posthumously awarded the Congressional Space Medal of Honour.

─────── Did You Know That? ───────

In an episode of the popular American animated sitcom *South Park* (entitled 'Summer Sucks'), Cartman, Kenny, Kyle and Stan pick up their instruments and play 'Nearer My God To Thee' amid the chaos created by the black snake.

A LETTER FROM RMS *CARPATHIA*

At a *Titanic* memorabilia auction held by Henry Aldridge & Son at The British Titanic Society's annual convention in Southampton on 12th April 2002, a very rare letter written by Captain Arthur Rostron on board the *Carpathia*, one of the ships which picked up *Titanic* survivors on 15th April 1912, was sold to an American collector of *Titanic* memorabilia for £3,100.

Did You Know That?

In 1999, Henry Aldridge & Son auctioned the Miss Clear Annie Cameron archive of letters for £60,000. Miss Cameron was a second-class passenger on *Titanic* and a small photograph taken of her before she left for New York was sold to a private buyer for £7,700 against fierce competition from bidders in the room and on the telephone.

TITANIC HITS BROADWAY

The *Titanic* disaster was made into a Broadway musical, *Titanic*, written by Peter Stone with music and lyrics by Maury Yeston. The musical ran from 23rd April 1997 to 21st March 1999, winning 5 Tony Awards in its inaugural year including Best Score, Best Book and Best Musical. The show ran for 804 performances and 26 previews and has been translated into five languages: Japanese, French, Dutch, German and Finnish.

SS FRANKFURT

Over the years since the *Titanic* sank, some have claimed that the North German Lloyd Steamship Company's steamer SS *Frankfurt*, was very close to *Titanic's* position. On 24th April 1912, nine days after *Titanic* sank, a newspaper published in Bremerhaven, Germany carried a story that Captain Hattorff of the *Frankfurt* claimed that his ship was the first ship to receive *Titanic's* CQD appeal for help, doing so at 12:10 am on 15th April 1912, which was just half an hour after *Titanic* collided with an iceberg. At the time *Titanic* gave her position as 41.54 latitude and 50.24 longitude which was 140 nautical miles away from the *Frankfurt*. However, Captain Hattorff said his ship did not reach the scene of the disaster until 10.00am on Monday 15th April 1912, some 7 hours and 40 minutes after the leviathan sank. Captain Hattorff stated that he had seen three huge icebergs en route to and in the area of the disaster, one which measured 120 feet high and 900 feet long, including an iceberg which *Titanic* may have struck and which reportedly bore evidence of the collision.

TITANIC READY FOR SEA

Titanic was finally completed on 1st April 1912 and ready to sail from Belfast to Southampton. However her departure from the Harland & Wolff Shipyard was postponed until the following day due to a strong north-west wind.

TELLING THE SISTERS APART

From an external view *Titanic* can be most readily distinguished from her sister ship, *Olympic*, by the forward end of A Deck which was enclosed to protect her passengers from windblown spray, which proved bothersome on the *Olympic*.

■ THE MOVIE TRIVIA ■ ■ ■ ■ ■ ■ ■ ■ ■ ■ ■ ■ ■

The ship was built to full scale but the lifeboats and funnels were shrunk by 10%.

UNDER THE HAMMER

A second-class passenger list from the *Titanic* was sold for £42,000 at an auction held by Henry Aldridge and Son on 18th April 2009. At the sale, a letter from SS *Minia*, one of the four Canadian recovery ships chartered by the White Star Line after the sinking of the *Titanic*, fetched £17,500 and a rare *Titanic* promotional poster printed by the Liverpool Printing and Stationery Company made £29,500. Other important pieces included: a piece of *Titanic* wreck wood from the Grand Aft Staircase was sold for £23,500; a letter from a *Titanic* crewman who was writing to his father from the *Carpathia* on 19th April 1912 (which fetched £11,100); and two *Titanic* postcards (one sent by Richard Smith and the other sent by Herbert Denbuoy) which made £10,000 and £8,200 respectively, the latter having been sold only months before at a London saleroom for £1,200. The last *Titanic* survivor, Millvina Dean, consigned several pieces from her personal collection to the auction – nothing from the ship itself but including a suitcase given to the Dean family by the people of New York a few days after the sinking. This was sold for £10,800 together with a selection of *Titanic* relief fund letters that made £11,000 and a selection of limited edition prints which fetched £9,250.

Did You Know That?

When the English bidder who purchased Millvina's suitcase went up to pay for it, he handed over the money and told the auctioneer to give the suitcase back to Millvina.

TITANIC'S GENERAL CHARACTERISTICS

Class and type:	Olympic Class ocean liner
Tonnage:	46,328 gross register tons (GRT)
Displacement at load draft:	52,310 tons
Length:	882 ft 9 inches (269.1m)
Beam:	92 ft 6 inches
Height:	175 ft (Keel to the top of her funnels)
Draught aft:	34 ft 7 inches
Draft forward:	34 ft 6 inches
Passengers & crew (fully loaded)	3,547
Staterooms	835 First-class: 416 Second-class: 162 Third-class: 257
Decks:	11 – Boat Deck, the Promenade (A) Deck, B, C, D, E, F, G, Orlop, Lower Orlop Deck and the Tank Top

TITANIC GUINNESS TV AD BANNED

In 2004, a Guinness television advertisement focusing on the *Titanic* was banned by the Advertising Standards Authority for Ireland (ASAI) after it was considered to be insensitive and in bad taste after a number of complaints were received by the ASAI. The advertisement featured two men talking about 'the best pint of Guinness'. One of the men says that the best pint is always the last and proceeds to order a drink for his friend, asking the barman to put it on his tab. The viewer then sees the sign '*RMS Titanic*' as the on-screen shot tilts to the side. Many of the complainants said that the use of the sinking of the *Titanic* as a setting for an advertisement was offensive while several of the complaints that were received were lodged by people who were children or grandchildren of those who lost their lives in the tragedy. In response the advertisers, Diageo Guinness and the Irish International Agency, said it was never their intention to cause offence or produce an advertisement in bad taste.

THE FINAL MEAL

The final meal served on *Titanic* on the evening of 14th April 1912, was recreated at a special event hosted by Liverpool's Lord Mayor, Councillor Steve Rotheram, on 14th July 2008. The special event saw representatives from five of the cities connected with the ship's doomed maiden voyage (Belfast, Cherbourg, Cobh, Liverpool and Southampton) gather to discuss how one of the worst maritime disasters that has ever occurred should be commemorated in the run-up to the centenary of the sinking. The Lord Mayors of Belfast, Cobh and Southampton attended the special event and were served:

****
Consommé Olga (clear soup garnished with scallops and cucumber)
****
Filet Mignons Lili (fillet steak medallions with Madeira sauce)
****
Courgette Farci (stuffed courgette with wild mushrooms)
****
Boiled potatoes, Parmentier potatoes, creamed carrots and petit pois
****
Chocolate and Vanilla Paris-Brest
****
Coffee and Petit Fours
****

Before the special menu was served, the representatives signed a Memorandum of Understanding, outlining their commitment to planning and organising the programme of events marking the 100th anniversary of *Titanic's* sinking.

WHEN GOD CAME FIRST

On the same day that the *Titanic* struck an iceberg, Sunday 14th April 1912, Captain Smith cancelled a lifeboat drill because the conditions were too windy. Boat and fire drills for crew members on board ships were customarily held once a week on Sundays, weather permitting. Passengers did not participate in either.

A *TITANIC* FLOP

In 1980, it cost the film and television company ITC $30 million to make *Raise The Titanic*. It was released the same year as *The Empire Strikes Back,* the second part of George Lucas's blockbuster *Star Wars* series, cost twice as much to make but made nowhere near the revenues which Lucas's movie pulled in at the box offices. Despite backing *Raising The Titanic* Sir Lew Grade, founder of ITC, is said to have later remarked: 'It would have been cheaper to lower the Atlantic.'

UNFILLED LIFEBOATS

At the British Board of Trade Inquiry following the sinking of the *Titanic*, some of the crew members who were responsible for loading the lifeboats claimed that the lifeboats did not appear to them to be strong enough to be lowered with 65 people in them. However, the lifeboats had been rigorously tested in Belfast on 25th March 1912 with over 70 men being lowered in some of them. None of *Titanic's* officers were informed of the test.

TITANIC – THE ARTIFACT EXHIBITION

On 3rd October 2009, *Titanic: The Artifact Exhibition* opened at the Louisville Science Center, 727 West Main Street, Louisville, Kentucky, USA and featured 150 artefacts recovered from the world's most famous passenger liner. The exhibition focuses on *Titanic's* compelling human stories as best told through the artefacts. Each visitor is given a 'Boarding Pass' when they enter the exhibition with the name of a passenger printed on the ticket who sailed on Titanic's doomed maiden voyage. At the end of the exhibition, the visitors enter the 'Memorial Gallery' where they can inspect the Memorial Wall to discover if their passenger survived or perished. The exhibition is produced by the Atlanta-based company, RMS Titanic, Inc.

Did You Know That?

RMS Titanic, Inc. is the only entity in the world permitted by law to recover objects from the wreck of the *Titanic*.

SS *NOMADIC* SAVED

On 16th September 2009, it was announced that a £7 million restoration of SS *Nomadic*, a ship purpose-built as a tender to ferry passengers from Cherbourg Harbour out to RMS *Titanic* ahead of its ill-fated maiden Atlantic voyage, was to begin in the spring of 2010 after the project secured a £500,000 cash injection. The grant was given by the Northern Ireland Tourist Board (NITB) to the Nomadic Trust, the government-appointed charitable trust to oversee the restoration of the ship, and pushed the total raised to refit the ship past the £4 million mark.

Did You Know That?

The *Nomadic* was saved from a wrecker's yard in France in 2006 by the Stormont Executive.

A DISTURBING DREAM

It is reported that Anna Lewis, a 14-year old girl, had a dream on 12th April 1912 in which she saw herself walking towards Trentham Park in Stoke-on-Trent, England. In her dream she claimed that she suddenly saw a very large ship a short distance away as if it was actually inside the park. Anna said that she saw several figures walking about on the ship and could hear people screaming before the ship lowered at one end and disappeared.

Did You Know That?

Anna's uncle, Senior Fourth Engineer Leonard Hodgkinson, was on the *Titanic* when it struck an iceberg two days after she experienced her dream and he went down with the ship.

TITANIC'S AUNT ON HER WAY

The *Baltic,* a White Star Line vessel built in 1903 by the Harland & Wolff Shipyard, Belfast was one of the ships in wireless radio contact with the Marconi Radio Station at Cape Race after *Titanic* struck an iceberg at 11:40pm on Sunday 14th April 1912. About half an hour later the Marconi Radio Station notified several vessels, including the *Baltic,* that the *Titanic* had issued a distress signal. The *Baltic* was approximately 200 miles from *Titanic* and expected to be on the scene of the disaster around 12.00 noon on Monday 15th April 1912. Three years prior to being asked to assist her older relative the *Titanic,* the *Baltic* was involved in a similar rescue operation. At 5.30 am on 23rd January 1909, while the *Titanic* was still under construction, the White Star Line's *Republic,* outward bound from New York for Mediterranean ports, collided with the *Florida,* a steamship owned by the Lloyd Italiano Line bound for New York. The collision occurred 250 miles from New York and just 26 miles southeast of the Nantucket Lightship in the foggy waters of the Atlantic.

Did You Know That?

In 1904, the first radio distress signal CQD was adopted. Interestingly, this signal was used for the first time five years later when the *Republic* and the *Florida* collided.

TITANIC STOUT

The Titanic Brewery was founded in 1985 in Burslem, Stoke-on-Trent, England. Most of their excellent range of beers have names that relate to a nautical theme including: 'White Star', 'Iceberg', 'Anchor', 'Lifeboat', 'Captain Smith's', 'Steerage', and 'Titanic Stout'. Titanic Stout is a dark beer which has a 4.5% ABV rating and is brewed using Maris Otter pale malt, wheat malt and roasted barley as well as Northdown, Yakima, Galena and Goldings hops.

Did You Know That?

The brewery took its *Titanic* name because it is located a short distance from Etruria, the birthplace of Captain Edward John Smith, *Titanic's* captain.

TITANIC HAT RIBBON

On 11th April 2003, a sailor's hat ribbon which was rescued by a young boy when the *Titanic* was slowly sinking on 15th April 1912, was sold at auction at the Hilton Hotel, Southampton for £34,000. The embroidered hatband bears the name RMS *Titanic* in gold thread, and is widely believed to be the only such souvenir from the doomed liner. Marshall Brines Drew was an 8-year-old passenger on *Titanic* and he took the ribbon with him as he was lowered in Lifeboat No. 10 alongside his aunt.

Did You Know That?

At the time *Titanic* set sail souvenirs and assorted toiletries aboard ships were sold by the ship's barbers. There were no proper shops of any sort aboard passenger ships until sometime after World War I.

THE *TITANIC* QUARTER

Almost 100 years after RMS *Titanic* sank on her maiden voyage, the site of Europe's biggest riverside regeneration project, The Titanic Quarter, was opened in Belfast in January 2009 at the very same slipway where the famous vessel was launched. The Titanic Quarter is situated at the edge of the River Lagan and the initial plans for the site included approximately 1,000 luxury private flats, a purpose-built college of further education for 16,000 full-time and part-time students, a three-star hotel, a banking centre, a multimedia hub and a Titanic Museum. The museum is to be partly modelled on the shape of the Guggenheim Museum in Bilbao, Spain.

THE UNWILLING PASSENGER

In early 1912, Benjamin Hart decided to emigrate to Canada with his family and booked himself, his wife Esther and their daughter, Eva, on *Titanic's* maiden voyage to New York. However, Mrs Hart had reservations about sailing on the *Titanic* after the family's original plans to travel to the USA on the *Philadelphia* were cancelled as a result of a coal strike at the time. But Mr Hart reassured his wife that everything would be fine as *Titanic* was deemed to be 'unsinkable'. Esther and Eva Hart survived the disaster but Benjamin lost his life. Many years later, Eva spoke about her mother's foreboding on the ship and the look on her father's face when he returned to their cabin after visiting the Boat Deck shortly after *Titanic* struck the iceberg. Mr Hart placed his wife and daughter in a lifeboat before going down with the ship.

ISMAY FORCED TO RESIGN

On 30th June 1913, in the midst of public ridicule and rumours surrounding the *Titanic* disaster 14 months earlier, J. Bruce Ismay was forced to step down from his position as President of the International Mercantile Marine Company (IMMC). Ismay had already announced his retirement as head of the White Star Line, which was owned by IMMC.

--------- Did You Know That? ---------

Ismay died a 74-year old recluse in 1937.

SHIP OF FOOLS

Many people aboard the *Titanic* did not believe that the ship was actually sinking after she struck the iceberg. At first they simply did not understand the gravity of the situation and, for that matter, neither did many of the stewards, stewardesses and other crew members who dealt directly with the passengers. Certainly, no one was telling the passengers that the ship was about to founder and the calm demeanour of the crew tended to work against those loading the boats by breeding complacency amongst the passengers. Faced with the choice of forsaking the solid decks, bright lights and warmth of a ship which was said to be 'practically unsinkable' for a small open boat and a long drop down to the freezing and pitch-black Atlantic below, many passengers elected to stay aboard the *Titanic*. For many their decision not to get into one of the ship's lifeboats cost them their lives.

SOUTHAMPTON REMEMBERS *TITANIC*'S DEAD

On Sunday 14th April 2002, an open-air service was held in Southampton on the eve of the 90th anniversary of the sinking of RMS *Titanic*. Approximately 400 people attended the commemoration at the Titanic Engineers' Memorial. Christine Kelly, the Mayor of Southampton, laid a wreath at the Memorial in memory of the engineers who gave their lives by remaining at their posts as well as the 549 people from the city who died on the world's most famous ship. Maritime organisations and members of the public also laid wreaths, including one in the colours of the White Star Line, *Titanic's* owners. As the wreaths were being laid, singer, Emma Scott-Copeland sang the hymn 'Nearer My God to Thee'. In her address to those in attendance, Mayor Kelly said: 'Ninety years ago an event took place that meant that in some streets in Southampton every household lost a family member.' Mayor Kelly went on to say that although the story of the Titanic had become a blockbuster movie, 'We want to remember the sinking, not the spectacle, not the entertainment.'

■ THE MOVIE TRIVIA ■ ■ ■ ■ ■ ■ ■ ■ ■ ■ ■ ■ ■

Most of the decor on the ship used in the movie was reconstructed by, or under the supervision of, the original companies which furnished the *Titanic* during its outfitting in Liverpool in 1911.

PLAYING TWO ROLES

The model ship used in the 1980 movie *Raise The Titanic*, was also used in a 1991 European six-hour TV mini-series about *Titanic's* sister ship, HMHS *Britannic*. In 1980, the model cost the movie studio £3 million to make and when it was completed, it was discovered there was no tank deep enough to accommodate it. Alongside the shallow water tank in Malta (one of the locations where the movie was filmed), teams constructed a new tank at a cost of £1 million. The European mini-series was called *Gluhender Himmel*.

Did You Know That?

In 1980, *Raise The Titanic* was the most popular movie to be shown during flights for airline passengers. In June 1980, ITV, a British television company, paid £500,000 for the rights to show the movie on TV.

GET THE FACTS RIGHT

In his best-selling novel *Raise The Titanic!* the author, Clive Cussler, has the first funnel of *Titanic* breaking off during the sinking, which is historically correct. However, in the 1980 movie *Raise The Titanic*, adapted from his book, we see the second funnel breaking off first, which is historically incorrect. The producers of the movie thought that if they depicted the second funnel of the ship breaking off first it would make the movie more dramatic and believed that many viewers wouldn't even notice that the first funnel was missing. How wrong they were! *Titanic* enthusiasts all over the world pointed out the obvious error.

■ THE MOVIE TRIVIA ■ ■ ■ ■ ■ ■ ■ ■ ■ ■ ■ ■ ■

Most of the ocean which the extras jumped into during filming was a mere 3 feet deep.

THE FORTUNE TELLER

Constance Willard was 20 years old when she boarded the *Titanic* as a first-class passenger at Southampton for the ship's maiden voyage. It is claimed that prior to *Titanic* setting sail, Miss Willard had her fortune told and was informed that she would die before her 21st birthday. When *Titanic* struck the iceberg, Miss Wallace thought that the spooky premonition was about to come true but she survived after being placed in one of the ship's lifeboats.

———————— Did You Know That? ————————

Miss Willard died in California on 25th April 1964, exactly
one week after the 52nd anniversary of her safe arrival in New York
onboard RMS *Carpathia*.

RMS *TITANIC* VISITS LONDON

On Friday 16th May 2003, in excess of 200 artefacts taken from the sunken wreck of the *Titanic* were placed on show at the Science Museum in South Kensington, London. Among the items on display were the ship's bell, a section of the ship's hull, passengers' jewellery, clothes, china and banknotes. The items were loaned to the Science Museum by RMS Titanic, Inc. which recovered more than 6,000 artefacts from the wreck site over six expeditions from 1987 to 2000.

WASHINGTON, D.C.'S *TITANIC* MEMORIAL

The Titanic Memorial is a granite statue which can be found in Washington, D.C. designed by Gertrude Vanderbilt Whitney and sculpted by John Horrigan. The statue stands 13 feet high and depicts a partly-clad male figure with his arms outstretched. It was erected by the Women's Titanic Memorial Association and was unveiled by Helen Herron Taft, the widow of President William Howard Taft, on 26th May 1931. In James Cameron's 1997 blockbuster movie *Titanic* we see Kate Winslet imitating the statue's pose on the bow of the ship. A replica of the head of the memorial, carved in marble and exhibited in Paris in 1921, was purchased by the French government for the Musée du Luxembourg in Paris. The inscription on the base of Washington's Titanic Memorial reads:

TO THE BRAVE MEN
WHO PERISHED
IN THE WRECK
OF THE TITANIC
APRIL 15 1912

THEY GAVE THEIR
LIVES THAT WOMEN
AND CHILDREN
MIGHT BE SAVED
ERECTED BY THE
WOMEN OF AMERICA

HOCUS POCUS

Some *Titanic* writers have argued that a reading of the stars (as practised by astrologers not astronomers) indicated that the planets were aligned in a way that foretold that *Titanic's* maiden voyage was doomed to disaster. Others claimed that strange birds were seen flying over the Harland & Wolff Shipyard in Belfast when the ship was launched.

GEORGIA ON MY MIND

In 1994, RMS Titanic, Inc. based in Atlanta, Georgia, USA was granted Salvor-in-Possession rights to the wreck of the *Titanic* by a United States Federal Court and has conducted numerous research and recovery expeditions to the wreck of the ship, recovering more than 5,500 artefacts. RMS Titanic, Inc. is a wholly-owned subsidiary of Premier Exhibitions Inc.

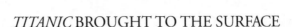

TITANIC BROUGHT TO THE SURFACE

On 10th August 1998, a large section of the *Titanic's* hull was raised to the surface despite protests by survivors and relatives of victims that the world's most famous ship is a sea grave and should be left alone. The hull was salvaged by RMS Titanic Inc., the company which has sole salvage rights for the wreck, and which at the time had already recovered in excess of 5,000 *Titanic* artefacts. The section of hull, known simply as 'The Big Piece,' was recovered from 2.5 miles below the North Atlantic, 370 miles off Newfoundland, Canada. It took just 40 minutes to raise the 20 ton, 14ft by 23ft steel section onto the deck of the salvage vessel *Abeille*. RMS Titanic Inc. had attempted unsuccessfully to raise the same piece of hull in 1996. Defending the salvage operation amid the storm of protests, Charles Haas, a historical advisor to RMS Titanic Inc., said: 'The Titanic has not revealed human remains in more than 130 dives by four different organisations.' However, in response Dan Conlin, the Curator of the Nova Scotia Maritime Museum, said: 'It's not a question of actually finding a bone. There are human remains in one form or another around that wreck, as well as all sorts of shattered lives directly associated with it. That does mean extra special care.'

Did You Know That?

The 'Big Piece' belonged to the C Deck on *Titanic's* starboard side. The portholes belonged to first-class cabins C-79 and C-81, neither of which were known to have been occupied.

TITANIC'S GRAVE

Most of the *Titanic's* 1,523 victims were never found and remain in their watery grave at the bottom of the Atlantic. Many of the bodies picked out of the Atlantic after the *Titanic* sank were brought to Halifax, Nova Scotia, Canada where they were stored in the Halifax Curling Rink, which was quickly made into a temporary morgue. The four vessels dispatched from Halifax recovered 328 bodies (SS *Mackay-Bennett* found 306 bodies, CS *Minia* found 17 bodies, CGS *Montmagny* found 4 bodies and SS *Algerine* found 1 body). Three other ships in the area of the disaster picked a further 8 bodies out of the freezing cold waters of the North Atlantic (RMS *Carpathia* – 4, RMS *Oceanic* – 3, SS *Ilford* – 1 and SS *Ottawa*-1). Almost one in three bodies (119) recovered by the seven ships were buried at sea, some too decomposed to preserve and others because regulations at the time permitted only embalmed bodies to be brought ashore. When the *Mackay-Bennett* ran out of embalming materials the ship's captain had to bury a number of the bodies at sea. A total of 150 bodies of passengers and crew members that were brought to Halifax are buried in three graveyards there. Fairview Lawn Cemetery holds the highest number of victims with 121 buried there; 19 were buried in the

Mount Olivet Catholic Cemetery; and the remaining 10 were buried in the Baron de Hirsch Jewish Cemetery. Visitors to Halifax can freely visit the graves at both the Fairview Lawn Cemetery and the Mount Olivet Catholic Cemetery but an appointment must be made to visit the Baron de Hirsch Jewish Cemetery. In total, 209 bodies were transported to Halifax with 59 claimed and taken elsewhere for burial. Of the 150 victims laid to rest in Halifax, a total of 42 have never been identified.

Did You Know That?

Of the 328 bodies recovered after the *Titanic* sank, including those buried at sea, 118 remain unidentified. Those unidentified victims have only a number on their tombstone with a date reading 15th April 1912.

FIRE ON THE *TITANIC*

When the *Titanic* left Belfast on 2nd April 1912 for Southampton, a fire had broken out in one of the ship's massive coal bunkers. It took a few days for successive watches of firemen to dig away at the surrounding coal in order to extinguish the fire. Some writers have suggested that the fire may have weakened a part of the hull which may then explain why the hull broke up so easily after it collided with the giant iceberg. But in reality any damage to the shell plating and frames in the area of the fire would not have compromised the structural integrity of the ship in any way that contributed to the flooding or break-up.

LUCKY FRANK

An urban legend claims that Frank Lucks Tower survived the sinkings of *Titanic* (April 1912), the *Empress of Ireland* (May 1914) and the *Lusitania* (May 1915). However, none of the crew lists from the three vessels show the name of Frank Lucks Tower as ever having served aboard them despite some stories claiming that he was a stoker on *Titanic* when she sailed on her maiden voyage to New York.

A HUNGRY SHIP

Titanic's coal bunkers held 6,611 tons of coal to feed the ship's 29 coal-fired boilers plus an additional 1,092 tons that could be held in the No. 3 (Bunker) Hold in place of cargo if necessary.

COUPLE MARRIED ON *TITANIC*

On 28th July 2001, a couple from New York, USA made history by getting married on the wreck of the *Titanic* inside a submersible. The pair, David Leibowitz and Kimberley Miller, descended 2.4 miles (4km) to the wreck beneath the North Atlantic in one of the submersibles used in James Cameron's 1997 movie *Titanic*. The newlyweds, keen scuba divers, had to remain on their knees throughout the marriage ceremony because the submersible was so small. Mr and Mrs Leibowitz strongly rejected allegations that their wedding was in bad taste and an insult to the 1,523 people who lost their lives in the disaster.

WORKERS TRAPPED IN *TITANIC*'S HULL

Another *Titanic* urban legend tells the story of workers trapped in the hull of the ship whilst it was being built at the Harland & Wolff Shipyard. However, the story is a complete myth and more than likely came about as a result of the inspections carried out to *Titanic's* hull at the end of each working day. Inspectors would check the work of the shipyard's riveters by tapping on the rivets from within the body of *Titanic's* hull to test their strength and to calculate whether or not any bonuses were due to the men for piece-work. Some riveters who heard the tapping sound as they stood outside on the dry dock would tease the young apprentices by telling them to go and get a bucket of sparks as there was someone trapped inside the ship's hull.

MILLVINA AND SOUTHAMPTON HONOUR *TITANIC*

On Monday 15th April 2002, *Titanic* survivor Millvina Dean commemorated the 90th anniversary of the ship's demise at a special event in Southampton. Miss Dean unveiled a plaque at the former headquarters of the ship's owners, the White Star Line, in Canute Road. At the time, Miss Dean was one of only four survivors of the disaster still alive. She was just 9 weeks old when the great ship sank. Miss Dean also opened a revamped exhibition of the *Titanic* at Southampton's Maritime Museum and launched web pages on the tragedy.

--- Did You Know That? ---

Miss Dean's father, Bertram, drowned when the *Titanic* sank but her mother, Georgetta, and her older brother, Bertram junior, were rescued by the *Carpathia*.

TITANIC'S PLANNED ROUTE

Belfast – Southampton, England ....471 miles

Southampton – Cherbourg, France ....84 miles

Cherbourg – Queenstown, Ireland ....307 miles

Queenstown – New York, USA ....2,825 miles

Did You Know That?

Titanic's planned return route was
New York – Plymouth – Cherbourg – Southampton.

TITANIC'S CLOTHING COMPANY CLOSED

In May 2009, Stephen Simpson Limited of Preston, England, a clothing firm established in 1827, closed down. The company once employed hundreds of people at the Gold Thread Works in Manchester Road, Avenham, Preston and most famously embroidered the uniforms for *Titanic's* staff.

TITANIC UNDER THE HAMMER

In June 2007, 18 lots of *Titanic* memorabilia including letters, postcards, telegrams from survivors and photographs of passengers went under the hammer at Christie's in New York. In total the artefacts fetched $193,140. A deck log from the *Mackay-Bennett* that searched for bodies after the *Titanic* sank sold for $102,000 (having had a pre-sale estimate of $30,000 – $50,000). The auction also included *Titanic's* first-class passenger list bearing the names of several prominent New York families such as the Astors, the Guggenheims and the Strauses. It fetched $48,000 and an eight-page handwritten description of the sinking written by 16-year old Laura Marie Cribb, of Newark, New Jersey who survived the disaster, was sold for $16,800. Laura was a third-class passenger rescued by the *Carpathia*, the first ship which arrived on the scene after *Titanic* sank, but her father died in the disaster. In her story Laura recalls the moment when *Titanic* struck the iceberg and how she watched the ship's many lights go out followed by the 'most terrible shrieks and groans from the helpless and doomed passengers who were left on the wreck of the great ship'.

THE ADDERGOOLE FOURTEEN

On 11th April 1912, a total of 113 third-class passengers boarded the *Titanic* at Queenstown (Cobh), Ireland. Fourteen of these passengers, three men and eleven women, were from Addergoole Parish (Lahardane), County Mayo, Ireland and were hoping to begin a new life in the USA. One of the women, Annie McGowan, had been born in America but later returned to Ireland with her parents as a child. Three others, Mary Mangan, Catherine Bourke and Catherine McGowan had emigrated several years ago and were returning to Chicago after a visit home. Just three days after leaving Queenstown, eleven of these fourteen died when the *Titanic* sank. These fourteen passengers are known locally as The Addergoole Fourteen. The eleven who died were: Catherine Bourke, John Bourke, Mary Bourke, Mary Canavan, Pat Canavan, Bridget Donohue, Nora Fleming, James Flynn, Catherine McGowan, Delia Mahon and Mary Mangan. Only Mary Mangan's body was found (recovered by the *Mackay-Bennett*) and then buried at sea after it had been identified, while some of her personal effects were eventually returned to her family. Meanwhile, the three survivors were all women – Anna Katherine (Annie Kate) Kelly, Delia McDermott and Annie McGowan. Annie Kate Kelly became a nun (she took the name of Sister Patrick Joseph Kelly) and the other two women married. All three lived long lives. Only Annie Kate Kelly paid a visit back to Mayo, when her mother died. The Addergoole Titanic Society was founded in 2002 by a small group of local residents, including relatives of The Addergoole Fourteen. Lahardane in Addergoole parish is known as 'Ireland's Titanic Village' and each year since 2002 the Timoney Bell in Saint Patrick's Church, Lahardane is tolled for one hour commencing at 2.20 am on 15th April to commemorate The Addergoole Fourteen. The bell ringing begins with slow knells for the eleven lives lost in the disaster followed by fast joyous rings for the three who survived. A large crowd attends this poignant ceremony each year while there is also a memorial in the church dedicated to Addergoole's *Titanic* passengers.

THE LUCK OF THE IRISH

In April 1912, two 18-year-old women from Lack, Turlough, Castlebar, County Mayo, purchased tickets for *Titanic's* maiden voyage and were scheduled to board the famous ocean liner when it stopped off at Queenstown (Cobh), Ireland en-route from Southampton to New York. However, Norah Callaghan from Lack East, Turlough did not use her *Titanic* ticket and instead boarded the White Star Liner RMS *Celtic* the day after the *Titanic* sailed. Meanwhile, Annie Jordan from Lack West, Turlough cancelled her planned trip as she had a facial rash at the time. The Ellis Island Records note that Norah arrived safely in New York on 20th April 1912.

Did You Know That?

Two members of *Titanic's* crew were also from Castlebar, County Mayo: William Duffy and Francis Young both lost their lives in the disaster.

◼ THE MOVIE TRIVIA ◼◼◼◼◼◼◼◼◼◼◼◼◼◼

The only real decks used in the movie were the boat deck and A deck, with a facade of plating and lighted portholes completed only on the starboard side of the ship.

TORONTO'S *TITANIC* LINK

In January 2008, twelve Toronto, Canada 5-cent streetcar tickets recovered from the shipwreck of the *Titanic* during a salvage expedition in 1987 went on display at the Ontario Science Centre in Toronto. The tickets belonged to Major Arthur Godfrey Peuchen, a first-class passenger who was travelling back to his home in Toronto on the ocean liner's ill-fated maiden voyage.

AN EXPENSIVE PASSENGER LIST

An extremely rare list of second-class passengers, which was carried off the *Titanic* by Mrs James Watt as the ship was sinking, was sold at auction at Christie's in New York on 25th June 2008 for $56,250.

Did You Know That?

A facing slip from a postal clerk on the *Titanic* fetched $21,250 at the same auction. RMS was never used as an abbreviation for Royal Mail ships collectively. RMS was only used in the singular form as part of the name for individual ships. Facing slips were used on Royal Mail ships to mark bundles of mail by their destination.

THE FIRST MEMORIAL

On 3rd May 1912, eighteen days after the *Titanic* sank, memorial services were held at St. Mary's Cathedral and the Brunswick Street Methodist Church in Halifax, Nova Scotia. During the services, 50 bodies were taken to the Fairview Cemetery for interment. A total of 150 victims from the *Titanic* disaster are buried in three separate graveyards in Halifax, Nova Scotia (121 of them in Fairview Cemetery).

GERMANY'S *TITANIC*

Some 33 years after RMS *Titanic* met her untimely end, the greatest marine disaster of all time took place on 30th January 1945. In excess of 9,000 people lost their lives when the Nazi flagship, MV *Wilhelm Gustloff*, packed with German refugees, was torpedoed in the Baltic Sea off Poland by the Soviet submarine *S-13*. There is an intriguing link between the *Titanic* and the *Wilhelm Gustloff*. In 1942, Adolf Hitler's Reichsminister of Propaganda, Joseph Goebbels, commissioned a movie to be made about the *Titanic*. The movie was filmed in Gdynia, Poland using the large German luxury liner *Cap Arcona* as a stand-in for the *Titanic*. During her life the *Wilhelm Gustloff* saw many incarnations: ocean liner, hospital ship, navy ship and rescue ship. The *Wilhelm Gustloff* was named after the assassinated German leader of the Swiss Nazi Party.

--- Did You Know That? ---

The *Wilhelm Gustloff* was originally to be named the *Adolf Hitler*.
However, following the assassination of Gustloff in Switzerland on 4th
February 1936, the Nazi propaganda machine saw an opportunity to
create a Nazi martyr. Hitler, being superstitious, asked Gustloff's wife
during her husband's memorial service if she would like the ship to be
named in honour of her late husband and she agreed. Ironically, Gustloff
was born on 30th January 1895, exactly 50 years prior to the sinking of
the ship named after him.

THE ROCK OF ICE

At one of the subsequent inquiries which followed the sinking of RMS *Titanic*, evidence given by one survivor described the iceberg which *Titanic* struck as: 'looking like the Rock of Gibraltar but a mirrored version'.

TITANIC'S RESCUE SHIP IS FOUND

On 6th September 1999, a group of treasure hunters found the wreck of RMS *Carpathia*, which rescued 705 survivors from the sinking *Titanic*. Graham Jessop, from the company Argosy International, said the *Carpathia* was found in 600 feet of water, 185 miles west of Land's End, Cornwall, England, using a sonar probe. The *Carpathia* was sunk by a German U-Boat in 1918 off Ireland's south coast while travelling from Liverpool to America. Five people died while 215 survived.

HITLER AND *TITANIC*

The *Titanic* and Adolf Hitler are the most popular archive newsreel downloads at the British Museum, London. Footage of the *Titanic* setting sail from Southampton on her doomed maiden voyage to New York is the most popular film downloaded from the *Pathe News* online archive. Meanwhile, Adolf Hitler's election as German Chancellor sits second in the Top 5 listings while *Titanic* also makes No.4.

Pathe News Top 5 Downloads		
1	*Titanic* sets sail on her maiden voyage	(1912)
2	Adolf Hitler is elected Chancellor of Germany	(1933)
3	D-Day	(1944)
4	The sinking of the *Titanic*	(1912)
5	The Beatles win the Radio Caroline Award	(1965)

TWO EXPENSIVE MARCONIGRAMS

Miss Elisabeth Walton Allen was 29 years old when she boarded *Titanic* in Southampton as a first-class passenger. She was making her way back home to St. Louis prior to her forthcoming marriage to a British doctor, Dr James B. Mennell. She was accompanied on the ship by Mrs Robert (her aunt), Miss Madill (her cousin) and Mrs Robert's maid, Emilie Kreuchen. All four women were placed in one of the last lifeboats to leave, Lifeboat No. 2, under the command of Fourth Officer Joseph G. Boxhall and were rescued by the *Carpathia*. Whilst onboard the *Carpathia* Miss Allen received a Marconigram dated 17th April 1912 which read: 'Have wired Belmont reservation for you and to furnish any funds needed/Marill.' The telegram, along with a small photo of Miss Allen and a list of the passengers in Lifeboat No. 2, was sold at auction at Christie's in New York on 25th June 2008 for $8,125. A Marconigram sent on 18th April 1912, by a *Titanic* survivor named Helen after being rescued by the *Carpathia*, simply reading: 'Safe on Carpathia/Helen' realised $6,250 at the same auction.

LAST KNOWN PHOTO OF *TITANIC* ICEBERG

In August 2002, the only known photograph of the iceberg believed to have sunk the *Titanic* went on display in the UK for the first time. The sepia picture was one of several taken by Stephan Rehorek of two icebergs on 20th April 1912, just five days after the *Titanic* sank. The photograph belongs to Henning Pfeifer, a collector of *Titanic* memorabilia, and was a key exhibit at Europe's largest ever *Titanic* exhibition which was held in Dundee from 10th–18th August 2002. Rehorek was a Czech sailor on the German cruise ship MS *Bremen*, which had been en route from Bremerhaven to New York but was requested to divert her course to the scene of the *Titanic* disaster to assist. However, the *Bremen* was not needed as the *Mackay-Bennett* and three other Canadian vessels had been chartered by the White Star Line to retrieve bodies from the wreck site and were only two hours away. Upon his arrival in New York on 25th April 1912, Rehorek sent a postcard home. The front of the postcard depicted a photograph of the *Titanic* and he wrote the following on the reverse side: 'Dear Mother and Father. Best wishes from New York. I am sending you a picture of an ocean liner which sank on its maiden voyage. It was the biggest in the world. Two days away from New York it collided with an iceberg and the ship was severely damaged on one side. Almost 1,600 people drowned and about 670 were rescued. I have a photograph of the iceberg and will send it to you. I also saw the bodies of the drowned and the wreckage from the ship. It was a dreadful sight.' A few weeks later Rehorek paid for his photographs of the two icebergs to be reprinted on to postcards and he posted one of them to his mother and father from Cherbourg. On the reverse side of the postcard he wrote: 'Dear Mother and Father. This card is a view of the iceberg that collided with and sank the Titanic liner. I will send a card to Josef too.'

THE PRICE OF A LIFE

A life preserver from the *Titanic* comprising twelve rectangular cork-filled stitched canvas panels with shoulder rests and side straps was sold at auction at Christie's in New York on 25th June 2008 for a staggering $68,500. The life preserver was recovered from the scene of the *Titanic* disaster by John James Dunbar from North Lake (Cape Breton), Nova Scotia, Canada who is believed to have been aboard one of the ships which left Halifax, Nova Scotia to recover bodies out of the water from the wreckage of the *Titanic*.

GOD WAS ON HIS SIDE

When the *Titanic* set sail from Southampton for New York on 10th April 1912, the Reverend John Stuart Holden was unable to use his first-class ticket after his wife became ill the previous day. Instead, he remained in England to care for his wife and when the *Titanic* sank five days later he mounted the ticket in a cardboard frame on which he wrote: 'Who redeemeth thy life from destruction.' He then hung the frame on a wall in his study to remind him of his lucky escape. Sometime after his death, the precious ticket was donated to Liverpool's Merseyside Maritime Museum. However, the ticket was considered too valuable to place on display and was instead safely housed in the museum's archive. In September 2003, the ticket finally went on public display at the Maritime Archives and Library.

BELFAST PROUD

In April 2002, Belfast marked the 90th anniversary of the launch of the *Titanic* with a week-long celebration in the city where the ship was built. 'Titanic – Made in Belfast' commenced with actors playing the crew and passengers of the ship in the grounds of Belfast City Hall. As part of the anniversary Belfast City Council unveiled a plaque at the home of the ship's designer, Thomas Andrews, while Belfast Lord Mayor, Jim Rodgers, opened an exhibition of *Titanic* memorabilia in the City Hall. The Belfast Titanic Society staged a gala ball in full Edwardian costume and a replica seven-course meal from *Titanic's* menu at Belfast City Hall. A spokesman for the Council said: 'The city was very proud of her, and we're trying to recapture that pride.' Meanwhile special tours of *Titanic's* place of birth, Harland & Wolff Shipyard, were also made available to the general public.

THE *TITANIC* ANGLE

When some 38,000 tons of water filled her bow and pulled it under, *Titanic's* stern rose out of the water, resulting in the ship breaking in two. To this date there is ongoing debate about the exact nature of how the ship broke in two. However, the most recent analyses indicate that the ill-fated ocean liner most likely broke apart at a much shallower angle than initially believed, possibly 11 degrees.

POPE PRAYS FOR *TITANIC*'S LOST SOULS

Pope Saint Pius X (who served as Pope from 5th August 1903 – 20th August 1914) held a mass at St. Peter's Basilica at the Vatican in Rome for all of those who lost their lives in the *Titanic* disaster.

THE QUEEN OF THE OCEAN

Some of the White Star Line's posters advertising *Titanic's* first return voyage from New York to Southampton described the luxury liner as 'The Queen of the Ocean'.

ILLEGAL ALIENS LAND IN NEW YORK

In 1912, US law specifically stipulated that all ships arriving at a port in the United States of America were responsible for ensuring that all non-US citizens on board were admissible to the country under US law. If someone was deemed to be an illegal alien then he/she would be prevented from entering the USA while the owners of the ship he/she travelled to the USA on were fined and forced to take the person back at the expense of the shipping line. Needless to say the latter could prove to be quite costly to companies such as the White Star Line and therefore many shipping lines required their passengers to complete immigration forms at the time they were booking their passage to America. These 'alien' passenger manifests contained various pieces of information about the passenger including: name, age, sex, marital status, occupation, nationality, last permanent address, destination, names and addresses of friends or relatives at both the past permanent address and the intended destination address. These forms along with the passenger manifest were then certified by a US Consul prior to embarkation from the foreign port and delivered to US immigration authorities prior to disembarkation at the US port. Before the passengers were permitted to set foot on American soil, the forms and passenger manifest would be examined by US Immigration Inspectors before being handed over to clerks to compile entry statistics. Accountants at the US Immigration Service would then use the passenger manifest as a basis for calculating the monthly 'head tax' bills it sent to the various shipping companies or for handing out fines for any breaches of US Immigration Law. And finally, the US Naturalisation Service would use the passenger manifest to verify legal admissions to the country for naturalisation purposes. However, when the *Carpathia* arrived at Pier 54 in New York at 9.25 pm on 18th April 1912, the US Immigration Authorities were faced with a major problem because *Titanic's* passenger manifest and immigration forms lay at the bottom of the Atlantic. However, when the *Carpathia* was making her way to New York a solicitor acting for the White Star Line wrote to Daniel J. Keefe, the Commissioner-General of Immigration in Washington DC, asking him to make special arrangements for the survivors of the *Titanic* and help ease their smooth passage into the USA. Indeed, the Purser of the *Carpathia* attempted to compile a passenger list detailing *Titanic's* survivors as he knew only too well just how strict US Immigration Laws were at the time. Thankfully for *Titanic's* survivors the US Immigration Service looked favourably on the White Star Line's request and when the *Carpathia* off-loaded the survivors, the Immigration Service's New York Commissioner of Immigration, William Williams, and his team of Immigration Inspectors, were on hand at Pier 54 to look after

them. As Ellis Island was closed for the night, the normally strict entry rules to the USA were not adhered to on this occasion as Commissioner Williams was under specific written instructions from Mr Keefe to interpret the USA's Immigration Laws as liberally as possible.

Did You Know That?

The Statue of Liberty situated on Liberty Island in New York Harbour and passed by *Titanic* survivors on the *Carpathia*, has a bronze plaque which is located on the second floor of its pedestal. It is inscribed with Emma Lazarus's famous sonnet 'The New Colossus', and includes the famous lines: 'Give me your tired, your poor, your huddled masses, yearning to breathe free.'

TITANIC'S BOXING CONNECTION

The legendary blues musician and singer, Huddie William Ledbetter (aka *Lead Belly*), referenced boxer Jack Johnson in a song he wrote about the *Titanic* simply entitled 'The Titanic'. In 1969, Jamie Brockett, the American folk singer, rewrote Lead Belly's song and made it into a satirical talking blues song called 'The Legend of the USS Titanic'. When the *Titanic*, the most luxurious passenger liner of its time, sank on 15th April 1912, Jack Johnson was the reigning World Heavyweight Boxing Champion, the sport's first black champion.

AN INEVITABLE DISASTER

On 24th April 1912, *Titanic* survivor Charles Dahl gave an interview to the *Chicago American* newspaper in which he said that the *Titanic* disaster was inevitable. Dahl said that the area where the *Titanic* sank was full of large icebergs and that when the *Carpathia* arrived at the scene of the disaster, she had to slowly zig-zag her way through them as she collected survivors. Dahl went on to say that no ship in the world could have driven a straight course through the ice pack and cited *Titanic's* 'high speed' at the time as one of the major reasons why she was unable to avoid the iceberg which ultimately caused her demise. Dahl said that in the early hours of the morning he counted as many as 19 icebergs near the lifeboat he was in, while one of the giant icebergs appeared to be as much as 5 miles long. He booked himself on *Titanic's* maiden voyage and boarded the luxury liner at Southampton as a third-class passenger (Ticket No. 7598, Price: £8 1s). He was rescued in Lifeboat No. 15 and returned to Norway in 1914 where he died on 13th February 1933.

TITANIC'S LUCKY SAILOR

On 25th April 1912, a story appeared in the *Chicago American* about a father and daughter who were on the Canadian Pacific steamship *Mount Temple* when RMS *Titanic* sank at 2.20am on 15th April 1912. Mr John Mlynarczyk and his daughter, Nellie, were en route from Antwerp to Boston and a few hours after the *Titanic* sank the *Mount Temple* was in the area where the disaster occurred. Mr Mlynarczyk said that he could hear the creaking of chains as three of *Mount Temple's* lifeboats were lowered into the Atlantic to help search for survivors. Mr Mlynarczyk claimed that when the three lifeboats returned they had found only one man alive, a member of *Titanic's* crew. However, to this day no one has any knowledge of this lucky sailor.

■ THE MOVIE TRIVIA ■■■■■■■■■■■■■■■■

The last line spoken by the *'old'* Rose in the movie is: 'He exists now only in my memory.' This is also the last line spoken in the 1981 movie, *Mad Max 2*.

NEW YORK READY FOR SURVIVORS

When the *Carpathia* arrived in New York at 9.25pm on 18th April 1912 with 705 *Titanic* survivors onboard, she was met by Mayor Gaynor of the city and Police Commissioner Waldo along with a fleet of ambulances from nearby hospitals. The ambulances were on standby to take the survivors to a number of hospitals including Bellevue, Flower Hospital, Kings County Hospital in Brooklyn, Lebanon Hospital in the Bronx, Metropolitan Hospital on Blackwell's Island, New York Hospital, St. Luke's and St. Vincent's. Meanwhile, The Charities ferryboat, *Thomas S. Brennan*, was equipped as a hospital boat with doctors and nurses on board and was ready to be called to Pier 54 where the survivors disembarked. Various other establishments in New York offered to take in survivors, among them the Irish Immigrant Society, the Italian Society, the Salvation Army and the YMCA. The 69th Regiment of the National Guard of New York (NGNY) offered the use of the Regiment's armoury to the White Star Line to temporarily house survivors.

———— Did You Know That? ————

One very generous man, Mr D. H. Knott of 102 Waverley Place, New York informed the Mayor's office that he was willing to take care of 100 of *Titanic's* survivors and give them food and lodging at three hotels he owned in the city: the *Arlington*, the *Earl* and the *Holly*.

FAT CATS

It is estimated that *Titanic's* first-class passengers were collectively worth in excess of $500 million, while the wealthiest person onboard, John Jacob Astor IV, was believed to have amassed a personal fortune of $30 million. It is also believed that *Titanic's* passengers had an estimated $6 million in cash, bonds, securities and jewellery on the ship.

THE MILLIONAIRE'S BOAT

At 1.00am on Monday 15th April 1912, starboard Lifeboat No.1 was lowered into the Atlantic from the *Titanic* by First Officer, William Murdoch. Despite the fact that it could hold up to 65 persons only 12 people were placed in the lifeboat: 5 first-class passengers (Sir Cosmo and Lady Lucy Duff-Gordon along with their maid and personal secretary, Miss Laura Mabel Francatelli, Mr Saloman and Mr Stenger) and 7 members of *Titanic's* crew. When they were rescued by the *Carpathia*, Sir Cosmo Duff-Gordon gave each one of the 7 crew members a hand-written bank draft for £5.00. The press later dubbed the lifeboat 'The Millionaire's Boat' and claimed that the 12 in it ignored the cries for help from many of their fellow passengers who were struggling in the freezing water. Sir Cosmo Duff-Gordon was also heavily criticised for paying the crew and despite his claims that he was only compensating the crew for their losing their kits; he never really ever managed to clear his name.

—————— Did You Know That? ——————

Lady Duff-Gordon was one of Britain's leading fashion designers in the late 19th and early 20th centuries and is credited with, amongst other things, introducing the modern runway-style fashion show.

TITANIC'S MEMORIAL GARDEN

On 15th April 1995, exactly 83 years to the day after the *Titanic* was claimed by the North Atlantic, 98-year old Edith Eileen Haisman (née Brown) along with fellow survivor, Eva Hart (aged 90), attended the opening of a Memorial Garden at the National Maritime Museum in Greenwich, London. A massive granite monument commemorating the 83rd anniversary of the liner's sinking was also unveiled at the ceremony.

LEGAL CLAIMS SETTLED

In December 1915, *Titanic's owner*, the White Star Line, agreed to pay out a total of $664,000 to settle all outstanding legal claims against the company. Approximately $500,000 was distributed among American claimants, $50,000 went to British claimants and $114,000 was set aside for interest and expenses in connection with the numerous law suits. In 1914, a Claimants Committee representing the families of those who lost their lives when the *Titanic* sank, estimated that the total claims would amount to $2,500,000 and therefore, this settlement meant that the claimants received approximately 26% of what they were originally seeking.

SCOTLAND ROAD

The vast majority of the crew members on the *Titanic* hailed from Liverpool, England. Indeed, there were so many people from Merseyside on the ship that the long corridor on E Deck where they bunked was nicknamed 'Scotland Road', after the famous road in Merseyside which was opened in the 1770s and was part of the stagecoach route to Scotland. Scotland Road was the hub of working-class life in North Liverpool at the turn of the 20th Century and was home to various migrant communities including the Irish, the Italians, the Scots and the Welsh. Jeffrey Hatcher wrote a play entitled 'Scotland Road' and in it he refers to the lower-deck corridor of the *Titanic*.

THE COURAGEOUS OFFICER

At 1.30am on 15th April 1912, Lifeboat No.14 on the port side of *Titanic* was lowered into the Atlantic under the command of Fifth Officer, Harold Lowe. The lifeboat could accommodate up to 65 people but had 58 people in it. Just as it was descending several men attempted to get into it prompting Lowe to fire three shots from his revolver to get the men to remain aboard the ship. Shortly after the ship went down Lowe quickly gathered together Lifeboats Nos. 4, 10, 12 and Collapsible D in the water. He then spread the passengers from his lifeboat into the other four and returned to the scene of the disaster to search for more survivors. However, at first he only found four men, one of whom was William Hoyt who died shortly after being rescued from the freezing water. Then just after dawn he noticed Collapsible Lifeboat A and after pulling up alongside it he transferred its occupants into Lifeboat No.14. Lowe's lifeboat was the only one to return to the scene of the wreckage in the hunt for survivors.

Did You Know That?

Fifth Officer Harold Lowe was only 14 years old when he ran away from his home in Llanrhos, North Wales to begin a career at sea and worked as a ship's boy aboard the Welsh coastal schooners.

TITANIC'S HOME PORT

Although Liverpool was *Titanic's* Port of Registry and therefore her 'home port', she never had the opportunity to visit Liverpool.

Did You Know That?

Although a ship's Port of Registry is the name that appears on her stern, it is not necessarily the port from which the ship regularly sails (which in the case of *Titanic* would have been Southampton).

LIVERPOOL'S *TITANIC* MEMORIALS

A memorial dedicated to the brave engineers who stayed at their posts while the *Titanic* was sinking is situated between Princes Dock and the Liver Building in Liverpool. The memorial's original design was changed midway through its construction to include a tribute to those men who lost their lives at sea during World War I. Another tribute, dedicated to the memory of *Titanic's* eight courageous musicians who continued to play on while panic surrounded them, is situated at the Philharmonic Hall in Hope Street. One of the eight, the bass violist Fred Clarke, was from 22 Tunstall Street, Smithdown Road, Liverpool.

Did You Know That?

The eight members of *Titanic's* band were employed by music agents CW and FN Black of 14 Castle Street, Liverpool.

EQUIPPING *TITANIC*'S GALLEYS

Henry Wilson & Company, Cornhill Works, Liverpool supplied the majority of the stoves, ovens and cooking/food preparation equipment for *Titanic's* galleys.

THE LIVERPOOL CONNECTION

The Captain of the *Titanic*, Captain Edward John Smith, and J Bruce Ismay, Chairman of the White Star Line, both had Liverpool connections. Captain Smith lived in Waterloo, near Liverpool for nearly 40 years before moving to Southampton in 1908. J Bruce Ismay owned a house at Sandheys, Mossley Hill in South Liverpool. The bridge and engine room telegraphs on the *Titanic* were made by J. W. Ray & Co. from Liverpool. Stonier's, a firm in Liverpool, supplied 50,000 pieces of bone china to the *Titanic*, including the quite distinctive cobalt blue dinner plates used in first class. Meanwhile, Captain Lord of the *Californian* lived and died in Wallasey near Liverpool.

COMPENSATION

The Liverpool and London Steamship Protection and Indemnity Association Limited was based in Water Street, Liverpool when the *Titanic* sank on 15th April 1912 and was the body responsible for settling compensation claims from passengers and crew members after the sinking. The Association was founded in 1881 by the legendary White Star Line Chairman, Thomas Ismay, along with other steamship owners from Liverpool and London.

TITANIC'S DOUBLE MARRIAGE

In James Cameron's 1997 blockbuster movie 'Titanic', the role of Sir Cosmo Duff-Gordon was played by Martin Jarvis while the role of Lady Lucy Duff-Gordon was played by Rosalind Ayres. Jarvis and Ayres were married in Ealing, London on 23rd November 1974.

ICEBERG RIGHT AHEAD!

At exactly 11.39pm on 14th April 1912, Frederick Fleet, one of *Titanic's* lookouts, rang the crow's nest bell and telephoned the bridge. Sixth Officer Moody answered the call and was informed by Fleet: 'Iceberg Right Ahead!' Moody acknowledged the warning and relayed the message to Murdoch who apparently had seen the iceberg for himself by the time the warning was relayed by Moody. Murdoch rang 'STOP' for both engines and ordered 'Hard a-starboard'. Quartermaster Robert Hitchins, who was at the helm, put the wheel hard over. *Titanic* turned to port and at 11:40pm struck the iceberg.

A KEEN PAIR OF EYES

The White Star Line followed a practice of hiring men specifically as lookouts, unlike many other companies where lookout duty was assigned to seamen who also had other responsibilities.

■ THE MOVIE TRIVIA ■ ■ ■ ■ ■ ■ ■ ■ ■ ■ ■ ■ ■ ■

In 2007, the American Film Institute ranked *Titanic* as the No.83 Greatest Movie of All Time.

NEWSREEL OF *TITANIC* SURVIVORS UNEARTHED

In August 2004, an old piece of newsreel showing survivors from the *Titanic* disaster was discovered in an old garden shed. This was after the death of its owner who used to work as a cinema projectionist. It shows survivors from RMS *Titanic* arriving in New York on 18th April 1912 aboard the *Carpathia* which rescued them, just three days after she collided with an iceberg and sank. Hundreds of people turned up at Pier 54 to help them. Quartermaster Robert Hitchins, who was at the helm of the ship when she struck the iceberg, was also featured in the newsreel.

RULE BRITANNIA

When the *Titanic* sailed under her own steam through the Victoria Channel and out of Belfast Lough on 2nd April 1912, an estimated crowd of 100,000 was on hand to watch the world's biggest and most luxurious passenger liner set sail for Southampton to embark on her maiden voyage. Many in the crowd waved their handkerchiefs in the air and sang 'Rule, Britannia!'

TITANIC FALLING APART

In August 2003, Captain Alfred McLaren, who visited the wreck of the *Titanic* in July, said he was shocked to see how badly the ship was decaying. McLaren first visited the wreckage in 1999 but was horrified to see how much deterioration had occurred in the following four years. 'I couldn't see anything but rusticles, everywhere we looked,' said McLaren. At the time scientists estimated that the world's most famous ship was losing up to 270kg of metal each day, meaning it would completely disappear within the following 20 years.

THE BRAVE YOUNG SOULS

Included among the hundreds of heroes who lost their lives when *Titanic* sank were several young men who worked on board as bell boys and lift attendants. After the disaster Quartermaster Sidney James Humphreys, who was in command of Lifeboat No. 11, recalled the last time he saw several of these young brave souls. Humphreys said the boys were called to their regular posts in the 'First Cabin' and told to remain there. Then when Captain Smith informed his crew that it was 'every man for himself', Humphreys recalled him seeing the boys smoking cigarettes and joking with the passengers. None of them even attempted to enter a lifeboat and they all lost their lives including:

Name	Age	Occupation
F. Allan	17-years-old	lift attendant
A. Barrett	15-years-old	bell boy
C.H. Harris	16-years-old	bell boy
A. King	18-years-old	lift attendant
R.J. Pacey	17-years-old	lift attendant
C. Turvey	16-years-old	page boy (*A la Carte Restaurant*)
W. Watson	14-years-old	bell boy

TITANIC LICKED

In 2005, the Irish artist Vincent Killowry had his Irish postage stamp design for the *Titanic* included as part of an exhibition depicting postage stamp designs at Cork City Hall to commemorate the city's year as the European Capital of Culture (2005).

IN THE LIFEBOATS

Despite reports that not all of the lifeboats lowered from *Titanic* were provisioned before launching, a biscuit tin and water beaker were standard equipment for each lifeboat. A detailed inventory of *Titanic's* lifeboats following their recovery shows that they were so equipped. Lanterns were also part of the standard equipment, although most of the boats left before the Lamp Trimmer got them filled and brought them out to the boats.

--- Did You Know That? ---

Each of *Titanic's* lifeboats was also equipped with a mast and a sail.

A ONE IN 21 CHANCE

On board *Titanic* was an 18-year old Finnish woman named Anna Turja. Anna was one of 21 children born of two mothers and one father in Oulainen, Finland. Her sister's husband paid for her passage in third-class accommodation on *Titanic* for the journey to the USA where he promised her a job working for him. Anna's family back in Finland thought she had lost her life when the *Titanic* sank when for some unknown reason her name appeared on a list naming lost passengers. However, a little more than five weeks after Anna was rescued by the *Carpathia*, her family received a letter from her informing them that she was safe and well.

THAT'S MY GRANDA

In August 2005, more than 93 years after the *Titanic* sank, the grave of one of the ship's stokers, William McQuillan, was discovered by his family. William's granddaughter, Marjorie Wilson, was at home in Belfast with her husband, Victor, who was watching BBC Newsline's 'Journey to Remember' documentary about Mike McKimm's dive to the wreckage of the ill-fated liner. Marjorie was shocked when Victor told her that he had just seen the headstone to grave No.183 from Fairview Cemetery, Halifax, Nova Scotia, Canada with the words 'W. McQuillan, Died April 15th 1912' engraved on it. When Mike mentioned that William was from 79 Seaview Street, Belfast and was just 26 years old when he lost his life in the *Titanic* disaster, Marjorie looked at Victor and said 'That's my Granda.' His body was found floating in the bleak and unforgiving North Atlantic and brought ashore to Halifax by one of the ships which was dispatched to recover the bodies. At the time of the sinking William's family thought his body lay on the ocean floor. An article which appeared in the *Belfast Telegraph* on 4th May 1912 stated that William did not survive the disaster and that the bodies of the missing Belfast firemen who stoked the ship's boilers 'lay in a sailor's grave, two miles beneath the ocean'. However, just two days after the article appeared in the newspaper, William's body was buried in Canada. William's name appears on the *Titanic* statue in the grounds of Belfast City Hall and until Victor saw his grave on television all the family had to remember him by was a photograph. Marjorie subsequently visited her grandfather's grave in Halifax and said that he should never have been aboard *Titanic's* maiden voyage. A friend of William's was selected for the job but when his wife became ill he asked William if he would take his place so as he could stay at home and care for his wife. William kindly agreed, a decision that cost him his young life.

TAKE THAT!

When *Titanic's* Chief Wireless Operator, Jack Phillips, was busy sending messages to other vessels seeking their assistance, one of *Titanic's* crew (possibly a stoker), attempted to steal his lifejacket. Harold Bride, Phillips's assistant, punched the unruly crew member, knocking him out cold.

─────────── Did You Know That? ───────────

In 1912, only four vessels carried two wireless operators: RMS *Lusitania*, RMS *Mauretania*, RMS *Olympic* and RMS *Titanic*.

NEW YORK STOCK EXCHANGE HANDOUTS

The New York Stock Exchange sent a committee of representatives to Pier No.54 in New York to greet the survivors of the *Titanic* disaster as they disembarked from the *Carpathia*. The committee was headed by Mr R. H. Thomas who held a black box in his hands which contained $5,000 in small bills. Mr Thomas and his fellow committee members handed out money to *Titanic's* third-class passengers as they filed by.

■ THE MOVIE TRIVIA ■■■■■■■■■■■■■

Work first began on the movie in 1995 when James Cameron shot footage of the real wreck of the *Titanic*. He then managed to persuade 20th Century Fox to invest in the movie.

TITANIC'S PLUMBING

On 8th April 2005, *Titanic* specialist auctioneers, Henry Aldridge and Son, sold an original blueprint of the *Titanic's* plumbing system at a British Titanic Society convention in Southampton for £12,000. The blueprint was owned by William Wilson, a naval architect on *Titanic's* maiden voyage. However, luckily for Mr Wilson he disembarked the ill-fated liner at Cherbourg and took the blueprint with him as he was required to help repair another vessel. Other items sold at the auction included a 12-minute nitrate film of the *Titanic* in Belfast which realised £15,000, and a White Star Line brochure was sold for £5,000. Alan Aldridge was delighted with the success of the auction and said that the 10-foot-long plans were thought to be the only ones in existence.

OLD TOMMY AND THE JINXED SHIP

A story was often told by workers at Belfast's Harland & Wolff Shipyard that just prior to *Titanic's* completion they often heard a faint knocking sound on the other side of a bulkhead, suggesting that a fellow worker had got trapped inside one the of the large metal walls. It was claimed that the knocking went on for a few days before finally dying out completely. Workers are said to have claimed that the knocking was being done by 'Old Tommy' who had been hammering rivets into *Titanic's* boiler room one day when planks of wood fell on top of him and killed him. However, many consider this piece of *Titanic* folklore to be nothing more of an embellishment of a similar piece of folklore about the *Great Eastern*. The *Great Eastern* was designed in 1854 by the legendary British engineer, Isambard Kingdom Brunel, and when it was launched on 31st January 1858, it was the largest ship ever built, six times bigger than anything before it and could carry 4,000 passengers from England to Australia without refuelling. The ship was built in Millwall, London and during its construction a riveter and his apprentice went missing. Rumours among the workforce abounded with tales of how the pair had been accidently sealed up in a compartment of the ship while their cries for help were drowned out by the noise of the riveters' hammers. Four years after the *Great Eastern* was launched it struck an uncharted rock which tore open her hull but the ship was saved from sinking as it had been constructed with a double hull. After expensive repairs to her were carried out, she was finally purchased for conversion into a cable-laying ship, a role in which she was successfully employed for a number of years. Following her stint as a cable ship, her owners tried unsuccessfully to sell her before eventually disposing of her in 1889 for scrap. It is claimed that men involved in demolishing the *Great Eastern* found two skeletons in her hull, a story repeated in a 2003 BBC documentary about Brunel's ship which formed part of the BBC's 'Seven Wonders of the World' series. The *Great Eastern* will go down in history as the ship that helped lay the first transatlantic telegraph cable in 1865.

THE MOVIE TRIVIA

James Cameron did not want any song in the movie including a song over the closing credits. However, the composer James Horner secretly worked with lyricist Will Jennings and the Canadian singer Celine Dion, and wrote 'My Heart Will Go On'. A demo tape of the song was presented to Cameron which he liked, and the song went on to win an Oscar.

TITANIC'S LOVERS

In early 1912, Henry Samuel Morley, a 39-year-old married sweetshop owner living in Worcester, England and Kate Florence Phillips, his 19-year-old shop assistant were having an affair. The lovers booked a second-class crossing on RMS *Titanic's* ill-fated maiden voyage in the hope that they could begin a new life together in the United States of America. Henry and Kate used the names Mr and Mrs Marshall when they booked their voyage. Their illicit love affair is believed to be the inspiration for the characters of Jack and Rose (played by Leonardo DiCaprio and Kate Winslet) in James Cameron's 1997 blockbuster movie *Titanic*. When they were on the *Titanic* Henry gave Kate a sapphire necklace which has been on display in various *Titanic* exhibitions and is believed to be the inspiration behind the 'Heart of the Ocean' necklace featured in Cameron's movie. The young Kate was one of the last passengers to leave *Titanic* before the great liner sank but her lover died. His body if ever recovered was never identified. However, Kate had conceived and gave birth to a daughter, Ellen, on 11th January 1913 at her grandparent's home in Worcester, exactly nine months to the day when *Titanic* stopped off at Queenstown, Ireland. Mrs Ellen Walker (née Phillips) died aged 92 in October 2005 and in her will she left the majority of her estate to the Royal National Lifeboat Institution (RNLI) and asked for her ashes to be scattered at sea. On 1st November 2006, a memorial service was held for Ellen aboard the *Spirit of Padstow*, a Tamar Class lifeboat off Cataclew Point, near Padstow, Cornwall and honouring her last wish the crew of the lifeboat scattered her ashes on the surface of the Atlantic. During her lifetime Ellen was very supportive of the work of the RNLI and never forgot how her mother had been rescued by the *Carpathia* from one of *Titanic's* lifeboats. Her son, 70-year old Robert Farmer, said: 'I think that she wanted to be in the same place as her father because she had never been close to him or known him. All I knew as a child was her father died on the Titanic.'

Did You Know That?

When Henry eloped with Kate he left behind a wife and a 12-year-old daughter. He told his wife that he was going to Los Angeles, California to recuperate from a recent illness.

TITANIC'S OLDER SISTER LIVES ON

The *Olympic*, *Titanic's* older sister, was launched on 20th October 1910 and on 31st May 1911 the pride of the White Star Line brought visitors to Belfast to see the *Titanic* being launched at Harland & Wolff Shipyard. When the *Olympic* was scrapped in 1937, some of the ship's fittings were purchased at auction by the White Swan Hotel in Alnwick, England.

THE QUEEN SINKS WITH THE *TITANIC*

On Christmas Day 2001, the BBC paid £6m to show James Cameron's 1997 blockbuster movie *Titanic*. A total of 9.9 million viewers tuned in to watch the story of the doomed luxury liner's doomed maiden voyage from Southampton to New York. This was 100,000 more viewers than watched the Queen's 10-minute broadcast to the nation which was shown on BBC1 and ITV at 3.00 pm. However, the movie was beaten on the day by *Coronation Street*, *EastEnders*, *Who Wants To Be A Millionaire* and the *ITV News*. The BBC issued a statement in which it said it was delighted with the movie's pulling power but some executives at ITV were only too happy to point out that the BBC received around 9.8 million viewers on Christmas Day 2000 when it screened *Jumanji* starring Robin Williams but only paid £1m for that movie.

SS *NOMADIC*'S FAMOUS PASSENGERS

Some of the most notable passengers transferred to the *Titanic* at Cherbourg by the purpose-built tender, *Nomadic*, included John Jacob Astor IV, Molly Brown and Benjamin Guggenheim.

TITANIC'S ASSISTANT SURGEON

John Edward Simpson, aged 37 and a former Captain of the Royal Army Medical Corps, was the assistant surgeon to Dr O'Loughlin on *Titanic*. He was responsible for looking after the second-class and third-class passengers. He died in the sinking of the *Titanic* and his body, if ever recovered, was never identified. John Edward Simpson left behind his wife, Annie, and their son, John Ralph Simpson. A memorial to Simpson, who was born in Belfast in 1875, can be found at Bangor Abbey, Northern Ireland.

--- Did You Know That? ---

Before *Titanic* arrived at Queenstown, Ireland, John Edward Simpson wrote a letter to his mother in which he stated that some money had been stolen from his trunk in his cabin.

A HEALTHY SHIP

A fruit and vegetables store situated in the Oakley Building at the bottom of Southampton's High Street supplied the *Titanic* with fresh provisions prior to her maiden voyage. RMS *Titanic* set sail from Southampton with 36,000 apples, 16,000 lemons and 13,000 grapefruits on board.

A FAMOUS MEMBER OF *TITANIC*'S EXCLUSIVE CLUB

Commodore Ronald Warwick, the former Master of the *Queen Mary 2*, is a member of the exclusive club of people who have dived to the wreck of RMS *Titanic*. When asked about the impact the sinking of the *Titanic* had on shipping and the world he said: 'It tells us we can never be complacent, especially as far as technology is concerned. Ships are something man creates but one always has to have respect for the sea, rough weather, calm weather, ice conditions, fog and snow.'

TITANIC'S CHINESE SAILORS

When *Titanic* left Southampton harbour on 10th April 1912 for her maiden voyage, eight Chinese sailors (all believed to be from Hong Kong) were on board but were travelling as third-class passengers. Six of them survived the *Titanic* disaster although very little is known about their true identity. When the sailors arrived in New York on 18th April 1912 on RMS *Carpathia*, they were interviewed by the US Immigration Service's Chinese Inspector. On 19th April 1912, the six joined the British steamship *Annetta* as seamen (possibly gaining work as Stokers) and left on board her when she set sail back across the Atlantic the next day.

LOST BUT NOT FORGOTTEN

At the Victoria Cemetery, Carrickfergus, Northern Ireland one of the many crew members who lost their lives in the *Titanic* disaster is remembered. Tommy Millar is remembered on his wife, Jeannie's, grave with the inscription: 'In memory of our dear father, lost in the Titanic disaster, April 1912.'

THE WHITE STAR DOCK

Titanic sailed from Berth No.44 at Dock Gate 4, the White Star Dock, Southampton on 10th April 1912 for her maiden voyage. The White Star Dock was built to house the three great liners built by the Harland & Wolff Shipyard (*Olympic*, *Titanic* and *Gigantic*, later *Britannic*) and was surrounded by various outbuildings and workshops.

Second Class passengers promenade along the after section of *Titanic's* boat deck during her stop at Queenstown. (*Cork Examiner* photo/Jonathan Smith collection)

AND THE BAND PLAYED ON

It is a known fact that the band of *Titanic* bravely played on as the passengers were being placed into lifeboats. A total of eight musicians lost their lives in the disaster. Violinist John Law Hume hailed from Dumfries and was just 21 years old when he joined his fellow band members aboard the famous ship. He lost his life along with Thomas Mullin who was a steward in third class and who came from nearby Maxwelltown. A poignant memorial to their memory was unveiled in 1913 in Dock Park, Dumfries with the inscription reading: 'In memory of John Law Hume, a member of the band, and Thomas Mullin, steward, natives of these towns, who lost their lives in the wreck of the White Star liner Titanic, which sank in the mid Atlantic on the 14th day of April 1912. They died at the post of duty.' The back of the memorial bears the following inscription: 'Erected by the people of Dumfries and Maxwelltown at home and abroad.' Both of their bodies were recovered from the wreck site and are buried in Fairview Lawn Cemetery in Halifax, Nova Scotia, Canada.

———————— Did You Know That? ————————

During an interview in the early 1970s, Edith Louise Rosenbaum Russell, a *Titanic* survivor, said that the band did not play as the ship went down.

WHO LOVES YA BABY?

Telly Savalas, who played the leading role in the 1970s US TV crime drama 'Kojak', (with his most famous lines: 'Who loves ya baby?' and 'Coochy Coo') hosted a live television show entitled 'Return To The Titanic Live' in October 1987 in which he famously opened what was believed to be the purser's safe from the *Titanic* live on television. The safe had been recovered from the wreckage of the *Titanic* by RMS Titanic, Inc., a company which recovered over 1,800 artefacts during 32 dives to the wreck between July and September 1987. The safe contained a leather bag, some banknotes ($10 and $50 bills), some papers, gold coins and jewellery. The show also included interviews with survivors of the *Titanic* disaster including Eva Hart. Also recovered from the wreck site were a number of 60-lb chunks of coal which were broken-up and sold to *Titanic* memorabilia collectors as souvenirs.

WEE BERTIE

The Belfast YMCA building, situated at Wellington Place, has a historical link to Bertie 'Wee Bertie' Ervine, a 19-year-old working-class Bible student who was the youngest member of the engine crew on the *Titanic* when he went down with the ship.

TITANIC GOES ON DISPLAY

On 10th April 2004, the German architect Peter Davies-Garner's magnificent 1:48 scale (18ft) model of *Titanic* went on display at Belfast City Hall. The model was part of a 7-day 'Titanic at Home Exhibition' organised by the Belfast City Council. Peter constructed his model from the original working drawings of the Harland & Wolff Shipyard's architects who worked on designing *Titanic*. Davies-Garner's diary describing step-by-step how he made the model was later published under the title *RMS Titanic: A Model Maker's Manual*.

A MOST POIGNANT MEMORIAL

Holy Rood Church, High Street, Botley, Southampton houses one of the most significant of the city's *Titanic* memorials. It is dedicated to the crew, firemen and stewards from Southampton who lost their lives in the *Titanic* disaster. A large number of staff on the ship when she sank hailed from the local area: Chapel, Freemantle, Northam, Shirley and St Mary's.

TITANIC THE SMELLY SHIP

In 1912, the perfume market in the USA was absolutely booming and 47-year-old Adolphe Saalfeld, a self-made businessman who was born in Germany in 1865 but living with his wife Gertrude in Manchester in 1912, was Chairman of the chemists and distillers '*Sparks, White, and Co. Ltd*'. Saalfeld had a vision of capturing a huge slice of the perfumery market in the USA when he boarded RMS *Titanic* in Southampton as a first-class passenger on 10th April 1912 (Ticket No.19988, costing £30, 10 shillings, Cabin C-106). Saalfeld survived the sinking of the *Titanic* but the 65 vials containing his fragrance samples went down with the great ship. However, 88 years later they were discovered lying on the ocean floor in leather satchels and on 10th April 2004, the 92nd anniversary of the *Titanic* setting sail on her maiden voyage, scientists were able to recreate one of Saalfeld's perfumes. His 'Rose and Violet' creation was reproduced using a 'fingerprint' of the original chemical composition after one of the vials was opened and the scientists found that the scent had been preserved. Visitors to the Edinburgh International Science Festival were among the first people to smell one of Saalfeld's creations in nearly a century

■ THE MOVIE TRIVIA ■■■■■■■■■■■■■■

Only the starboard side of the exterior set was completed. Consequently in the scenes showing the ship at Southampton dock, all shots were reversed to give the appearance of the port side of the ship, to resemble the way in which Titanic was actually docked in Southampton in April 1912. The latter process involved the painstaking construction of reversed costumes and signage to complete the illusion, which was then achieved by reversing the image in post-production.

THE FRENCH CONNECTION

Prior to the Department of Social Development in Northern Ireland purchasing *Nomadic* at auction in January 2006 for £171,320, the little tender ship which once famously ferried passengers from Cherbourg out to the *Titanic*, was moored on the River Seine, Paris (opposite the Eiffel Tower). Before arriving back home in Belfast in July 2006, the *Nomadic's* previous owners used her as a restaurant and conference centre.

─────── Did You Know That? ───────

The *Nomadic* is the last surviving member of the world famous
White Star Line fleet.

THE *TITANIC* MEMORIAL LIGHTHOUSE

On the corner of Fulton Street and Water Street in New York, and in front of the entrance to the South Street Seaport Museum, stands the *Titanic Memorial Lighthouse*. The memorial is dedicated to those people who perished in the *Titanic* disaster and was paid for by public donations in 1915. Between 1915 and July 1968 the memorial stood above the East River on the corner of the old Seaman's Church Institute at the corner of South Street and Coenties Slip. The time ball at the top of the lighthouse would drop down the pole to signal 12.00 noon to the ships in the nearby harbour. The time ball mechanism was activated by a telegraphic signal which was sent from the National Observatory in Washington, D.C. The inscription on the plaque reads:

TITANIC MEMORIAL LIGHTHOUSE

This lighthouse is a memorial to the passengers, officers and crew who died as heroes when the steamship Titanic sank after collision with an iceberg.

LATITUDE 41°46' NORTH

LONGITUDE 50°14' WEST

APRIL 15, 1912

TWO VERY SPECIAL GUESTS

J. Bruce Ismay, Chairman and Managing Director of the White Star Line, and Thomas Andrews, *Titanic's* principal designer, stayed at The Southwestern Hotel situated on Canute Street, Southampton on 9th April 1912, one night before RMS *Titanic* set sail on her doomed maiden voyage. Indeed, Ismay stayed at the hotel during *Titanic's* entire stay in Southampton. He kept up a punishing schedule, arriving aboard *Titanic* early each morning and finally disembarking late in the evening after a gruelling day's work.

──────────── Did You Know That? ────────────

Most of *Titanic's* third-class and emigrant-class passengers stayed in a hotel located on Albert Road, Southampton before boarding the ship. The name of the hotel was 'The Atlantic Hotel' but it was nicknamed 'Emigrants' House'.

TITANIC SONGS

In 1998, an album entitled *Titanic Songs* was released comprising 18 songs recorded by their original artists between 1912 and 1948, each one about the doomed ocean liner. The CD was mastered from original 78s recordings of the songs and includes artists such as: Vernon Dalhart ('Sinking of the Great Titanic'), the Dixon Brothers ('Down With The Old Canoe'), Blind Willie Johnson ('God Moves On The Water') and Lead Belly ('The Titanic').

HOME TO *TITANIC*'S CREW

On 6th April 1912, 17 young men left the Seaman's House in Oxford Street, Southampton and boarded the *Titanic*. Many orphans were brought up in the Seaman's House before embarking on a life at sea. Of the 17 who set sail on *Titanic* a remarkable 15 survived the disaster.

A BAD OMEN

Some people have alleged that when *Titanic* left Southampton on 10th April 1912, a cockerel was heard crowing during the day, something which many of the ship's sailors believed to be a bad omen. It is also rumoured that around 20 people who were booked on *Titanic's* maiden voyage cancelled their travelling plans to New York at the last minute after dreaming that the ship would sink.

THE LUCKY SIX

On 9th April 1912, the Slade brothers, Alfred, Bertram and Thomas were out for a night's drinking at The Grapes pub in Oxford Street, Southampton along with William Nutbean, the latter's watch-mate, John Podesta, and a trimmer named Penney. All six *Titanic* crew members knew they had to be back at the ship in time for her 12.00 noon departure for Queenstown, Ireland the next day. Nutbean and Podesta just made it back to the docks in time but a passing train resulted in all three Slade brothers and Penney missing *Titanic's* departure. Nutbean and Podesta were both on duty the night *Titanic* struck the iceberg but their watch ended at 8.00 pm when they went to the ship's mess room for dinner. When the great ship collided with the iceberg at 11:40 pm, Nutbean and Podesta were lying in their bunks and after feeling the impact they went up to the Boat Deck and helped lower Lifeboat No.7 into the icy sea before assisting passengers off the ship and into the safety of other lifeboats. When Second Officer Murdoch realised that the ship could not stay afloat much longer before it would sink, he ordered Nutbean and Podesta to abandon the ship and they safely entered one of the lifeboats. The pair were picked up several hours later by the *Carpathia* and taken on to New York before returning to England on the *Lapland*.

DOLL FACE

Robinson's Bar in Belfast is one of the city's oldest public houses and contains some very prized and interesting items of *Titanic* memorabilia. These include the famous Philomena doll which was recovered from the wreck site shortly after the sinking. The bar faces Belfast's famous Europa Hotel and also has the brass nameplate from *Titanic's* Lifeboat No.12 on display as well as various letters and postcards sent by passengers aboard the ship when she stopped off at Queenstown en route to New York.

THE *TITANIC* ROOMS

The Lord Mayor's suite at Belfast City Hall is also known as 'The Titanic Rooms' in honour of the craftsmen who worked on the suite as well as on *Titanic's* interior and fittings.

TITANIC DOWN UNDER

In the sleepy little town of Broken Hill, New South Wales, Australia stands 'The Titanic Bandsmen's Memorial'. The memorial can be found in the town's main park and was commissioned shortly after the *Titanic* disaster. There is another memorial paying tribute to *Titanic's* brave bandsmen in Ballarat, Victoria, Australia. Broken Hill and Ballarat were two of Australia's biggest mining centres at the beginning of the 20th century and like most mining towns they had a local band. The memorials were paid for by local bandsmen in tribute to their lost brothers.

THE MATCHSTICK *TITANIC*

In June 2006, Mark Colling, a father-of-four, went into the record books for making a model of a ship using the greatest number of matchsticks. He built a 19-feet long (5.8m) replica of the *Titanic* using 3.5 million matchsticks, which weighed almost a ton. Mark persuaded a Hollywood film studio to allow him to borrow a blueprint of the *Titanic* to build his model. He began his mammoth project in his workshop in Llanelli, South Wales in 2004, spending as many as eight hours each day working on it. His superb model includes hundreds of tiny details such as deckchairs and lifeboats and he even included a 2.5 m iceberg for added realism. His masterpiece cost him £4,500 to build and he regularly takes it to *Titanic* exhibitions.

TITANIC'S MISSING DIAMONDS

In July 2000, an article appeared in the press stating that a team of divers from the salvage company which owns the rights to the wreckage of the *Titanic* were preparing to dive to recover a treasure trove of diamonds and items of jewellery. Newspaper reports at the time of the disaster suggested that two Swiss brothers were carrying diamonds on the ship when she sank, believed to be worth in the region of $250m today. The salvage company, RMS Titanic Inc., believed that one of the ship's officers packed the valuables into leather pouches and placed them in the first-class purser's office for safekeeping just minutes before the ship sank. Although various items of jewellery have been recovered from the floor of the Atlantic Ocean where the wreck of the *Titanic* rests, no Swiss diamonds have ever been recovered.

-------- Did You Know That? --------

A crew member from the *Mackay-Bennett*, one of four ships which recovered bodies out of the water after *Titanic* sank on 15th April 1912, informed a reporter that when he was searching the pockets of the body of one man for identification, 12 loose diamonds spilled on to the deck of the ship. The dead man was later identified as Austin Blyler van Billiard.

■ THE MOVIE TRIVIA ■■■■■■■■■■■■■

Before he announced a statement that he was going to make a movie about *Titanic*, Director James Cameron shot footage of icebergs off Nova Scotia under the pretence that he making a film called *Planet Ice*.

WHERE IT ALL BEGAN

The Harland & Wolff Shipyard in Belfast has been at the core of European heavy engineering for nearly 150 years. In 1858, Edward James Harland, General Manager of the Hickson Shipyard in Belfast, bought the yard from his employer and in 1861 he went into partnership with his assistant Gustav Wilhelm Wolff. Both very young and ambitious, neither knew they had formed the core of what was to become the world's largest shipyard. Harland & Wolff used innovation in ship design and manufacturing processes to great effect; their designs were cheaper to build, more reliable, gave greater carrying capacity and improved sea keeping. No wonder Harland & Wolff became the world's shipyard of choice during the first three decades of the 20th century. In the second half of the 20th century, competition from lower cost nations around the world had a detrimental effect on

European shipbuilding. To compete, Harland & Wolff upped the technology stakes and diversified into the offshore oil and gas market, building oil rigs, FPSOs and drillships. In recent years Harland & Wolff have adapted this vast experience to execute a wide range of renewable energy projects, such as offshore wind farms and wave and tidal energy devices.

Did You Know That?

The largest-ever cruise ship to sail into Belfast is the *Crown Princess*. When the 113,000 gross registered tons, 951 feet long (290m), 3,080 passengers (1,200 crew members) ocean liner arrived in Belfast in August 2009, she docked beside Harland & Wolff's Thompson Graving Dock, home of the *Titanic* during the famous White Star Line leviathan's construction period.

A MUTUALLY BENEFICIAL PARTNERSHIP

Following an after-dinner game of billiards at the Liverpool home of the shipping financier, Gustav Christian Schwabe in 1869, Edward Harland and Thomas Ismay forged their historic alliance. Ismay agreed to have all of his ships constructed by the Harland & Wolff Shipyard on a cost plus basis with an agreement that the Belfast shipyard would not build any vessels for Ismay's competitors. Schwabe's role was to organise the finances necessary to build the ships. The White Star Line-Cunard Line rivalry was born.

NOSTRADAMUS PREDICTS THE SINKING OF *TITANIC*

It is often said that Michel de Nostredame, better known as Nostradamus, predicted the sinking of *Titanic*. Nostradamus was a French apothecary and reputed prophet who published collections of prophecies which are very well known. In 1555, the first edition of his book entitled *Les Propheties* (*The Prophecies*) was published. However, depending on how one interprets the numerous quatrains he wrote, he can be credited with predicting many major world events including the reigns of Napoleon, Hitler and Stalin; the sinking of *Titanic*; both World Wars; the atom-bomb attacks on Hiroshima and Nagasaki; the assassination of President John F. Kennedy; the death of Princess Diana and the 9/11 attacks in the USA. However, Nostradamus never mentioned any names, places or more importantly definitive dates in his quatrains and therefore while many people believe his prophecies actually did come true, many also are highly sceptical of them.

PRONI

The Public Records Office Northern Ireland (PRONI) has an extensive archive of *Titanic* material. Indeed PRONI's Harland & Wolff archive comprises some 2,000 files, approximately 200 volumes and in the region of 16,000 documents covering the period 1861–1987.

WHITE STAR LINE'S OWNER RESCUES THE UNITED STATES

When the US Treasury almost ran out of money in 1893, they asked John Pierpont Morgan, the American tycoon, for a loan of $65 million. It was J. Pierpont Morgan and his International Mercantile Marine Company (IMMC) who purchased the White Star Line for £10 million on 2nd May 1902.

——————— Did You Know That? ———————

J. Pierpont Morgan detested being photographed as he had a large bulbous purple nose, the result of a chronic skin condition called rosacea.

A MODERN NOAH

Lord William James Pirrie was nicknamed 'A Modern Noah'. Indeed, it was the English journalist William T. Stead who once said that Lord Pirrie was: 'the greatest shipbuilder the world has ever known', a man who 'built more ships and bigger ships than any man since the days of Noah'.

ABOVE ALL OTHERS

Captain E. J. Smith was being paid £105.00 per month to command *Titanic* whilst Captain Arthur Rostron of the *Carpathia*, the ship which brought all 705 of *Titanic's* survivors safely to New York after the *Titanic* sank, was in receipt of £53.00 per month.

THE CHOCOLATE SHIP

The chocolatiers Fassbender & Rausch located at the Gendarmenmarkt, Berlin, Germany is one of the most favourite meeting places in the world for connoisseurs of chocolate. This chocolate emporium is unparalleled when it comes to offering its visitors a variety of choices. The *Pralinentheke* offers a choice of handmade truffles, pralines, and sweets of the highest quality and freshness. The famous chocolate house also features an impressive display of chocolate models including the Berlin Reichstag, the Brandenburg Gate and even *Titanic*.

One of *Titanic's* massive reciprocating engines photographed in the Engine Works
at Harland & Wolff. (Ulster Folk and Transport Museum/Jonathan Smith collection)

TITANIC'S RADIO MESSAGES

The following table lists in detail the messages sent and received by the *Titanic* following her collision with an iceberg at 11:40 pm on Sunday 14th April 1912:

Time	Message(s)

Sunday 15th April 1912

12·15 am	CQD (6 times) DE (this is) MGY (6 times) position 41.44 N. 50.24 W.
	The French steamer *Provence* and the German vessel *Frankfurt* were the first ships to receive *Titanic's* first distress signals.
	Titanic sends position to the *Frankfurt*. *Frankfurt* replies: 'OK STBI (standby)"
	Jack Phillips, *Titanic's* Chief Wireless Operator, informs Harold Bride, *Titanic's* Second Wireless Officer, that the *Frankfurt* had answered his call and asked him to take the information to the bridge. Captain Smith then asked for the *Frankfurt's* position.
12·15am	The Canadian Pacific Line's *Mount Temple* hears *Titanic* sending CQD stating she requires assistance.
12·15am	Cape Race Coast Radio Station hears *Titanic* giving her position as 41.44 N. 50.24 W.
12·18am	The SS *Ypiranga*, a German-registered cargo-steamer owned and operated by the Hamburg-America Line, hears CQD from *Titanic*. *Titanic* gives her position as 41.44 N. 50.24 W. and requires assistance (calls about 10 times).
12·25am	*Carpathia* calls *Titanic* and asks: 'Do you know that Cape Cod is sending a batch of messages for you?'
	Titanic replies: 'Come at once. We have struck a berg. It's a CQD OM [it's a distress situation old man]. Position 41.46 N. 50.14 W.'
	Carpathia asks: 'Shall I tell my Captain? Do you require assistance?'

Time	Message(s)
	Titanic replies: 'Yes, come quick.'
	Phillips advises Captain Smith that the *Frankfurt* did not acknowledge her position, merely stating that she would see *Titanic* in a few minutes.
12-25am	Cape Race hears MGY (*Titanic*) give corrected position of 41.46 N. 50.14 W. Calling him, no answer (Titanic's Fourth Officer Boxhall had just provided a corrected position to the radio room).
12-25am	MGY (*Titanic*) sends message: 'CQD. Here (is my) corrected position 41.46 N. 50.14 W. Require immediate assistance. We have collision with iceberg. Sinking. Can hear nothing for noise of steam (engineers releasing excess steam pressure from boilers to minimise risk of explosion).' The message was sent about 15 to 20 times to the *Ypiranga*.
12-26am	The North German Lloyd ocean liner *Prinz Friedrich Wilhelm* calls MGY (*Titanic*) and gives position at 12 am 39.47 N. 50.10 W.
	MGY (*Titanic*) replies: 'Are you coming to our rescue? We have collided with an iceberg. Sinking. Please tell Captain to come.' Prinz Friedrich Wilhelm replies: 'O.K. will tell."
12-27am	*Titanic* sends the following message: 'I require assistance immediately. Struck by iceberg in 41.46 N. 50.14 W.'
12-30am	The *Caronia*, a Cunard ocean liner, sends a CQ message (message addressed to all ships) to the *Baltic* (a White Star Line vessel) and CQD (i.e.: a distress relay message): 'MGY (*Titanic*) struck iceberg, require immediate assistance.'
12-30am	*Mount Temple* hears 'MGY' sent by the *Titanic*. *Mount Temple's* Captain turns his ship around to go to *Titanic's* aid.

Time	Message(s)
12-34am	*Mount Temple* hears *Frankfurt* give MGY (*Titanic*) her position 39.47 N. 52.10 W.
	Titanic replies (to Frankfurt): 'Are you coming to our assistance?"
	Frankfurt replies: 'What is the matter with you?"
	Phillips, perhaps feeling stressed, replies to *Frankfurt*: 'You are a fool, keep out!' It is unclear if the *Frankfurt* thought this message was advising them to actually stay away from the Titanic.
12-45am	*Titanic* calls her sister ship, *Olympic*, which is 500 miles away en route to England. 'SOS.' This was the first use of 'SOS' by *Titanic* with Harold Bride jokingly suggesting to his fellow Marconi operator, Jack Phillips, that it may be his last chance to use the new distress call.
12-50am	*Titanic* calls CQD and replies: 'I require immediate assistance. Position 41.46 N. 50.14 W.' The message was received by another White Star liner, *Celtic*.
12-53am	The *Caronia* to the *Baltic*: 'MGY (RMS *Titanic*) CQD in 41.46 N. 40.14 W. Wants immediate assistance.'
1-00am	MGY gives distress signal. SS *Cincinnati* replies: 'MGY's position 41.46 N. 50.14 W. Assistance from *Cincinnati* not necessary as RMS *Olympic* answered the distress call."
1-00am	*Titanic* replies to the Olympic and gives his position as 41.46 N. 50.14 W., and states: 'We have struck an iceberg.'

Time	Message(s)
1-02am	Titanic calls SS *Asian* and states: 'Want immediate assistance.' The *Asian* replied immediately and received *Titanic's* position as 41.46 N. 50.14 W., which was immediately taken to the bridge. Captain Wood of the *Asian* instructs his wireless operator to have *Titanic's* position repeated.
1-02am	The *Virginian* calls *Titanic* but gets no response. *Cape Race* informs the *Virginian* to report to his Captain that the *Titanic* has struck iceberg and requires immediate assistance.
1-10am	*Titanic* to *Olympic*: 'We are in collision with berg. Sinking head down. 41.46 N. 50.14 W. Come soon as possible."
1-10am	*Olympic* to *Titanic*: 'Get your boats ready. What is your position?"
1-15am	*Baltic* to *Caronia*: 'Please tell RMS *Titanic* we are making towards her."
1-20am	*Virginian* hears Cape Race inform *Titanic*: 'That RMS Baltic is going to her assistance. RMS *Baltic's* position is 170 miles N. of RMS Titanic."
1-25am	*Caronia* notifies *Titanic*: 'RMS *Baltic* is coming to your assistance."
1-25am	*Olympic* sends position to *Titanic* at 4-24 am G.M.T. '40.52 N. 61.18 W,' and asks: 'Are you steering southerly to meet us?'
1-27am	*Titanic* replies to *Olympic*: 'We are putting the women off in the boats."
1-30am	*Titanic* informs *Olympic*: 'We are putting passengers off in small boats. Women and Children in boats, can not last much longer."
1-35am	*Olympic* asks *Titanic* what the weather is like at her location. *Titanic* replies: 'Clear and calm."

Time	Message(s)
1-35am	*Baltic* hears *Titanic* stating: 'Engine room getting flooded.' (Captain Smith had just visited the *Titanic*'s wireless room and advised this to Phillips and Bride).
1-35am	The *Mount Temple* hears the *Frankfurt* ask *Titanic*: 'Are there any boats around you already?' There is no reply.
1-37am	*Baltic* advises *Titanic*: 'We are rushing to you."
1-40am	*Olympic* to *Titanic*: 'AM LIGHTING UP ALL POSSIBLE BOILERS AS FAST AS CAN."
1-40am	Cape Race replies to the *Virginian*: 'Please tell your Captain this: 'The RMS *Olympic* is making all speed for RMS *Titanic*, but his (RMS *Olympic's*) position is 40.32 N. 61.18 W. You are much nearer to RMS *Titanic*. The RMS *Titanic* is already putting women off in the boats, and he replies the weather there is calm and clear. The *Olympic* is the only ship we have heard say, 'Going to the assistance of the RMS *Titanic*. The others must be a long way from the RMS *Titanic*."
1-45am	Last signals heard from *Titanic* by the *Carpathia*: 'Come as quickly as possible old man: the engine-room is filling up to the boilers."
1-45am	*Mount Temple* hears *Frankfurt* calling *Titanic*. There is no reply.
1-47am	Caronia hears *Titanic* but is unable to decipher the signals.
1.47am	*Virginian* hears *Titanic* calling very faintly. It is evident that *Titanic*'s power is being greatly reduced.
1-48am	The *Asian* hears *Titanic* calling SOS and answers *Titanic* but receives no reply.

Time	Message(s)
1-50am	The *Caronia* hears *Frankfurt's* contact with *Titanic*. The Frankfurt is 172 miles from *Titanic* when the first SOS was issued.
1-55am	Cape Race contacts the *Virginian*: 'We have not heard RMS *Titanic* for about half an hour. Her power may be gone.'
2.00am	Captain Edward Smith visits *Titanic*'s wireless room for the last time and speaks to Bride and Phillips: 'Men, you have done your full duty. You can do no more. Abandon your cabin. Now it's every man for himself."
	Bride and Phillips continue sending calls for help.
2-10am	*Virginian* hears two 'V's' signalled faintly in spark similar to *Titanic*'s. It is believed that Phillips was transmitting a test signal whilst Bride adjusted the main transmitter motor-generator field regulators to compensate for the loss of power supply from the engine room.
2-17am	*Virginian* hears *Titanic* call 'CQ' (a call to all ships). *Titanic*'s signals end very abruptly as if the ship had lost all power.
	At this point the wireless room had lost all power and Bride and Phillips made their way up to the Boat Deck where Bride helps launch Collapsible Lifeboat B.
	The *Virginian* attempts to contact *Titanic* and suggested she should try her emergency set. No reply is received.
2-20am	*Virginian* contacts the *Olympic*: 'Have you heard anything about RMS *Titanic*?' *Olympic* replies: 'No. Keeping strict watch, but hear nothing more from RMS *Titanic*. No reply from her.'

Time	Message(s)
	This was the official time the *Titanic* foundered in 41.46 N. 50.14 W. as given by the *Carpathia* in a message to the *Olympic*.
2-35am	*Mount Temple* hears *Carpathia* send the following message: 'If you are there we are firing rockets.'
2-40am	*Carpathia* attempts to contact *Titanic*.
2-58am	The Russian American Line's SS *Birma* thinks she hears *Titanic* and responds: 'Steaming full speed for you. Shall arrive with you at 6.00am. Hope you are safe. We are only 50 miles away now.'
3-00am	*Carpathia* once again attempts to call *Titanic*.
3-28am	*La Provence* sends the following message to *Celtic*: 'Nobody has heard the RMS *Titanic* for about 2 hours.'
4-24am	The *Birma* replies: 'We are 30 miles S.W. off RMS *Titanic*.'
6-40am	The Allan Line steamship SS *Parisian* hears weak signals from *Carpathia* or some radio station saying *Titanic* had struck an iceberg and that the *Carpathia* had rescued many of *Titanic*'s passengers from lifeboats.
6-40am	The *Asian*, with a German oil tanker in tow bound for Halifax, Nova Scotia asks if there is any news of *Titanic*.
7-40am	*Mount Temple* hears MPA (*Carpathia*) report that she rescued 20 boat loads of *Titanic*'s survivors.
8-07am	The *Baltic* sends the following message to the *Carpathia*: 'Can I be of any assistance to you as regards taking some of the passengers from you? Will be in position about 4-30. Let me know if you alter your position.'

Time	Message(s)
8-40am	*Mount Temple* hears *Carpathia* call CQ and say, no need to assist her.
8-45am	The *Olympic* sends a message the White Star Line in New York via Sable Island saying: 'Have not communicated with RMS *Titanic* since midnight.'
8-55am	*Carpathia* replies to *Baltic*: 'Am proceeding to Halifax or New York full speed. You had better proceed to Liverpool. Have about 800 passengers on board.'
9-00am	The *Carpathia* to the *Virginian*: 'We are leaving here with all on board about 800 passengers. Please return to your Northern course."

NB. *Message Table courtesy of Glenn Dunstan, Webmaster: http://www.hf.ro/*

WORLD RECORD-BREAKING *TITANIC* AUCTION

On 17th October 2009, Henry Aldridge and Son held an auction of *Titanic* and White Star Line memorabilia at their Devizes Rooms. A remarkable lot containing an Omega pocket watch, luggage tag and unique studio portrait belonging to third-class passenger Malcolm Johansson, sold for £155,000. Another striking item offered was an oil on canvas painting depicting first-class survivor Eleanor Widener (née Elkins) circa 1880's. Mr and Mrs George D. Widener boarded *Titanic* at Cherbourg with their son, Harry Elkins Widener, Edwin Keeping (Mr Widener's manservant) and the Wideners' maid, Amalie Gieger. They occupied first-class staterooms C80/C82. The oil painting fetched £14,500. Postcards and photographs from the *Titanic*, her passengers and crew are always very highly sought-after at *Titanic* auctions. Leading the way at auction in this respect was a painting of Rev. John Harper and his family which sold for a world record £19,500. Other notable prices included £9,500 for a launch photo of *Titanic* and £7,000 for a photograph of first-class passengers Mr and Mrs J. J. Astor. A two-tier table made from wood salvaged from the wreck site of the *Titanic* sold for £6,000 and a postcard written on board the ill-fated White Star Line vessel by first-class passenger Stanley May sold for £9,500.

———————— Did You Know That? ————————

The Wideners are known for having hosted the dinner for Captain Smith on the night of the disaster.

TITANIC AND THE DRAGONS

Aboard *Titanic* when she finally came to rest at the bottom of the North Atlantic Ocean were 76 cases of 'Dragon's Blood' which were being shipped to New York by Brown Brothers & Company. Dragon's Blood is a bright red resin that is obtained from various plants including *Croton draco, Daemonorops* and *Pterocarpus*. It was a highly popular resin at the turn of the 20th century which had a number of uses: dye, incense, medicine, printer's ink and varnish.

HARLAND & WOLFF'S TRANSFORMATION

Founded	– 1861
Nationalised	– 1977
Privatised	– 1989

———————— Did You Know That? ————————

In 1880, the average output at Harland & Wolff Shipyard was 1,000 tons and rose to 100,000 tons during the mid-1890s.

A HARD TASKMASTER

Edward James Harland, a 23-year old Yorkshireman, was already a hard taskmaster when he was appointed manager of Robert Hickson's shipyard situated at Queen's Island, Belfast in 1854. Shortly after taking up his position he introduced a smoking ban at the yard which hardly endeared him to the workforce. He would often be seen walking around the shipyard with a piece of chalk in his hand marking off what he considered to be inferior workmanship. Indeed, his drive for perfection at the yard almost resulted in a strike before the workforce realised that his management style benefitted everyone. Had it not been for his drive and enthusiasm, the world may never have seen the magnificent *Titanic*.

SISTERS SWAP OVER

The very same day that the *Olympic* was officially delivered to her owners, the White Star Line, the *Titanic* was launched in Belfast – 31st May 1911.

———— 127 ————

CHRISTMAS ONBOARD THE *TITANIC*

When *Titanic* left Southampton harbour, on board was a Mr H. Christmas, aged 33 from Southampton. Mr Christmas worked on the ship as an assistant steward and his body, if ever recovered from the freezing cold waters of the North Atlantic, was never identified. Prior to working on *Titanic*, Mr Christmas worked as an assistant steward on the White Star Line's RMS *Oceanic*.

ROYAL RESPECT

Within hours of the devastating news reaching England that the *Titanic* had sank after colliding with an iceberg, King George V and Queen Mary, sent their sincere condolences and sympathies to the White Star Line. King George V's cousin and Queen Victoria's first grandchild, the German Emperor, Wilhelm II, also sent his condolences.

THE CALL SIGNS

A number of ships and shore stations were in wireless radio contact with the *Titanic* after she struck an iceberg. At the time *Titanic's* call sign was **MGY** whilst the other vessels which *Titanic* was in touch with had the following call signs:

DFT	SS *Frankfurt*
DKF	SS *Prinz Friedrich Wilhelm*
MBC	RMS *Baltic*
MGN	SS *Virginian*
MKC	RMS *Olympic*
MKL	SS *Asian*
MLC	RMS *Celtic*
MLQ	SS *Mount Temple*
MPA	RMS *Carpathia*
SBA	SS *Birma*

Meanwhile the call signs for the two shore stations were:

MCC	Cape Cod
MSE	Cape Race

Titanic's Collapsible D lifeboat, photographed as it came alongside the *Carpathia*.
(Jonathan Smith collection)

MALCOLM'S STORY

On 17th October 2009, Henry Aldridge and Son, held an auction of *Titanic* and White Star Line memorabilia at their Devizes Rooms. In excess of 270 lots went under the hammer with prices ranging from £50 to £60,000. One of the most outstanding items on offer was a remarkable collection of material belonging to Malcolm Johansson, a third-class passenger on *Titanic*. Johansson was 33-years old when the icy cold waters of the North Atlantic claimed the great leviathan. Although he was born in Sweden, he lived and worked in Minneapolis, USA and owned a successful construction business there. In early 1912, he decided to return home to Sweden where he planned to purchase the farm he grew up on as a boy in Bjorkaryd. However, his attempt was an unsuccessful one and he decided to return to the USA. It is believed that Malcolm travelled from Sweden to England on SS *Calypso* before booking his passage on *Titanic* for £7. 15 shillings, boarding her at Southampton on 10th April 1912. Like so many others he was due to travel to the USA on the White Star Line's RMS *Adriatic* but as a result of the 1912 coal strike in Britain, and a very cruel twist of fate, he was transferred to the *Titanic*, the *Adriatic* being unable to make the voyage, her coal stocks having been transferred to the *Titanic*. Malcolm travelled along with fellow Swedes, Gustaf Joel Johansson and Oscar Hedman. Malcolm died in the sinking and his body, No.37, was recovered by the *Mackay-Bennett*.

After he lost his life in the *Titanic* disaster, Malcolm's brother and family stated he had over $1,000 in dollar bills sewn into his socks prior to leaving the USA, presumably the funds he never used to purchase his farm. His brother, Wilhelm Nilsson, wrote to the authorities in New York several times to find out what had happened to the money but his enquiries came to nothing.

WHEN BELFAST RULED THE WORLD

Remarkably at one time in its illustrious history, Harland & Wolff Shipyard, Belfast produced one eighth of the world's total shipping output.

AVERAGE COAL PRICE IN SOUTH WALES IN 1912

Year	Average Selling Price per Annum per Ton of Large Coal		Average Price per Annum per Ton at Pit-mouth	
	s	d	s	d
1912	15	6	11	2

In April 1912, Britain was in the midst of a coal strike and as a result, the White Star Line cancelled the transatlantic sailings of the *Adriatic* and the *Oceanic* and transferred their crew, passengers and coal to the *Titanic*. *Titanic* consumed on average a mammoth 650 tons of coal each day of sailing.

NICE AND COSY

When the *Titanic* was moored in Berth No.44 at the White Star Dock in Southampton on Friday 5th April 1912, beside her rested RMS *Oceanic* in Berth No. 38 and the *City of New York* in Berth No. 39. Across the water from *Titanic's* berth sat the American Line's SS *Philadelphia* and SS *St. Louis* and the White Star Line's SS *Majestic*. Just as *Titanic* was leaving Southampton on 10th April 1912 she sailed past Berth No. 39 and the suction caused by her passing caused the *City of New York* to become torn away from her moorings. Captain Smith quickly ordered *Titanic's* port propeller to be put in reverse and a collision was only just avoided thanks to the very quick actions of a nearby tug captain who managed to get a line on the *City of New York* and prevented her drifting into *Titanic's* side. The near mishap resulted in a one-hour delay to *Titanic's* departure.

FIRST TO HEAR *TITANIC*'S CRY FOR HELP

The Compagnie Générale Transatlantique's (CGT French Line) *La Provence*, one of the first ships in contact with *Titanic* after the ill-fated liner struck an iceberg, was the largest and fastest French steamer when she entered service in 1906. *La Provence* was also the first CGT steamer equipped with wireless telegraphy. In 1914, she was converted into an auxiliary cruiser and renamed *Provence II* and in 1915, she was converted into a troopship. On 16th February 1916, she was torpedoed and sank 65 miles (115 km) off Cape Matapan in the Mediterranean by the German submarine *U-35*, with the loss of 930 lives (870 were rescued). Ironically, the Commander of *U-35* was Arnauld de la Péreire, a distant relative of CGT's founders, Emile and Isaac Péreire.

THE TAXI CONNECTION

The last time Captain Smith's wife saw her husband was when he waved goodbye to her from the taxi which took him from their home on Winn Road, Highfield, Southampton to Southampton harbour where he boarded RMS *Titanic* at 7.00 am on Wednesday 10th April 1912. Captain Smith died five days later when the ship sank. After her husband's death, Captain Smith's widow, Eleanor Sarah Smith, remained in Southampton for a while before moving to London. On 28th April 1931, she was knocked down by a taxi outside her London home and died.

BRAVE TO THE VERY END

Shortly after Captain Edward Smith visited *Titanic's* wireless room for the last time around 2.00am to inform his two Marconi wireless operators, Jack Phillips and Harold Bride, to abandon their posts and save themselves, the pair went up to the Boat Deck and noticed a few members of crew attempting to launch a Collapsible Lifeboat on the port side. It is believed that Phillips decided to return to his station one last time in an attempt to let the *Carpathia* know that the great leviathan's engine room was flooded and her dynamos were going out. That was the last time Bride saw his friend and when the collapsible lifeboat landed on the freezing cold water it capsized leaving Bride and its other occupants trapped underneath it. *Titanic* sank less than 10 minutes later and it was a further 30 minutes before another lifeboat came to the rescue of Bride and those with him. Phillips lost his life when *Titanic* sank but no one knows for sure if he went down with the ship or if he died from exposure aboard the collapsible boat which Bride was on. In his testimony at the subsequent American and British Inquiries held to investigate the *Titanic* disaster, Bride stated that he had never seen Phillips on the lifeboat and was only told that he had been on it by someone else.

Did You Know That?

At both inquiries held following the disaster, Harold Bride said that the *Frankfurt* was the first ship to respond to *Titanic's* distress calls. Bride also said the signal received by *Titanic* from the *Frankfurt* was the strongest signal out of all of the ships he was in contact with after colliding with the iceberg. The latter testimony either meant that the *Frankfurt* was very close to *Titanic* or else the German liner possessed a very powerful wireless device.

HARLAND & WOLFF'S BEST CUSTOMER

The White Star Line was Harland and Wolff Shipyard's best customer. In 1911, the Harland & Wolff Shipyard in east Belfast employed around 15,000 men, 6,000 of whom worked on the construction of the *Titanic*. Amazingly, it is often said in and around the houses and pubs of east Belfast that between 1869 and 1919, there was never a single day that went by when the Harland & Wolff workforce was not building a ship for the White Star Line.

TITANIC AND THE CHINESE CALENDAR

1912 was the Year of the Rat in the Chinese calendar. Coincidentally, traditional Year of the Rat attributes/associations include:

Attribute		
Zodiac Location	1st	(*Titanic* was on her maiden voyage)
Ruling Hours	11.00 pm–1.00 am	(*Titanic* struck an iceberg at 11:40 pm)
Direction	North	(*Titanic* sank in the North Atlantic)
Motto	'I Rule'	(*Titanic* was the largest ship in the world)
Fixed Element	Water	(*Titanic* was built to cross the Atlantic)
Colours	black, red & white	(*Titanic's* colours were predominantly black and white)

Did You Know That?

Harland & Wolff Shipyard was nationalised in 1977, 116 years after its formation in 1861. Twelve years later in 1989, the shipyard was privatised.

THE BLACK GANG

Titanic's firemen, greasers and trimmers were nicknamed 'The Black Gang', a term collectively given to these workers on any ship at the time.

NO APRIL FOOL

Titanic's planned sea trials for Monday 1st April 1912 (April Fool's Day) in Belfast had to be cancelled because of strong winds.

THE ILL CHAIRMAN

Lord William James Pirrie, Chairman of the Harland & Wolff Shipyard, was unable to participate in *Titanic's* sea trials on Tuesday 2nd April 1912 as he was suffering from pneumonia. As a consequence *Titanic's* designer and Pirrie's nephew, Thomas Andrews Jnr., took his place. Meanwhile, J. Bruce Ismay, Chairman and Managing Director of the White Star Line, was also unable to attend due to a previously arranged family engagement. The White Star Line sent Harold Sanderson in Ismay's place.

CAPTAIN SMITH'S LAST-MINUTE CHANGE OF PLANS

On the morning of Tuesday 2nd April 1912, *Titanic* was boarded by the 8 Officers who would conduct her sea trials that day – Captain Edward John Smith, RNR, Chief Officer William McMaster Murdoch, RNR, First Officer Charles Herbert Lightoller, RNR, Second Officer David Blair, Third Officer Herbert John Pitman, Fourth Officer Joseph Groves Boxhall, RNR, Fifth Officer Harold Godfrey Lowe and Sixth Officer James Pell Moody. However, at the last minute, Captain Smith decided to bring aboard Henry Tingle Wilde, who at the time was the Chief Officer of *Olympic*, *Titanic's* older sister. The last-minute inclusion of Wilde as his new Chief Officer meant that Murdoch now became the ship's First Officer and Lightoller was demoted to Second Officer, resulting in Blair missing *Titanic's* maiden voyage. In a strange twist of fate, Blair was the only officer who knew where the binoculars for the Second Officer were kept and when he walked off *Titanic*, no one could find them. Popular belief holds that the key he had in his pocket was used to lock a cabinet where the missing binoculars were stored. Whether this is true or not, *Titanic's* fate would not have hinged on these missing binoculars. Although the Second Officer's pair had been loaned to the lookouts on the Belfast-Southampton trip (there was no specific pair issued to them), it has been well established that they would have been of no use in spotting the iceberg earlier than the lookouts did, and several experienced captains even condemned their use by lookouts at the post-sinking inquiries. Indeed, on Day 5 of the US Senate Committee inquiry into the *Titanic* disaster, Second Officer Charles Lightoller was questioned by Senator Bourne about the use of lookouts aboard *Titanic*. During questioning Lightoller said that he never personally relied on a lookout, preferring instead to keep a lookout himself and went on to say that many other officers aboard ships adopted the same policy. However, Lightoller was quick to point out that this was not a vote of no confidence in the abilities of lookouts; in fact he said they were very smart men but as with many other officers he took his duties very seriously and tended to keep a lookout whilst he was on watch.

TITANIC'S FIRST BREAKFAST

The first breakfast was served on *Titanic* on Wednesday 3rd April 1912, as the liner was making her way to Southampton for provisioning and to board passengers for her maiden voyage to New York. The breakfast consisted of:

Calves' Liver and Bacon
****
Marmalade
****
Fillets of Whiting
****
Cold Meat
****
Fried and Poached Eggs
****
Grilled Ham and Grilled Sausage
****
Strawberry Conserve
****
Kippered Herrings
****
Rolls and Scones
****
Minced Chicken and Watercress
****
Omelettes
****
Quaker Oats Mashed and Sauté Potatoes
****
Toast
****
Tea, Coffee and Fruit Juice

UNCLE GEORGE HELPS *TITANIC* OUT

On Thursday 4th April 1912, whilst en route from Belfast to Southampton *Titanic* passed the Isle of Wight where she met with the Nab Light vessel. Captain George Bowyer, Southampton's senior harbour pilot, boarded the *Titanic* at the lightship from the pilot boat and at 12.00 midnight the leviathan arrived at Berth No.44, the White Star Line Dock at Southampton. The 53-year old Bowyer was affectionately nicknamed 'Uncle George'.

■ THE MOVIE TRIVIA ■■■■■■■■■■■■■■

The full-size exterior replica of *Titanic* was constructed in a tank on a beach south of Rosarito, Baja California, Mexico. Ironically, the work began on 31st May 1996, exactly 85 years after the great ship was launched at the Harland & Wolff Shipyard in Belfast. The set was oriented to face into the prevailing wind so that the smoke from the funnels would blow in the correct direction. The entire movie set was mounted on hydraulic jacks and could be tilted up to 6° intact within the depth of the tank. Indeed, all of the scenes from the movie where there is an exterior sunset shot were filmed at the set in Mexico.

TITANIC'S UNION MEN

It is estimated that approximately 200 members of the British Seafarer's Union and 100 members of the National Sailor's Union and the Fireman's Union signed on aboard *Titanic* for work. All 300 crew members were only too happy to secure work at a time when a national coal strike was gripping Britain.

TITANIC GOOD TO GO

Following *Titanic's* 8 hours of sea trials on Tuesday 2nd April 1912 under the supervision of Board of Trade inspector Francis T. Carruthers, the White Star Line was issued a certificate which permitted her to carry passengers 'for one year from today 2nd April 1912'.

■ THE MOVIE TRIVIA ■■■■■■■■■■■■■■

The filming of the departure scene was shot on a green screen in a parking lot.

AS SHINY AS A NEW PIN

On Saturday 6th April 1912 (Easter Saturday), countless boatloads of coal were delivered to Berth No. 44 of the White Star Dock at Southampton harbour to load onto *Titanic* ahead of her maiden voyage to New York. Some 4,500 tons of coal arrived at the port from various coaling and shipping ports at a time when Britain was in the middle of a national coal strike. Indeed, there was so much coal that it took the workers a full day to load it onto *Titanic*. When the final load of coal was being transferred to the ship's bunkers, the men from *Titanic's* Deck Department were left with the arduous task of removing all of the coal dust that had landed on various parts of her during the delivery process. These men scrubbed the boat decks and cleaned the portholes. The interior clean-up was performed by stewards who vacuumed the carpets and polished the fixtures and fittings leaving *Titanic* in pristine condition.

HOW *TITANIC* GOT HER NAME

Olympic, Titanic and *Gigantic* (later renamed *Britannic*), the White Star Line's three giant sister ships, are the adjectival forms of *Olympus, Titan* and *Giant* respectively. The Greek Gods of Mount Olympus, led by Zeus, defeated the Titans, led by Atlas, in a 10-year war, imprisoned many of the Titans in Tartarus and exiled the others. Many years later a group of Giants, enraged by the exile of the Titans, rebelled against the Olympians but they were all killed in battle by the Olympians.

SPORT OFF THE FRONT PAGES

Exactly three weeks after the *Titanic* disaster, the fifth Olympic Games (Olympiad V) were officially opened on 5th May 1912 by King Gustav V in Stockholm, Sweden. At the time the sinking of the *Titanic* on 15th April was very much still in the headlines as the US inquiry into the disaster was still ongoing. The hearings commenced on 19th April at the Waldorf-Astoria Hotel, New York, the day after the *Carpathia* arrived back in New York with 705 *Titanic* survivors on board, and were conducted by a special sub-committee of the Senate Commerce Committee, chaired by Senator William A. Smith. After the first week of the hearings in New York they moved to a new location, the new caucus room of the Russell Senate Office Building in Washington, D.C. In total, 82 witnesses testified that ice warnings received by the ship's wireless operators were either not passed on or acted upon; that the White Star Line vessel did not have enough lifeboats to accommodate all of the passengers onboard; that *Titanic* was travelling at full speed despite entering an area where there was known to be ice and a ship in close proximity to *Titanic* (said to be the *Californian*) apparently failed to respond to the numerous distress rockets she fired. The hearings concluded on 28th May 1912 and the findings were published in a 1,100-page Senate Document No. 726, 62nd Congress, 2nd session document entitled: '*Titanic' Disaster: Hearings before a Subcommittee of the Committee on Commerce, United States Senate, Sixty-Second Congress, Second Session, Pursuant to S. Res. 283, Directing the Committee on Commerce to Investigate the Causes Leading to the Wreck of the White Star Liner 'Titanic.'*

TITANIC II TO BE BUILT IN BELFAST

In July 1999, the Harland & Wolff Shipyard in Belfast announced plans to construct a £400 m housing, tourism and technology development on Queen's Island in Belfast. The plans included the construction of a replica of the yard's most famous ship, RMS *Titanic*.

PLAYFUL PASSENGERS

Passengers on *Titanic* passed the day playing a variety of games including board games, cards and shuffleboard. Shuffleboard was played by sliding discs along the deck at a target area which was marked out with boxes numbered 1–10, with 10 the highest score. Ladies were permitted to stand slightly closer to the score target to compensate for restrictions in movement resulting from tight corsets.

A TALE OF WHISKERS

Reports following the sinking of the *Titanic* stated that there were a number of animals aboard the ship when she struck an iceberg. It has been claimed that there were 30 cockerels, 9 dogs (5 of which were with their owners in their cabins), 4 hens and roosters, 1 yellow canary and the ship's cat named Jenny. Only 3 of the dogs and the canary survived the sinking of the giant liner. The cost for a passenger to bring a pet aboard *Titanic* for the ship's maiden voyage was the same price for a child to sail on her, half fare.

Did You Know That?

During *Titanic's* maiden voyage two second-class passengers, Mrs Nellie Hocking and Edwina Trout, claimed that their sleep was disturbed by the sound of a rooster crowing, which both ladies believed to be a sign of bad luck.

TITANIC'S ILLUSTRIOUS RELATIVES

RMS *Titanic* was just one of nearly 2,000 ships built at the world famous Harland & Wolff Shipyard in Belfast.

THE PERFECT MARRIAGE

Edward James Harland's British technology and Gustav Wilhelm Wolff's German efficiency created the perfect marriage when Harland made Wolff his partner in 1861. The pair began to draw up radical new ship designs, with steel decks as opposed to wooden decks and squarer hulls to accommodate larger loads. Meanwhile, a greater length to width ratio resulted in a much faster, sleeker, more efficient vessel. In 1868, just seven years after the company's formation, Harland & Wolff had racked-up losses of £16,000. However, the German shipping financier, Gustav Schwabe (Wolff's uncle), came to their rescue when he introduced them to the young Liverpool businessman Thomas Ismay who decided to buy the yard's yet unnamed ship given Yard No.44 which was under construction at the time. Schwabe had financed Ismay the sum of £1,000 to purchase the bankrupt White Star Line on 18th January 1868 and contributed 25% of the capital for Ismay's new company, still using the house flag of the White Star Line, to purchase Yard No. 44. Little did they know it at the time but the Harland & Wolff and Ismay partnership would soon dominate the lucrative world of transatlantic travel over the closing stages of the 19th century and the first decades of the 20th century. Harland & Wolff received their first orders for new ships from the White Star Line on 30th July 1869.

TITANIC, BELFAST AND HOME RULE IN IRELAND

The day after *Titanic* set forth on her maiden voyage from Southampton to New York, the Liberal British Prime Minister, Herbert Henry Asquith, introduced the Third Home Rule Bill which foresaw granting Ireland self-government. The Bill was passed by the House of Commons by a majority of 10 votes but rejected by the House of Lords, 326 votes to 69. However, two years later the Home Rule Act 1914 was passed.

THE OLYMPIC MUTINEERS

Just 9 days after *Titanic* sank, the firemen, greasers and trimmers on her older sister, RMS *Olympic*, went on strike on 24th April 1912 claiming that the ship's newly acquired 40 collapsible lifeboats taken from troopships in Southampton harbour were not seaworthy. *The New York Times* reported that the 276 strikers (180 firemen, 72 trimmers and 24 greasers) collected their kitbags and walked off the liner singing 'We're All Going The Same Way Home'. The strike resulted in the postponement of *Olympic's* scheduled departure from Southampton for New York and the leviathan lay off Spithead waiting for her crew members to return to duty. When the strikers left the ship the seamen on board became discontented and refused to handle the ship's ropes, leaving the stewards and White Star Line officers to perform this duty. The men dubbed the 'Olympic Mutineers', were supported

by 54 of *Olympic's* seamen, all of whom appeared in Portsmouth Magistrates Court on 4th May 1912 charged with mutiny. However, although the Magistrates agreed that the mutiny charge had been proved by the White Star Line, they stated that it would be inexpedient to imprison or fine the mutineers under the circumstances that had arisen prior to their refusal to obey orders and released all 54 in the hope that they would return to work.

THE MAIN RIVAL

Prior to the emergence of the White Star Line in the late 1860s the Cunard Line ruled the seas in terms of passenger liners. Samuel Cunard was born on 21st November 1787 in Halifax, Nova Scotia, Canada and when he was just 17 years old, he became the manager of his own general store. In 1839, he relocated to the United Kingdom in order to tender for the Royal Mail contract to provide a regular scheduled transatlantic mail service between Great Britain and the USA. The 52-year-old Cunard was awarded the tender and founded the British and North American Royal Mail Steam Packet Company (later to become the Cunard Line). On 4th July 1840, Cunard's first ship, RMS *Britannia,* commenced her maiden voyage. In January 1842, Charles Dickens travelled to the USA on the *Britannia.*

■ THE MOVIE TRIVIA ■■■■■■■■■■■■■■■

A total of 12 dives to the wreckage of *Titanic* were made during the movie. The deep-sea camera held only 12 minutes' worth of film although each dive took several hours. Therefore, to make the best use of the resources available to him, director James Cameron had a 1/33 scale model of the wreck constructed and used it to show the operators of the Russian sub exactly what shots he wanted.

MARCONI SPEAKS ABOUT *TITANIC*

On Wednesday 18th April 1912, when the world was still coming to terms with the devastating news that the *Titanic* had sunk just three days earlier, Guglielmo Marconi, the inventor of the wireless, made his first public appearance before an American audience. He gave a lecture in the Engineering Societies Building in New York under the auspices of the New York Electrical Society. During his speech he spoke about how wireless telegraphy helped save the lives of the *Titanic* survivors whilst a telegram from Thomas Alva Edison was read out in which he stated that he regretted his inability to be present at the lecture and congratulated Marconi upon the success of his wireless telegraph invention and the work his system had done in saving human life in disasters at sea.

JUST HOW DID CAPTAIN SMITH DIE?

There are several differing accounts of how *Titanic* Captain Edward John Smith died on 15th April 1912. One story claims that he swam to the overturned Collapsible Lifeboat B with a baby in his arms and after handing the baby to a female passenger he swam off in the freezing cold waters. Harold Bride, one of the two Marconi wireless operators onboard *Titanic*, said that he had seen Captain Smith dive into the sea from the open bridge just minutes before the final plunge began. Another report suggested that Captain Smith went down with his ship standing on the Boat Deck helping others to safety to the very end.

Did You Know That?

Captain Edward John Smith was first portrayed on the silver screen by the German actor, Otto Wernicke, in the 1943 Nazi propaganda movie *Titanic*.

TITANIC'S CAPTAIN NEMO

Many people consider Robert Ballard, the man who discovered the shipwreck of RMS *Titanic* in 1985, to be a modern-day Captain Nemo. (Captain Nemo is a fictional character who featured in Jules Verne's *20,000 Leagues Under The Sea*.) Ballard visited the wreck site of the *Titanic* in a submersible named *Alvin* whilst Captain Nemo roamed the sea in a submarine named *Nautilus*.

GONE FOREVER

By 2.00 am, 2 hours and 20 minutes after *Titanic* struck the iceberg, she was flooded with approximately 39,000 tons of water. Twenty minutes later she sank.

LOCKED BELOW?

John E. Hart was a steward in third class on the *Titanic*. On Day 9 of the British inquiry into the *Titanic* disaster he was questioned at length about 'locked barriers/gates' on the ship. The question as to whether or not locked gates prevented third-class passengers from gaining access to the Boat Deck after *Titanic* collided with an iceberg, thereby contributing to their deaths, remains a popular, yet highly debated subject on many *Titanic* websites to this day. Movies such as *A Night To Remember* and *Titanic* depict third-class passengers trapped behind locked barriers/gates as the cold waters of the North Atlantic rise within the ship. *Titanic* did have two sets of Bostwick (collapsible) gates on E Deck: one in the crew area and the other in the third-class area. Hart was asked what means were employed to prevent the third-class passengers during the voyage from straying into the first-

class and second-class decks and quarters of the ship (*Question No. 10151*). Hart replied that there were collapsible gates throughout the ship which could easily be opened. Despite further probing about the barriers and gates, Hart maintained that at no time during the period he spent on the *Titanic* had he ever seen any barrier or gate locked, nor had he ever observed it done on any of the other ships he had served on. It was testimony such as Hart's which eventually disposed of any concerns that third-class passengers on *Titanic* had been trapped within their own areas. Both the American and British inquiries into the disaster were satisfied over this issue, and no locked barriers have ever been found during any investigations of the wreck of the *Titanic*. In any event, class distinctions in place at the time would have effectively kept third-class passengers from crossing out of their own parts of the ship as effectively as any locked gates.

Did You Know That?

Although many third-class stewards abandoned their areas and left passengers to their own fates, John Hart and other stewards worked diligently to shepherd as many passengers as they could to safety in the limited time remaining to them.

HITLER SPYING ON *TITANIC*'S HOME PORT

During the 1970s, Bridget Hitler, the wife of Adolf's half-brother Alois, published her 'memoirs' which included a fanciful story about a 23-year-old Adolf Hitler spending six months in Liverpool in 1912, to avoid conscription to the Austro-Hungarian Army. It is claimed that Hitler stayed with Alois and Bridget in Upper Stanhope Street, Toxteth, Liverpool. Other accounts of Hitler's supposed stay in Liverpool included claims that he often visited the docks to make a note of the shipping using the port, *Titanic's* registered home port, for future reference should Germany ever go to war with Great Britain.

TITANIC'S MAN FROM UNCLE

In Roy Ward Baker's 1958 movie *A Night to Remember,* the role of *Titanic's* Assistant Wireless Operator Harold Bride was played by the Scottish actor David McCallum, who is best known for playing the role of Ilya Kuryakin, in the hit 1960s television series, *The Man From U.N.C.L.E.*

A GERMAN FAMILY'S LUCKY ESCAPE

In 1911, Philip Hohnstein emigrated to the United States of America from his home in Norka, a German colony in Russia. A year later his wife, Louise, followed him along with his grandfather, Henry, and his grandfather's two brothers, Alexander and George. His family were booked on *Titanic's* maiden voyage from Southampton to New York, but their trip was cancelled when one of his grandfather's brothers became ill and was too sick to travel. Consequently, they left for the USA a week later on 17th April 1912 aboard the steamship *Haverford*.

CAPTAIN SMITH'S MEMORIAL

On 29th July 1914, just six days before the world would witness the outbreak of World War I, a statue in memory of Captain Smith was unveiled by his daughter, Helen Melville Smith, in Beacon Park, Lichfield, England. The life-size bronze statue was designed by Lady Kathleen Scott and stands 7 feet, 8 inches high and sits on a 7 foot high plinth carved from Cornish granite. The memorial cost £740 to make. However, as Captain Smith was born in Hanley, Stoke-on-Trent, Stoke has made vain attempts to have the statue moved there. A plaque which was placed on Hanley Town Hall in his memory in 1913 was later moved to Etruria Middle School. The plinth on his statue bears the inscription:

CAPT. OF RMS TITANIC
COMMANDER
EDWARD JOHN SMITH, RD, RNR.

BORN JANUARY 27 1850 DIED APRIL 15 1912

BEQUEATHING TO HIS COUNTRYMEN
THE MEMORY AND EXAMPLE OF A GREAT HEART
A BRAVE LIFE AND A HEROIC DEATH

"BE BRITISH"

Did You Know That?

Lady Kathleen Scott (1870–1947) was the widow of
Captain Robert Falcon Scott, 'Scott of the Antarctic'.

EXEMPT FROM ANY BLAME

Although questions about *Titanic's* sinking were raised in the House of Commons concerning the insufficient number of lifeboats aboard the leviathan, no formal charge was brought against the White Star Line by the British Board of Trade. Meanwhile, the White Star Line did not pay any compensation to the families of the 1,523 souls who lost their lives in the North Atlantic on Monday 15th April 1912.

■ THE MOVIE TRIVIA ■■■■■■■■■■■■■■■

Titanic was the first film to be released on video (DVD/VHS) while it was still being shown in cinemas.

TITANIC'S SINKING RESULTS IN MAJOR CHANGE

After the sinking of *Titanic*, all ships including those under construction at the time, had to comply with newly introduced safety regulations. Many ships, including *Titanic's* older sister, *Olympic*, were refitted at Harland & Wolff in compliance with the new legislation. Indeed, there was so much work going on at the Belfast shipyard after the sinking that Harland & Wolff's profits shot up considerably by the end of 1912.

——————— Did You Know That? ———————

Whereas there were in excess of 2,200 people aboard *Titanic* there were only 8 people on Noah's Ark: Noah, his wife, his three sons (Shem, Ham and Joseph) and their three wives.

ABLE-BODIED BUT LOWLY PAID

Able-Bodied Seamen on the *Titanic* signed on for work on the ship on 6th April 1912 at a monthly wage of £5.00.

——————— Did You Know That? ———————

It is claimed that when some of Harland & Wolff's workforce heard the devastating news that the world's greatest and biggest ship which they had built in Belfast had sunk, they were so much in shock that some said: 'She was alright when she left here.'

THE FAMILY CURSE

On her sixth voyage and less than a year after making her maiden voyage HMHS *Britannic*, the younger sister ship to *Olympic* and *Titanic*, ran into a mine or was struck by a torpedo and sank within one hour. Although she was originally destined to travel on the Southampton to New York route, the *Britannic* never carried a fare-paying passenger on any of her voyages. She was the second of the famous three White Star Line's Olympic class liners to sink.

NOT SUCH A SLEEPY COUPLE

On 10th April 1912, Henry Sleeper Harper and his wife, Myra Haxtun Harper, boarded *Titanic* at Cherbourg. Mr Harper, a wealthy publisher (his grandfather started the Harper and Sons Publishing Company), and his wife were returning home to the USA after touring Europe and Asia. The Harpers were accompanied on board *Titanic* by their dragoman, Hammad Hassab, whose services they had secured when visiting Cairo, Egypt. A dragoman was a person who could serve as an interpreter, a translator and a guide in Middle Eastern countries. The Harpers travelled as first-class passengers on *Titanic* (Ticket No. PC 17572, £76 14s 7d) and occupied Cabin D-33. Henry brought his Pekinese dog named 'Sun Yat-Sen' with him (the dog had Contract Ticket No. 869 – £1 19s 7d.). Shortly after the call to launch the lifeboats was made by Captain Smith, the Harpers, Hassab and the dog were safely loaded into Lifeboat No. 3 and later rescued by the *Carpathia*. Myra died on 27th November 1923 and Henry died on 1st March 1944 at his home in New York City.

TITANIC'S SCULPTOR

Paul Romaine Chevré, a sculptor born in Brussels, Belgium of French parents in 1867, was aboard *Titanic* on her maiden voyage. He was on his way to Ottawa via New York to attend the unveiling of a bust he had carved of the Canadian Prime Minister, Sir Wilfrid Laurier, in the lobby of the Grand Trunk Pacific Railway's Château Laurier Hotel in Ottawa. The hotel was scheduled to officially open for business on 26th April 1912. Chevré was playing cards with three other gentlemen in the Café Parisien when the ship struck an iceberg and was rescued in Lifeboat No.7 by the *Carpathia*.

TITANIC IN 'A&E'

The Art and Entertainment television network, commonly referred to as 'A & E', featured a three-part mini-series on all aspects of the *Titanic* which it then released on DVD in January 2002. The documentary includes sections on the sinking of the *Titanic*, the legacy of the ship and the discovery of her wreckage.

■ THE MOVIE TRIVIA ■■■■■■■■■■■■■■

When James Cameron was writing the script for *Titanic*, his intention was for his main characters, Rose DeWitt Bukater and Jack Dawson, to be entirely fictitious. However, shortly after Cameron completed his script for the movie he learned that there had been a real J. Dawson who lost his life when the ship went down in 15th April 1912. Joseph Dawson was a trimmer whose body was salvaged and buried at Fairview Lawn cemetery in Nova Scotia with many other *Titanic* victims. Today, his gravestone (No. 227) is the most widely visited in the cemetery.

FOREVER LINKED

On the day that the *Titanic* was launched at the Harland & Wolff Shipyard in Belfast, 31st May 1911, Lord William James Pirrie, the chairman of Harland & Wolff, and his wife Lady Margaret Montgomery Carlisle Pirrie, celebrated their birthdays. Not long after the death of her husband on 19th June 1924, Viscountess Pirrie was appointed President of Harland & Wolff, a new position specifically requested for his wife by Lord Pirrie before his death. On many occasions Lord Pirrie made it publicly known that he had consulted his wife on numerous important decisions concerning the Belfast shipyard. There are many reported accounts of Lady Pirrie arriving at the yard around 6.00 pm every day in a chauffeur-driven Rolls Royce to help her husband finish off the day's business, which sometimes lasted until 9.00 pm. Lady Pirrie was a daughter of Professor John Carlisle of Belfast University and a sister of the Chief Naval Architect at Harland & Wolff in 1899, Sir Alexander Carlisle. Indeed, it was Sir Alexander Carlisle who designed RMS *Oceanic*, the largest ship in the world when she was launched at the Harland & Wolff Shipyard on 14th January 1899. It was Lady Pirrie who was charged with the responsibility of informing her husband of the sinking of *Titanic*. Lord Pirrie was extremely proud of the *Titanic* and was due to sail on her maiden voyage from Southampton to New York until he fell ill and allowed his nephew, Thomas Andrews, *Titanic's* designer, to take his place.

Did You Know That?

In 1910, Hugh Dickson of the Royal Nurseries in Belfast bred a new rose. 'The Lady Pirrie Rose'.

SHIPS CAPTAINED BY EDWARD JOHN SMITH

In total Captain Edward John Smith took command of 15 different vessels, commanding SS *Britannic* on four separate occasions. Interestingly, his first command, the *Lizzie Fennell* (May 1876–January 1880), was the only vessel he took charge of which was not in the White Star Line's fleet.

Name	Period	About the Ship
Lizzie Fennell	May 1876–Jan 1880	His first command was a sailing vessel.
SS *Republic*	Apr–Aug 1887	Temporary command.
SS *Baltic*	Apr–May 1888	
SS *Britannic*	June– Sept 1888	
SS *Cufic*	Dec 1888	Commanded this cattle transporter for her maiden voyage.
SS *Republic*	Jan 1889	His second time in command of the vessel.
SS *Celtic*	Apr–July 1889	
SS *Coptic*	Dec 1889–Feb 1890	In the Australian service.
SS *Adriatic*	Dec 1890–Feb 1891	Smith went back to the North Atlantic route.
SS *Runic*	Mar–Apr 1891	Cattle transporter.
SS *Britannic*	May 1891–May 1893	His second charge in command of the vessel.
SS *Adriatic*	June 1893	His second charge in command of the vessel.
SS *Britannic*	July 1893–Jan 1895	His third charge in command of the vessel.
SS *Cufic*	Jan 1895	His second charge in command of the vessel.
SS *Britannic*	Jan–Apr 1895	His fourth charge in command of the vessel.
SS *Germanic*	May–June 1895	
SS *Majestic*	July 1895–June 1904	When the Boer War started in 1899, Smith and the *Majestic* were called upon to transport troops to Cape Colony, South Africa. (He made two trips.) It was Smith's longest command of a vessel.

Name	Period	About the Ship
SS *Germanic*	Dec 1902–May 1903	Commanded the *Germanic* for a second time whilst the *Majestic* was undergoing a refit.
RMS *Baltic*	June 1904–Mar 1907	Commanded her maiden voyage from Southampton to New York on 29th June 1904.
RMS *Adriatic*	8th May 1907–Feb 1911	Commanded her maiden voyage from Liverpool to New York on 8th May 1907.
RMS *Olympic*	May 1911–Mar 1912	Commanded her maiden voyage from Southampton to New York on 14th June 1911. Collided with HMS *Hawke* on 20th September 1911.
RMS *Titanic*	1st Apr 1912–15th Apr 1912	Commanded her maiden voyage from Southampton to New York on 10th April 1912. She sank five days later after hitting an iceberg.

■ THE MOVIE TRIVIA ■ ■ ■ ■ ■ ■ ■ ■ ■ ■ ■ ■

The scenes during which Thomas Andrews is seen chastising Second Officer Charles Lightoller for lowering the lifeboats without filling them to capacity is the only scene in the entire movie in which the actors' breath was not digitally added in later.

Did You Know That?

Smith's first sea adventure was when he served as an apprentice aboard the three-masted sailing vessel *Senator Weber*, from 5th February 1867 to 8th February 1868.

COMPANIONS TO THE VERY END

Miss Malaki Attala, a 17-year-old servant from Syria, boarded the *Titanic* along with her Syrian companion, 30-year old Youssef Ibrahim Shawah, at Cherbourg as third-class passengers. Both died when *Titanic* sank, while their bodies, if ever recovered, were never identified.

———————————— Did You Know That? ————————————

The White Star Line reported Youssef Shawah as being saved in their
passenger list dated 9th May 1912.

LUCKY PRIEST RESCUED

Arthur John Priest was born in Southampton on 31st August 1889 and worked on
the *Titanic* as a fireman. On 20th September 1911, he was on the *Olympic*, *Titanic's*
older sister, when she collided with HMS *Hawke*. He signed on as a fireman on
Titanic just four days before she set sail from Southampton on her ill-fated maiden
voyage to New York. Arthur left the *Asturias* to work on *Titanic* having been aboard
her during her maiden voyage when she was involved in an accident: a sign of
things to come for the young fireman. It is believed that he was rescued from
Lifeboat No.15 by the *Carpathia* just hours after *Titanic* sank. However, Arthur's
luck at sea did not end with his experience on the *Titanic*. He served on the
Alcantra (a Royal Mail Steamship Packet Company vessel pressed into service by
the Royal Navy in April 1915 and converted into an Armed Merchant Cruiser)
during her closely-fought battle with the German raider *Greif* in the North Sea on
29th February 1916 (the *Alcantra* was sunk by a torpedo with the loss of 72 men
while Arthur survived, suffering a shrapnel wound). He then joined HMHS
Britannic, *Titanic's* younger sister, and survived her sinking after she hit a mine on
21st November 1916. His final ship (a hospital ship) was HMHS *Donegal* which
was sunk by a German torpedo on 17th April 1917. (He escaped with a very serious
injury to his head which ended his war service.)

———————————— Did You Know That? ————————————

Priest used to jokingly claim that he was forced to retire from the sea
because no one wished to sail on the same vessel as him given his
'unlucky' track record at sea.

TITANIC'S BELGIAN CONNECTION

Four Belgian men survived the sinking of *Titanic*: William DeMessemaeker,
Theodoor De Mulder, Jules Sap and Jean Scheerlinckx. A short while after the
sinking De Mulder, Sap and Scheerlinckx joined a travelling roadshow and were
promised $5.00 each per day to retell their story of what life had been like onboard
Titanic and the events that followed after she struck an iceberg. However, the owner
of the show then absconded with all of the money, without having paid them a
single cent.

■ THE MOVIE TRIVIA ■■■■■■■■■■■■■

The hands seen sketching Rose are not Leonardo DiCaprio's. In fact they are the hands of the director, James Cameron. However, as Cameron is left-handed the scene had to be mirror-imaged in post-production to make it look like Jack (DiCaprio) who is right-handed, was making the sketch. Indeed, Cameron drew all the pictures in Jack's sketchbook.

Did You Know That?

After William DeMessemaeker returned home to Belgium in 1931, two years after the Great Depression swept the USA, he turned his home in Aspelare into a roadside cafe and named it 'In den Titanic', ('In the Titanic').

THE ARROL GANTRY

Before work could even commence at the Harland & Wolff Shipyard in Belfast on the three Olympic-Class liners (*Olympic, Titanic* and *Gigantic*) ordered by the White Star Line, slipways had to be put in place to accommodate the building of these huge vessels. Sir William Arrol & Company, the famous Scottish civil engineering concern founded in Dalmarnock in 1873 by William Arrol, was contracted by the Belfast shipyard to construct a large gantry (the 'Arrol Gantry') in order that the construction of the first two of the three sister ships could commence (the *Olympic* and the *Titanic*). Between 1906 and 1908, William Arrol & Co designed and erected the huge gantry system and, like the liners that were to be constructed beneath the mammoth structure, the gantry itself was of an impressive scale. It towered 230 feet in height, 840 feet in length and 270 feet in width. The impressive steel structure weighed almost 6,000 tons and was one of the largest of its kind in the world, dominating the Belfast skyline for decades to come. The concrete base had a slight slope from the forward end of the gantry down to the river basin. Across the top of the gantry were cranes to help lift heavy steel plates into place during the construction of the leviathans. The original slipways Nos. 2, 3 and 4 at the shipyard were converted into shipways (Nos. 1 and 2) and the Arrol Gantry was constructed over them at a cost of £100,000. William Arrol was knighted in 1890 and passed away in 1913, but his company carried on trading under his name until 1969. Other notable achievements associated with the William Arrol name are the construction of the Forth Bridge in Scotland (opened in 1890) and the Nile Bridge, Cairo, Egypt (1908). However, Sir William's most famous construction stands proudly in London over the River Thames: Tower Bridge, built in 1894.

Did You Know That?

Prior to the outbreak of the First World War in August 1914, all of the White Star Line's ships, with the exception of one, were built in Belfast.

SIDE BY SIDE

On the same day (31st May 1911) that the *Titanic* was launched at the Harland & Wolff Shipyard in Belfast in a ceremony attended by the White Star Line Chairman and Managing Director, J. Bruce Ismay, and the ship's financial backer, J. Pierpont Morgan, *Titanic's* older sister, the *Olympic*, was delivered to her new owners, the Oceanic Steam Navigation Company (owners of the White Star Line). The *Olympic* sailed down the River Lagan with Ismay and Morgan on board to embark on her maiden voyage.

TITANIC DESIGNER RESIGNS

In April 1911, just one month before the ship he helped design, the *Titanic,* was launched, Alexander Carlisle resigned from his position as Managing Director at Harland & Wolf Shipyard, Belfast. He was 56 years old at the time and little is known about the exact reasons behind his departure from the yard, although it is widely believed that he had become dissatisfied with the way his brother-in-law, Lord William James Pirrie, was running the company. When he learned the devastating news that *Titanic* had sank, family and friends said it broke his heart. Two months before he died on 5th March 1926, he paid in advance for his funeral service and directed that his body be cremated at Golders Green, London and that the organist should play 'The Merry Widow Waltz' at his funeral. According to reports he chose this upbeat number saying: 'I am sure it will be more agreeable than the Dead March from Saul.'

LOOKING SHIPSHAPE

On 4th April 1912 (Holy Thursday) dockyard workers at Southampton harbour 'dressed' *Titanic* in a panoply of flags and pennants for the occasion of her maiden arrival at the port. Later that evening the flags and pennants were taken down. This was the only occasion the ship was ever dressed although many artists have depicted her with flags as she set sail on her maiden voyage. Good Friday 1912 (5th April) was the first recruitment day in Southampton for the ship's crew.

The *Titanic* dressed in flags at her berth in Southampton on Good Friday, 5 April 1912
(Jonathan Smith postcard collection)

WORLD'S LARGEST PASSENGER SHIPS BEFORE AND AFTER *TITANIC*

The following table lists a number of ships which preceded and succeeded *Titanic* as the largest passenger liner in the world:

Name	Owner	Period
RMS *Lucania*	The Cunard Line	1893–97
SS *Kaiser Wilhelm der Grosse*	Norddeutsche Lloyd (NDL)	1897–99
RMS *Oceanic*	The White Star Line	1899–1901
RMS *Celtic*	The White Star Line	1901–05
RMS *Baltic*	The White Star Line	1905–06
SS *Kaiserin Auguste Victoria*	Hamburg America Line	1906–07
RMS *Lusitania*	The Cunard Line	1907
RMS *Mauretania*	The Cunard Line	1907–11
RMS *Olympic*	The White Star Line	1911–12
RMS *Titanic*	The White Star Line	1911–12
RMS *Olympic*	The White Star Line	1912–13
SS *Imperator*	Hamburg-America Line	1913–14

--- Did You Know That? ---

The *Kaiser Wilhelm der Grosse* underwent three name changes, all with different owners: USS *Kaiserin Auguste Victoria* (1919, US Navy), SS *Kaiserin Auguste Victoria* (1920, The Cunard Line) and RMS *Empress of Scotland* (1921–30, Canadian Pacific Line).

TITANIC'S ZOO

In the cargo hold of *Titanic* there were various animal products which were being shipped to the USA including: 79 goat's skins, 15 cases of rabbit hair, 12 cases of ostrich feathers, 3 bales of sheepskins and 2 cases of horsehair.

TWO CLOSE FRIENDS

On 1st January 1910, two close friends, Henry Sutehall Jnr. and Howard Irwin, began a journey which would take them around the world from the USA to England to Australia to the Suez Canal to the Mediterranean with the intention of arriving back in the USA in early 1912. Henry was a qualified trimmer of leather upholstery and during their world tour the two friends often found work as trimmers but on occasion simply had to do whatever work was on offer to get by. They even worked on a peach farm in California, USA. Around mid-1911 they parted company, agreeing to meet again in England in April 1912 to set sail together on *Titanic's* maiden voyage from Southampton to New York, the last leg of their world tour. Howard arrived in England a few days before Henry and they both booked their passage back to the USA on *Titanic*. On the morning of Wednesday 10th April 1912, the scheduled day for *Titanic's* departure, Henry arrived at Southampton dock and stood around waiting for his friend. He had Howard's trunk with him. When it became apparent that Howard was not going to show up, Henry boarded *Titanic* and lost his life just five days later when she sank. Henry's body, if ever recovered, was never identified while his close friend died in 1953.

--- Did You Know That? ---

In 1993, RMS Titanic, Inc. recovered Irwin's trunk close to the wreckage of *Titanic* and sent it to France for the restoration of its contents. When the trunk was opened, among its contents was Irwin's diary from 1910 with the entry for New Year's Day setting out his and Sutehall's plan to tour the world.

THE FIRST WHITE STAR LINE SHIP TO SINK

In 1912, the *Titanic* was considered to be the pinnacle of naval architecture and technological achievement, deemed to be 'practically unsinkable' according to *The Shipbuilder* magazine. However, the same was said of another ship more than half a century earlier, a ship which would claim the unwanted tag of being the first White Star Line vessel to sink. RMS *Tayleur*, a fully-rigged iron clipper was the largest ship in the world when she set sail on her maiden voyage from Liverpool, her place of birth, to Melbourne, Australia on 19th January 1854. She was named after Charles Tayleur, the founder of the Vulcan Engineering Works, Bank Quay, Warrington, England. Just two days after she left Liverpool the *Tayleur* found herself caught in the middle of a dense fog in the Irish Sea off the east coast of the island of Lambay, Ireland, approximately five miles from Dublin Bay. She ran aground on the nearby rocks resulting in the loss of more than 250 lives. The disaster haunted the White Star Line for many years.

TITANIC'S COLOURS

Area	Colour	Comments
Cranes	White and white/brown	The cranes located in the well deck areas were white with the lower halves painted to match the brown of the well decks. All other cranes were entirely white. All had their bases painted light grey on top, with the operator's platforms and top rails painted black.
Deck chairs	Teak	The teak wood was unpainted. The centre section of the seat area was rattan, painted light tan.
Decks	Yellow pine with teak margin boards	The decks were natural wood, with a bleached white appearance when not wet.
Deck hardware (anchors, bitts, capstans etc.)	Black	The capstans had bronze tops.
Deckhouses	White with dark grey roofs	
Doors (exterior)	White outside	
Funnels (lower part)	Buff	Buff was a unique colour difficult to accurately describe but approximately a light tan with hints of yellow, peach and brown.
Funnels (upper part)	Black	
Hatch covers	Unpainted canvas	
Hull – above waterline	Black to top of well deck bulwarks; white above	
Hull stripe between black and white sections	Yellow	The hull stripe on White Star Line vessels was a colour called 'Yellow Chromate'.
Hull – below waterline	Dark brick-red	The paint below the waterline was called Antifouling and was designed to retard the attachment of marine growth.

Area	Colour	Comments
Lifeboats – exterior hulls and davits	White outside	
Lifeboats – covers	Unpainted canvas	
Masts and lower half of well decks	Light brown	The brown on the masts and 'dadoes' of the well deck was a unique shade best described as honey brown.
Railings	White with unvarnished teak top rail on passenger decks	
Skylights for grand staircases	White inside and out except for glass	
Stairs – exterior, except for short stairs to raised roofs on boat deck	White sides and railings with teak steps and brass step guards	The well deck stairs were made of steel.
Stairs – short stairs to raised roofs on boat deck	Teak sides and steps, white railings and brass step guards	These steps were made of teak, except for the railings which were steel.
Stays and shrouds for the masts and funnels	Shiny silver-grey	Made from galvanised steel wire rope
Vents and vent bases	White	
Winches	Green/black	*Titanic* had two different types of winches, electric and steam. All of the winches with the exception of those located on the forecastle deck were electric. These were painted in a colour known as 'Green Chromate', although the drums were painted black. The cargo winches on the forecastle deck were steam winches and were all painted black.

Area	Colour	Comments
Windows	Dark red-brown	*Titanic's* windows were made of brass and teak (depending on their location). With some exceptions, most of the windows on *Titanic* were made of varnished teak. The windows that were not made of teak were the officers' quarters, which were made of brass, and the forward-facing windows on A-deck (overlooking the bow), which were made of brass. These were believed to have been painted in a red-brown colour to match the varnished teak of the other windows.
Wooden benches	Teak	Unpainted slats of teak wood, with side and centre supports. The armrests were cast bronze.

PENSIONER CLAIMS OWNERSHIP OF THE *TITANIC*

On 26th November 2009, a story appeared in several newspapers about Douglas Faulkner-Woolley, aged 73 from Redbridge in Greater London, who claimed to own the wreck of the *Titanic*. Douglas, a retired caterer and *Titanic* fan, launched a legal challenge against *RMS Titanic Inc.*, the company to which the US Courts gave salvor rights of the wreck. Douglas said that he registered a claim for ownership of the White Star Line vessel in 1981, which according to Douglas has never been disputed in the UK since. Douglas went on to say that the American courts did not have any power over a British-made ship in international waters.

Did You Know That?

In 1970, Douglas Faulkner-Woolley formed the 'Titanic Salvage & Seawise Salvage Co.' and suggested that if the *Titanic* was found she could be raised to the surface by connecting huge bags filled with hydrogen to the ship's hull. Four decades later his dream remains unfulfilled.

50TH ANNIVERARY FOR BELFAST MEMORIAL

On Sunday 29th November 2009, the largest-ever gathering of *Titanic* descendants from Northern Ireland took place in the grounds of the City Hall, Belfast. Relatives and friends of seven men who lost their lives when the *Titanic* sank attended the 'Titanic Memorial' at the City Hall to commemorate the 50th anniversary of the monument's relocation.

TITANIC'S CHURCH

On Sunday 15th November 2009 the Reverend Chris Bennett was introduced into the newly created Titanic Parish in Belfast by the Bishop of Down and Dromore, the Right Reverend Harold Miller. The parish was formed at the request of the Bishop who wanted to ensure that the Church of Ireland had a presence in the Titanic Quarter. However, because there was no church building, the service took place in The Pump House Cafe at Titanic Dock. The Bishop conferred the title of 'Chaplain to the Titanic Quarter', on Chris.

TITANIC'S BOND GIRL

In Roy Ward Baker's 1958 movie *A Night to Remember,* the role of Mrs Liz Lucas was played by the English actress, Honor Blackman, who is best known for playing the role of Cathy Gale in the hit 1960s television series *The Avengers*, and the role of Bond girl Pussy Galore in the James Bond 007 movie *Goldfinger.*

—————————— Did You Know That? ——————————

No passenger by the name of Mrs Liz Lucas ever boarded *Titanic.*

NEW *TITANIC* SCULPTURE FOR BELFAST

On 30th October 2009, more than 100 years after *Titanic's* keel was laid at the Harland & Wolff Shipyard in Belfast, a scale replica of *Titanic's* component parts was unveiled in Belfast. The bronze sculpture, which stands 13.5 metres high, was designed by the English artist Tony Stallard, and he was assisted in its construction by engineers from the famous Belfast shipyard. Tony's work of art stands in the new 'Titanic Quarter' of the city on the former shipyards at Belfast Lough. The sculpture was simply named 'Kit' and at night-time it is lit up with blue and white phosphorus lighting. Tony's design was chosen in an open competition run by the charitable arts organisation, 'ArtSpark NI', while the project was jointly funded by the Titanic Quarter and Arts and Business NI.

TITANIC FLAGS – FACT AND FICTION

Various articles which have appeared in print have claimed that the 'Pilot Flag' was hoisted above RMS Titanic's bridge when she cast off her hawsers at Southampton dock on Wednesday 10th April 1912. However, the Pilot Flag does not appear in a single photograph of the famous White Star Line leviathan. Meanwhile, the 'Red Ensign' was flown on Titanic when she underwent her sea trials in Belfast on 2nd April 1912. This flag was flown from the ensign staff at the stern during daylight hours and identified the ship's nationality. The 'Blue Ensign' was flown from the ensign staff at the stern during daylight hours and could only be used upon issue of an Admiralty warrant which denoted that the captain and at least 10 ratings or officers were members of the Royal Naval Reserve (RNR). Photographs taken of the Titanic in 1912 show that the 15-foot 'Blue Ensign' of the RNR was flown from the ensign staff at her stern (Commander Smith of the Titanic had served as a Commander in the RNR). The 21-foot size version of this flag (not in use until after 1914) would have by tradition been known as the 'Sunday Ensign' or 'Holiday Ensign'. The Blue or Red Ensign was also flown from the foremast when the ship was dressed in British waters – as with Titanic on 4th April 1912 in Belfast Lough and on 5th April 1912 in Southampton when her crew dressed Titanic in a panoply of flags and pennants to celebrate the leviathan's impending maiden voyage. The 9-foot version was the flag normally used here. The White Star house flag flew from one of the flag halyards at the top of the mainmast from 8.00am to sunset.

The foremast flag of a ship is very frequently but incorrectly referred to as the 'Destination Flag'. However, while the flag on display at this location did in fact reflect the ship's destination prior to the ship leaving port, the flying of a 'courtesy flag' at this location always took precedence. A courtesy flag, or courtesy ensign, is the ensign of another country and is flown when entering that country's port and during the ship's entire time in a 'foreign' port. This was done as a means of marking the visit to that country. Failure to do so would have been a mark of the utmost disrespect. Therefore, the French and American ensigns were flown on Titanic as follows: the American ensign was flown at Southampton and continued to fly for the duration of her passage down Southampton water; the French ensign was then flown entering Cherbourg, and for the entire time in the French port until sunset. In Titanic's case, she arrived at Cherbourg approximately 15 minutes before sunset, so all of her flags were still flying when she anchored just outside the harbour. As Cherbourg was normally departed after dark, no flags were flown. The next morning, 11th April 1912, the American ensign was flown entering Queenstown (Cobh) and for the duration of her time anchored outside the harbour. The American ensign reflected *Titanic's* final destination, New York. As Ireland was not a sovereign country in 1912, it was not necessary for *Titanic* to display a courtesy ensign during her time in Irish waters. If *Titanic* had made it to New York then the American ensign would have been

raised a third time and flown daily from 8.00am to sunset during her entire time in port. Finally, as *Titanic* was a Royal Mail Steamship, the Royal Mail pennant flew leaving Southampton and arriving at Cherbourg and Queenstown and would have still been flying had *Titanic* reached New York.

––––––––––––––– Did You Know That? –––––––––––––––

The Blue Peter flag, the signal for the letter P in the International Code, was often flown by ships when leaving a port to announce that they were about to set sail. On the Olympic class ships this flag could be flown from one of the signal halyards off the bridge or from the second halyard at the foremast (the first being already in use for the courtesy ensign). A second Blue Peter could be flown from one of the mainmast halyards. No photographs are known to exist to indicate whether or not *Titanic* flew this flag prior to her departure from Southampton, Cherbourg or Queenstown.

■ THE MOVIE TRIVIA ■■■■■■■■■■■■■■

Titanic was the highest-grossing movie in Japan until Hayao Miyazaki released *Sen to Chihiro no kamikakushii* in 2001.

AN UNLUCKY TRIO

Many historians have noted that in a strange coincidence or twist of fate, two-thirds of the passengers and crew were lost when *Titanic* sank. This very same ratio has been cited with the sinking of RMS *Lusitania* and the sinking of RMS *Leinster*. However, whereas *Titanic* met her demise at the foot of a giant iceberg, the latter two ships were sunk by German U-Boats in World War I.

■ THE MOVIE TRIVIA ■■■■■■■■■■■■■■

Titanic was the first time the Best Song Oscar (for 'My Heart Will Go On') was won by a non-musical Best Picture winner. Best Song Oscar had been won by Best Picture winner only twice before ('Going My Way' in 1944 and 'Gigi' in 1958, both musicals).

COMMANDER SMITH OR COMMODORE SMITH?

Contrary to popular belief, Captain Smith of the *Titanic* never formally held the title of 'Commodore of the White Star Line Fleet'. Some reports claim that J. Bruce Ismay made his 'Millionaires Captain', Captain Smith, the company's Commodore in 1904 when Smith was given command of the White Star Line's new passenger liner, RMS *Baltic*, the largest ship in the world at the time. While there is no doubting the fact that Edward John Smith was the most senior captain employed by the White Star Line at the turn of the 20th century, there is no evidence to suggest that he ever held the distinction of Commodore. Indeed, according to the memoirs written by Sir Bertram Hayes in 1925, the White Star Line had suspended the rank of 'Commodore of the Fleet' as far back as 1882 after the resignation of Commodore Hamilton Perry. It is claimed that the White Star Line took this decision because Thomas Henry Ismay, the founder and chairman of the company and the father of J. Bruce Ismay, was of the opinion that the position of Commodore gave the holder the impression that he could instruct the company directors how best to run the company. It is, however, more likely that people confused Smith's rank of Commander in the Royal Naval Reserve with the White Star Line rank of Commodore, or perhaps some simply assumed that his position as senior captain of the fleet automatically accorded him that rank.

──────── Did You Know That? ────────

The White Star Line re-introduced the rank of Commodore (and with it the flying of the Commodore's flag) when SS *Bismarck*, which was launched in 1914, was given to the White Star Line and renamed RMS *Majestic*. Sir Bertram Hayes D.S.O., R.D., R.N.R., A.D.C. was made Commodore of the *Majestic*, the new flagship of the White Star Line's fleet and flew the Commodore flag for the first time on the occasion of *Majestic's* maiden voyage on 10th May 1922.

■ THE MOVIE TRIVIA ■■■■■■■■■■■■■

The staircase used on *Titanic* was slightly larger in the movie than it was on the real vessel. The main reason for this was because in general people at the turn of the 20th century were a little smaller than they were when the movie was being made and director James Cameron did not want many of his actors looking out of place.

A GAME OF LUCK

On Sunday 21st April 1912 the photograph of a Two of Hearts playing card appeared in the *New York Sun*. The playing card was signed by three of a group of four men who were all playing bridge in the Café Parisien on RMS *Titanic* when she struck the iceberg. The four men were Paul Chevré (a sculptor), Pierre Maréchal (son of the Vice-Admiral of the French Navy) and Alfred Omont (a cotton dealer), all French citizens and Lucian Smith, an American. The pack of cards was saved from the sinking by Pierre Maréchal. On Monday 20th April 1912, the day after they arrived safely in New York on RMS *Carpathia*, Chevré, Maréchal and Omont signed some of the cards and posted them to their friends in France. On the Two of Hearts they wrote – *Carpathia, 14 Avril 1912, 11 h 40*. Pierre Maréchal also took a volume of *The Memoirs of Sherlock Holmes* with him into Lifeboat No.7. Only Smith failed to survive the sinking of *Titanic* and his body, if ever recovered, was never identified.

Did You Know That?

The playing cards used aboard *Titanic* were made for the White Star Line by Goodall & Son Ltd, London. The Goodall business was founded in Soho in 1820 by Charles Goodall and printed playing cards and message cards. It was not until 1830 that Goodall started experimenting with 'court' card designs which gradually evolved into those we see all over the world today. The playing cards on *Titanic* were a gilt-edged variety of this now famous design.

THE DONKEYMAN AND *TITANIC*

Ernest Gill from Scotland Road, Liverpool was employed as second donkeyman (looking after the ship's auxiliaries, generators, donkey 'steam boiler', pumps, ballast and cooling water pumps) on the *Californian* when the *Titanic* struck the iceberg. On Day 8 of the United States Senate inquiry into the *Titanic* disaster, Gill was questioned at length by Senator William Alden Smith, Chairman of the Committee. Gill stated that he had been on duty from 8.00pm to midnight in the engine room and that at 11.56 pm he went up on deck. Gill said it was a calm peaceful evening as the *Californian* slowly drifted through an ice floe, her engines having been stopped at 10.21pm. Looking out across the North Atlantic he saw the lights of a large vessel about 10 miles away on the starboard side of the *Californian* which he assumed to be a German ship. At 12 midnight he went to his cabin and spoke to his friend, William Thomas, who could hear the *Californian* nudging various pieces of ice as she drifted. Thirty minutes later Gill

Artist's impression of the *Titanic* anchored at Cherbourg.
In reality, her lights would not have been as bright as shown here.
(*The Sphere*/Jonathan Smith collection)

still could not get to sleep and decided to go back up on deck and have a cigarette. He told Senator Smith that he saw a bright light flashing through the sky on the starboard side around 00.40 am, thinking it to be a shooting star. About seven or eight minutes later Gill said he saw another flashing light and thought immediately that they must be rockets fired by a ship in distress. Unknown to Gill, Fourth Officer Boxhall from the *Titanic* gave the order to fire the first rocket from *Titanic* at 00.45 am and over the following hour *Titanic* fired a further seven rockets. Amazingly, at the inquiry Gill said that it was not his business to report what he had seen to the bridge, claiming that there was no way the lookouts or the bridge could have failed to have seen the rockets.

■ THE MOVIE TRIVIA ■■■■■■■■■■■■■■■

Gloria Stuart, who played the aged Rose, was the oldest person ever to receive an Oscar nomination for her role in 'Titanic'. At the age of 87, she was also the only person on the set who was alive at the time of the real *Titanic* disaster.

Therefore, instead of raising an alarm that he saw a ship in distress he nonchalantly turned in for the night. At 6.40 am he was awakened by the Chief Engineer who informed him that the *Titanic* had sunk and instructed him to go up on deck to help out with the rescue of her survivors. Gill went on to testify that he heard the *Californian's* second (Mr J. C. Evans) and fourth (Mr Wooten) engineers talking with Evans saying that the third officer had reported seeing rockets going up in his watch. Gill said that Captain Stanley Lord had been informed about the sighting of rockets by the apprentice officer, Mr Gibson, who then told him to Morse to the vessel in distress. When Gibson saw further rockets being fired, Gill testified that once again Gibson reported this to Captain Lord. According to Gill, Captain Lord simply told Gibson to continue to Morse the ship until a reply was received. No reply was ever received and therein lies the *Californian's* apparent negligence: failure to go and assist *Titanic*, which was clearly in distress a mere 10 miles or so away, sank 2 hours and 35 minutes after firing her first rocket. Gill married Rose McIver on 19th April 1912 in Liverpool, four days after his return to England aboard the Leyland liner *Cestrian*, with Captain Lord claiming Gill was a deserter shortly after the *Californian* arrived in Boston, USA. Gill's return first-class fare was paid for by the British Consul in New York, Courtenay Bennett. Gill was also asked to give evidence at the British inquiry and did so on 4th June 1912.

ISMAY AND THE US SENATE COMMITTEE INQUIRY

On Day 1 (19th April 1912) of the United States Senate Inquiry into the *Titanic* disaster, J. Bruce Ismay was the first person to be questioned by the Committee. Senator William Alden Smith, Chairman of the Committee, questioned Ismay at length while Ismay informed the Committee that the White Star Line welcomed the fullest inquiry and had nothing to conceal or hide. Ismay informed Senator Smith that the *Titanic* was built in Belfast and that she was the latest thing in the art of shipbuilding with absolutely no money being spared in her construction. Ismay said that he was in bed when *Titanic* struck the iceberg. Senator Smith was anxious to learn of the ship's speed when she collided with the iceberg and Ismay informed him that the stories about the ship travelling at full speed through an ice field were simply not true. Ismay stated that *Titanic* never had been at full speed, pointing out that her full speed was 78 revolutions and that she had never exceeded 75 revolutions. Ismay also testified that not all of *Titanic's* boilers were lit when the collision occurred; none of the single-ended boilers had been lit.

Did You Know That?

After being rescued by the *Carpathia*, Ismay and the surviving officers from the *Titanic* disaster, arrived back in Liverpool, England onboard the *Adriatic*, a White Star Line vessel.

TITANIC'S LONE FEMALE SWIMMER

Mrs Rhoda Mary Abbott, aged 35, from Providence, Rhode Island, USA was the only female passenger on *Titanic* who survived after being pulled from the water and was one of the most badly injured. She was in bed in her cabin along with her two sons, Rossmore (aged 16) and Eugene (aged 13), when the ship collided with the iceberg. All three were on their way home having arrived in England in August 1911 on *Titanic's* big sister, the *Olympic*, where they lived with Rhoda's widowed mother in St. Albans. However, when the boys grew homesick and missed their friends in Providence, Rhoda, a soldier in the Salvation Army, decided to move back to the USA. They booked their passage on *Titanic's* ill-fated maiden voyage and boarded the ship at Southampton as third-class passengers. When *Titanic* was slowly sinking Rhoda, Rossmore and Eugene were all standing beside Collapsible Lifeboat C, the last lifeboat to be launched from the starboard side of the ship. However, the crew was only allowing women and children into the lifeboat and when they called for Rhoda to get in, she looked at her two sons before pulling them close to her as she stepped back, not wishing to be separated from her boys. The three of them jumped off the deck into the freezing cold water. Rhoda managed to make her way towards collapsible Lifeboat A and was hauled on to it. Sadly, Rossmore and Eugene went down with the ship. Those passengers and crew members on Collapsible Lifeboat A were picked up by Fifth Officer Harold Lowe in Lifeboat 14 and rescued by the *Carpathia*. Rhoda suffered burns to her legs after a boiler exploded when it struck the water and severe frostbite to her legs. She was admitted to Saint Vincent's Hospital in Manhattan when she arrived in New York and remained there for many weeks. Rhoda suffered from asthma and respiratory problems for the rest of her life following her ordeal in the North Atlantic.

Did You Know That?

Rhoda married Stanton Abbott, a former middleweight boxing champion, in 1895 but the couple parted in early 1911.

TITANIC STAND-IN

RMS *Asturias*, the second Royal Mail Line ship of that name, was built by Harland & Wolff Shipyard, Belfast. She was launched on 7th July 1925 and delivered to her owners, RMSP Meat Transports Ltd, on 6th February 1926. In 1939, at the outbreak of World War II, she was taken over by the Royal Navy and converted to an armed merchant cruiser. In 1943, she was torpedoed and badly damaged by an Italian submarine in the South Atlantic and towed to Freetown. She later served as a troop transport vessel and in 1957 was sold for scrap to Thomas W. Ward. However, before she was broken up Thomas H, Ward loaned her to the Rank Organisation for use in Roy Ward Baker's 1958 movie *A Night to Remember*. The port side of the *Asturias* was seen in the movie during the lifeboat-lowering scenes. Amazingly, as Baker was shooting his scenes workmen were busy on the starboard side of the ship dismantling her.

--- Did You Know That? ---

Kenneth More played Second Officer Charles Herbert Lightoller in the movie.

THE ISMAY FAMILY CONNECTION

Joseph Bruce Ismay, Chairman and Managing Director of the White Star Line when RMS *Titanic* set sail on her ill-fated maiden voyage, married Julia Florence Schieffelin on 4th December 1888. Later Julia's sister married C. Bower Ismay, the brother of Joseph. J. Bruce Ismay's son-in-law, George Cheape, was a brother of Mrs Albert Jaffray Cay, who lost her life when RMS *Empress of Ireland* sank after colliding in the fog with the Norwegian coal boat, SS *Storstad*, on 29th May 1914 in the Saint Lawrence River, Canada. It was Canada's worst-ever maritime disaster.

AN EARLY *TITANIC* MOVIE

In 1928, Victor Kendall made the movie *Atlantic* for British International Pictures Studios based on a play entitled *The Berg* by Ernest Raymond. The movie is essentially the story of the sinking of the *Titanic* 17 years earlier and includes the hymn 'Nearer Thy God To Thee'. The sequence in the movie when *Atlantic's* lifeboats were being lowered were filmed on an actual ocean liner which was docked on the Thames River in London. British International Pictures Studios at first called the movie *Titanic*, but soon changed the title to *Atlantic* after they were threatened with legal action by the White Star Line.

MEMORY LOSS

Jean Scheerlinckx, a farm hand from Haaltert, Belgium, boarded RMS *Titanic* at Southampton as a third-class passenger. He was going to the USA to take up employment during the sugar beet harvest near Detroit, Michigan. Because he told his story of the ship's sinking so many times, particularly after he arrived back home in Belgium where café owners gave him free drinks to talk about his experiences, it is not exactly known how he survived the disaster. In 1914, he was called up to serve in the Belgian Army and fought for his country during the First World War.

CREW MEMBER'S LEGAL ACTION AGAINST THE WHITE STAR LINE

Thomas Arthur Whiteley, aged 18, was employed as a steward on the *Titanic* having previously worked on her older sister, the *Olympic*. When it became evident that *Titanic* was slowly sinking, he jumped off the deck into the water and managed to swim to Collapsible Lifeboat B which was upturned. He was rescued by the *Carpathia* and taken to New York where he was admitted to Saint Vincent's Hospital in Manhattan suffering from a fractured leg. During his period in hospital he gave an interview to a local newspaper in which he alleged that officers aboard *Titanic* had ignored ice warnings and said that he was told this by *Titanic's* radio operator, Jack Phillips, who was with him on the lifeboat. In March 1914, he took legal action against the White Star Line claiming that officers had been negligent in steering the vessel through the ice field and that *Titanic* was not a seaworthy vessel. However, there is no record of the case ever being heard, leaving one to speculate that the White Star Line may have settled with Whiteley out of court to avoid any further bad publicity following the sinking of their most prized ocean liner.

Did You Know That?

Despite Whiteley's allegations of negligence on the part of *Titanic's* officers in ignoring several iceberg warnings, he was never called before the US Senate Committee inquiry or the British Board of Trade inquiry into the disaster.

■ THE MOVIE TRIVIA ■■■■■■■■■■■■■

Titanic became the second co-production between Paramount Pictures and 20th Century Fox to win the Best Picture Oscar, after Mel Gibson's *Braveheart* in 1995. Both studios were nearly bankrupted during production.

TITANIC'S HEROIC STEWARD

John Edward Hart, a former soldier who had fought in the Boer War (1899–1902), signed on to work aboard the *Titanic* in Southampton on 4th April 1912 as a third-class steward. When the ship struck an iceberg, the 31-year old Hart was fast asleep in bed on E Deck. However, the impact wakened him and a short time later James Kiernan, the Chief Steward for third-class passengers, told Hart and his fellow off-duty stewards to wake those passengers who were under their charge. Each steward on *Titanic* was given the responsibility for a number of cabins, with Hart in charge of 58 people who were located in Sections K and M on E Deck. Hart woke up all of his passengers and helped them put on their lifebelts, then gathered them at their muster station before receiving an instruction around 00.30 am to transfer the women and children up to the boat deck. Approximately 30 women and children were in his care and he took them up to the boat deck as ordered and helped them get into Lifeboat No.8. Although he was willing to go and help his fellow stewards assist other passengers, First Officer Murdoch ordered him into Lifeboat No.15 to help row it. All 58 passengers under Hart's charge were rescued by the *Carpathia* and he returned home to England on the White Star Line's *Celtic*. He went on to work on the White Star Line's *Oceanic* and died at his home in Devon on 15th January 1954.

ALL ON HIS OWN

Hudson Trevor Allison was born on 7th May 1911 in Westmount, Quebec, Canada and was just 11 months old when he boarded *Titanic* at Southampton with his father Hudson, mother Bess, sister Lorraine and his nurse Alice Cleaver. Hudson Jnr. had moved to England with his family shortly after he was born as his father had business interests there but in early 1912 the Hudson family decided to move back home to Canada. Hudson Jnr. lost his family when *Titanic* sank, but was saved from the disaster by his nurse, and after being rescued by *Carpathia* he was brought up in Canada by his Aunt Lillian and Uncle George. Sadly, he died at the age of 18, on 7th August 1929 of ptomaine poisoning and was buried beside his father in Chesterville, Ontario, Canada.

FIRST *TITANIC* BABY CONCEIVED

David Baclini was born on 28th January 1913, some 9 months and 13 days after the *Titanic* sank and is believed to be the first child conceived by a survivor of the *Titanic* disaster. David's father, Solomon, was in New York working and sent home money to Syria to allow his wife, Latifa, and his three daughters (Eugenie, Helene Barbara and Maria Catherine) to join him in the USA. The Baclini family boarded *Titanic* at Cherbourg and after the ship struck an iceberg, they were loaded into Collapsible Lifeboat C and rescued by the *Carpathia*.

Did You Know That?

The Baclinis were not supposed to travel to New York on *Titanic's* maiden voyage. They booked their passage to join Solomon in the USA on another ship leaving Cherbourg but had to cancel these plans at the last minute when Maria contracted conjunctivitis, delaying their planned departure. Solomon was unaware that his wife and girls were aboard *Titanic* until the *Carpathia* steamed into New York on 19th April 1912.

Did You Know That?

In *Titanic's* refrigerated stores area were two rooms for chilled beef; one named *Eastbound Beef* and the other *Westbound Beef*. The latter was much larger than the former as not many immigrants would be carried on the return trip.

A HEFTY BILL

During the *Olympic's* maiden voyage from Southampton to New York on 14th June 1911, J. Bruce Ismay, Chairman and Managing Director of the White Star Line, was aboard the company's first of a planned three Olympic class leviathans (RMS *Titanic* & RMS *Gigantic* were to follow). Whilst on board ship Ismay spoke freely to reporters and during one interview with a reporter from the *New York Times*, he was asked several questions about what was at the time, the biggest ship in the world. Ismay said that she had cost £1.5 million to build ($7.5m) and cost the company £35,000 ($175,000) to run per voyage.

Did You Know That?

When the White Star Line insured the *Olympic*, the company had to accept a £500,000 indemnity with the underwriters picking up the balance.

A COWARD OR A RELUCTANT SURVIVOR?

Much has been written about how J. Bruce Ismay, the Chairman and Managing Director of the White Star Line, survived the sinking of *Titanic*. Many stories claim that as soon as he knew that the ship would ultimately sink he forced his way into a lifeboat with no care or consideration for women and children around him. After the disaster Ismay was pilloried by the American press, which branded him a coward with one newspaper renaming him 'J. Brute Ismay'. However, when Ismay arrived back in Liverpool aboard the White Star Line's RMS *Adriatic*, he was

cheered by the waiting crowd as he walked down the gangway. An article appeared in the *Worcester Evening Gazette* on 20th April 1912 in which Mrs Charlotte Cardeza, who occupied one of the most luxurious first-class cabins on the ship, claimed that Ismay was one of the first people to get into a lifeboat and even chose his own crew to row it. Mrs Cardeza said that Ismay knew that her son, Thomas Drake Martinez Cardeza, was an excellent oarsman and beckoned him into the lifeboat. However, Thomas Cardeza gave a completely different account of events when he was interviewed by the *Washington Herald*. Thomas said that he had helped his mother into Lifeboat No.3 on the starboard side of the ship along with Mrs Astor and Mrs Widener and at one point there was not a single man in it. He then went on to say that one of the women asked for some of the men to be lowered into the lifeboat to row it with one woman in particular calling out for Ismay to get in. According to Mr Cardeza's statement to the newspaper he said that Ismay refused to take the place of a woman in a lifeboat and said that he would remain aboard his ship. Mr Cardeza said that after further pleas from several women aboard Ismay reluctantly got into the lifeboat. This is substantiated by testimonies of several crew members at the subsequent US Senate Committee inquiry and British Board of Trade inquiry into the *Titanic* disaster. Indeed, August Weikman, a barber on *Titanic,* in an interview with *The Philadelphia Evening Bulletin* on 19th April 1912, stated that he witnessed Ismay being forced into a lifeboat to help row it by a member of the ship's crew (believed to be Fifth Officer Harold Lowe) who had no idea who Ismay was. According to Weikman, who gave similar evidence to the US Senate Committee inquiry on Day 5 (24th April 1912), the policy of four women followed by one man to look after them was being adopted by the crew members responsible for loading the lifeboats where he was standing on the boat deck. Weikman went on to say that the charge of cowardice against Ismay was both unfair and untrue.

Day 5 of the US Senate Committee Inquiry also saw Second Officer Charles Lightoller give his testimony. He was questioned by Senator Smith, Chairman of the Senate Committee, about Ismay entering a lifeboat. Lightoller said that Ismay only got into the last lifeboat to be lowered on the starboard side, Collapsible Lifeboat C, after he was informed by Chief Officer Wilde that there were no more women or children aboard the ship. He entered the lifeboat at the same time as another male passenger, Mr William E. Carter from Philadelphia, USA. In an interview with *The Washington Times* on 22nd April 1912, Mr Carter said that after he helped his wife and children into a lifeboat on the port side, he went to the starboard side where he saw Ismay assisting officers to load a lifeboat with women and children. Carter said that most of the women were third-class passengers and that he, Ismay and some of the officers walked up and down the boat deck shouting out for any more women or children to come forward. When it was evident to all that there were no more women or children waiting to be placed in a lifeboat, Carter said that an officer asked him and Ismay to get into the lifeboat and help two seamen row it.

Albert Pearcey, a third-class pantryman on *Titanic*, gave evidence at the British Board of Trade inquiry, chaired by Lord Mersey, stating that he picked up two babies from the boat deck and was instructed to get into Collapsible Lifeboat C with them by Chief Officer William Murdoch. Pearcey stated that when he got into the lifeboat there were no women or children on the boat deck. On the other hand, Edward Brown who was a first-class steward on *Titanic*, informed the British inquiry that Ismay was in the lifeboat receiving women and children being lowered into it. Ismay informed the inquiry that Brown was mistaken and that he only got in at the last second. However, quite amazingly, Ismay never once mentioned that he had been 'forced' into a lifeboat against his own will at either inquiry into the disaster. And yet despite Ismay's innocence of the accusations against him, the public was either unwilling to believe this or unforgiving of the fact that he survived when so many others had perished in the disaster. With his reputation irreparably damaged, he was forced to retire from his position as Chairman and Managing Director of the White Star Line on 30th June 1913. The events of that fateful evening of Sunday 14th April 1912 and the early hours of Monday 15th April 1912, undoubtedly haunted him for the rest of his life.

Did You Know That?

J. Bruce Ismay died on 17th October 1937 at his home in Mayfair, London without ever making any further public statement about his beloved *Titanic* or his conduct than that which he told the US Senate Committee inquiry and Lord Mersey's British Board of Trade inquiry.

A NATION ONCE AGAIN

Just as the tender PS *America* was about to leave the quay at Queenstown, Ireland around 12.00 noon on Thursday 11th April 1912 and make her way out to the *Titanic*, one of the paddle-steamer's passengers decided to brighten up the occasion and play a tune on his traditional Uileann pipes. With so many at the quay in tears bidding farewell to loved ones, 29-year old Eugene Daly, a weaver and amateur musician from Athlone, played 'A Nation Once Again'.

Eugene Daly survived the sinking of the *Titanic* and arrived in New York on the *Carpathia*. He gave an interview to the *Evening World* in which he dramatically claimed that he saw an officer shoot and kill two men who attempted to force their way into a lifeboat before all of the women and children were safely loaded into boats. Daly said he then heard a third shot and saw an officer lying dead on the boat deck and assumed that he had committed suicide. Daly lodged a claim with the White Star Line in New York for the loss of his Uileann pipes and received $50.00.

A COSTLY MESSAGE – 'SHUT UP, I AM BUSY!'

Guglielmo Marconi gave evidence on Day 2 of the United States Senate Committee inquiry into the *Titanic* disaster. Senator Smith asked Mr Marconi what CQD meant and his response was that it was a conventional signal which was established by the Marconi Company to let other ships know that the sending ship was in danger. At this point, Mr Uhler asked Mr Marconi if CQD was an arbitrary signal. Mr Marconi said that it was an arbitrary signal but also a conventional one which everyone understood meant 'All other Stations stand to attention and reply'. Harold Bride, the Assistant Wireless Operator onboard the *Titanic*, was also present on Day 2 and concurred with Mr Marconi on the meaning of CQD. Senator Smith went on to ask Mr Marconi what the 'Silent Signal' was and when he replied that he did not know, Harold Bride said it was DDD. This signal meant: 'All other Stations must cease transmitting' or as candidly pointed out by Mr Marconi 'Shut Up'. The latter translation is important in that Jack Phillips, the Senior Wireless Operator on the *Titanic*, has been criticised by many writers about the *Titanic* for worrying more about dealing with the huge volume of Marconigrams he had to send on behalf of the ship's passengers than dealing with warnings of ice which were transmitted by several ships to the *Titanic*. Cyril Evans, the Wireless Operator on the *Californian* (the closest vessel to the *Titanic* when she struck an iceberg) was also questioned by the US Senate Committee. Evans stated that on the evening of the *Titanic's* collision with the iceberg he sent Phillips warnings of icebergs informing him that the *Californian* had stopped for the night in an ice field. He went on to testify that he called Phillips and said: 'Say, old man, we are stopped and surrounded by ice.' When asked what Phillips' reply was, Evans said: 'Shut up, shut up, I am busy; I am working Cape Race.' Evans then switched off the *Californian's* radio and retired for the night. If only Phillips had taken the time to answer Evans perhaps the huge death toll could have been significantly less.

NO NEED TO RUSH

Since *Titanic's* sinking many have claimed that Captain Smith and J. Bruce Ismay intended to beat the time set by *Olympic* on her maiden voyage and arrive in New York early, and that this led to an increase in speed and unwillingness by Ismay and Smith to slow *Titanic* down despite warnings of ice. In his book *The Olympic Class Ships: Olympic – Titanic – Britannic*, author Mark Chirnside offered a superb analysis of the estimated coal consumption onboard *Titanic*, and effectively proved that merely by maintaining her speed, *Titanic* would have arrived in New York at 9.50 pm on Tuesday 16th April 1912, thereby beating her older sister's, *Olympic*, maiden voyage transatlantic crossing time by some 4½ hours. Therefore, taking into consideration Mark's analysis (and this seems flawless), *Titanic* could have arrived in New York the night before she was actually due in with no additional push of speed necessary. However, the only person who could have truly set this matter to rest was Chief Engineer Joseph Bell or another senior engineer, as it would have required some definitive information on remaining coal stores and coal consumption, but neither he nor any of the other engineers survived the disaster. Consequently, J. Bruce Ismay may have indeed speculated about such things. Miss Elisabeth Lindsey Lines stated in an interview after the disaster that she overheard a conversation between Ismay and Smith in the First-Class Reception Room on D Deck on the afternoon of 13th April 1912 in which she claimed Ismay told Smith that Titanic would beat *Olympic*'s time and arrive early in New York. J. Bruce Ismay may have speculated about such things, but he was most certainly in no position to really know anything definitive.

A DISPROPORTIONATE LOSS OF LIFE

One of the most striking aspects of the *Titanic* disaster was the fact that third-class passengers perished in far greater percentages than their first and second-class counterparts. The American and British inquiries focused in part on this issue and whether locked gates prevented third-class passengers from leaving their areas of the ship. There was no evidence of locked gates heard, nor is there any evidence for them today, but that in itself does not explain the disproportionate loss of life in third class. Instead, there were several factors that contributed to the disproportionate loss of life in third class.

Firstly, in 1912 the typical third-class passenger would never presume to cross into a second or first-class area unbidden. A closed barrier, even one that was waist high and unlocked, signified 'you are not permitted in this area' and it would have been understood as such and obeyed. Secondly, there was no direct access to the boat deck from third-class areas. Unless they had courage, were resourceful and possessed a good sense of direction, not many third-class passengers were going to find the way on their own, on top of which they would have to go through areas where they did not belong as noted above. Thirdly, many, if not most, third-class passengers obediently expected that they would be told what to do, and waited for help that never came. A great number of stewards simply abandoned them. Although each steward was responsible for a certain number of cabins, that didn't necessarily extend to ensuring that all the passengers in those cabins were assisted to the lifeboats. Unlike today, an organised system of crew members stationed at various points in corridors, cabin checks etc. did not exist in 1912. However, some stewards such as John Hart displayed a laudable sense of decency in shepherding as many passengers up to the boat deck in the little time they had, but these were the exception. And finally, the lifeboats were closest to *Titanic*'s first-class areas. Consequently, those passengers arrived at the lifeboats first and got in first. And considering how so many of *Titanic*'s lifeboats were launched only partially filled, there really should not be any surprise that most third-class passengers were left behind.

Did You Know That?

Third-class passengers, although paying the lowest fares, provided
a significant amount of revenue for the steamship companies
and effectively subsidised the cost of building and operating such
immense ships.

FIRST SURVIVOR TO DIE

Miss Maria Nackid was born in May 1910, the first-born daughter of her Syrian
parents, Said and Mary Nackid. She boarded the *Titanic* at Cherbourg as a third-
class passenger with her mother and father, the family on their way to Waterbury,
Connecticut, USA. After *Titanic's* collision with an iceberg the Nackid family were
loaded into Lifeboat Collapsible C and rescued by the *Carpathia*. Sadly, young
Maria contracted meningitis and died on 30th July 1912, just 75 days after
surviving the *Titanic* disaster. Maria was the first *Titanic* survivor to die and was
buried in an unmarked grave at the Calvary Cemetery in Waterbury, Connecticut.

RECKLESS BEHAVIOUR OR STANDARD PRACTICE?

Many writers over the years have criticised Captain Smith for not slowing the
Titanic down on the night she struck an iceberg. On Day 12 of the British Wreck
Commissioner's inquiry into the *Titanic* disaster, Second Officer Charles
Lightoller was questioned at length about the speed *Titanic* was doing on the
Sunday evening. It was suggested to Lightoller during questioning (Question
No. 14414) that it was: 'recklessness, utter recklessness, in view of the conditions
which he described as abnormal, and in view of the knowledge he had from
various sources that ice was in Titanic's immediate vicinity, for Captain Smith to
allow Titanic to proceed at 21½ knots'. Lightoller in response said that if Captain
Smith was being reckless then all he could say was: 'that recklessness applies to
practically every commander and every ship crossing the Atlantic Ocean'. When
asked (Question No. 14416) if he thought Captain Smith was in his view
applying careful navigation, he responded: 'It is ordinary navigation, which
embodies careful navigation.' Further questioning seemed to be pressuring
Lightoller into admitting that the ship was travelling too fast: 'within the near
vicinity of a place which was reported to *Titanic* to be abounding in ice'
(Question No. 14416). However, to his credit, Lightoller maintained that
Captain Smith was not acting recklessly despite it being suggested to Lightoller
in Question 14425: 'that the conditions having been so dangerous, those in
charge of the vessel were negligent in proceeding at that rate of speed'. Lightoller
simply replied: 'No.' A little further on, the Attorney-General continued to press
Lightoller about the advisability of reducing speed, and in Question 14372,
whether or not it would have helped to avoid a collision. Clearly irritated over

---

being pushed into criticism of his captain, his response was: 'It is one way. Naturally, if you stop the ship you will not collide with anything.'

On Day 21 of the British Wreck Commissioner's inquiry Bertram F. Hayes (Master of the White Star Line's *Oceanic*) was questioned by the Attorney-General who specifically wished to focus on the reports of ice on the Sunday evening and *Titanic's* associated speed. When asked what precautions he took when approaching an ice region (*Question No. 21808*) he simply replied that he took precautions according to the weather and if the weather was clear then he would place a look-out in the crow's-nest and on the bridge and personally stay on duty. When pressed in Questions 21814 and 21815 if he would maintain the same rate of speed or make any alteration to the ship's course when approaching an ice region, he responded that he would not. When he was further asked if the latter was the practice in his Line (*Question No. 21816*) he said: 'It is the practice all over the world so far as I know – every ship that crosses the Atlantic.' He went on to add that: 'Ice does not make any difference to speed in clear weather and that you can always see ice then.' Hayes added the *Titanic* had encountered: 'abnormal circumstances which nobody had ever experienced before'. A clearly ruffled Attorney-General decided to press Hayes further and in Question *21820* put the following point to him: 'Now I want to ask you, at night – supposing you are steaming at night, and it is reported that along the course you are following you will come into an ice-field, according to your view would you make any reduction in the rate of speed?' Hayes replied: 'None, till I saw the ice.'

In the report published following the British Wreck Commissioner's inquiry, it was pointed out that it had been demonstrated that for more than 25 years, the practice of liners using the southern track which *Titanic* was on had been, when ice was in the vicinity at night, to maintain the ship's course and speed and keep a lookout on duty and trust the lookout to spot an iceberg in sufficient time to take action. Whilst the British Wreck Commissioner's inquiry accepted the latter as standard practice their report concluded that, based on the *Titanic* disaster, this practice was no longer acceptable when in the vicinity of ice. The report concluded that it could not hold Captain Smith to blame for the sinking of the *Titanic*, because he was merely following standard practice and generally doing what any other captain would have done on that fateful night.

THE AGE OF CHIVALRY

In 1912, it was common practice for gentlemen to formally offer their services to ladies travelling alone ('unprotected ladies') onboard a ship. Indeed, Colonel Archibald Gracie IV was one such gentleman who offered his services to three sisters who were returning to the USA on the *Titanic* following a family funeral in England. The three damsels who the Colonel knew well were Mrs E. D. Appleton, Mrs John Murray Brown and Mrs R. C. Cornell. A fourth lady, Miss Edith Evans, was also offered Gracie's services.

AMONG THE ICEBERGS

The Most Appalling Disaster in Maritime History.
The White Star Liner " TITANIC," sunk on her maiden voyage, off Cape Race, 15th April, 1912.

This overly dramatic postcard illustration erred in several respects: it showed heavy black smoke from all the funnels (including the fourth funnel, which was not connected to the boilers) and showed *Titanic* passing numerous icebergs close to the ship. Except for the iceberg that *Titanic* struck, none were seen this close until the following morning. (Jonathan Smith collection)

COBH'S PLACE IN *TITANIC*'S HISTORY

On 3rd August 1849, Cobh was renamed Queenstown to commemorate a visit by the reigning British Sovereign at the time, Queen Victoria, and retained the new name until Irish independence in 1922, established when Cobh formed part of the Irish Free State. Although famous for being *Titanic's* final port of call on her doomed maiden voyage, Cobh itself has another famous maritime connection. In 1838, it was the departure point for the inaugural crossing of the Atlantic by a steamship under steam only (as opposed to sail and steam). On 7th July 1998, The Irish Titanic Historical Society and The Titanic Historical Society unveiled a plaque in Pearse Square, Cobh commemorating those people who lost their lives in the *Titanic* disaster which reads: 'Commemorating R.M.S. Titanic and her last port of call on her maiden and final voyage. April 11, 1912. In special memory of the Irish emigrants and all those who lost their lives in this great tragedy.' Also inscribed on the memorial is: 'Ar dheis dé go raibh an anmacha', which in Irish means: 'At God's right hand are the souls.'

─────────── Did You Know That? ───────────

Memorials can also be found in Cobh to the Cunard Line's RMS *Lusitania*. The *Lusitania* sank on Friday 7th May 1915 after being torpedoed by the German U-Boat, *U20*, eight miles off the Old Head of Kinsale Lighthouse. *The Lusitania Peace Memorial* can be found in the city centre while many who lost their lives following the sinking of the *Lusitania* were buried in the local cemetery.

ONE BILLION RIVETS

In the early part of the 20th century arc-welding had not yet been invented and consequently, in excess of 1 billion iron rivets, more than 3,500 tons of them, were used in the construction of the three famous sister ships – RMS *Olympic*, RMS *Titanic* and HMHS *Britannic*.

─────────── Did You Know That? ───────────

It took almost 23,000 tons of tallow, soap and grease to ease the *Titanic* down the slipway and into the water. Once afloat, the workers at Harland & Wolff gathered-up the tallow and soap and took it home in buckets to use as a source of cheap toiletry.

PUTTING ON WEIGHT

Once afloat the fitting-out process practically doubled the weight of the *Olympic* and the *Titanic* and took almost one year each to complete.

COMFORT FOR ALL

Most third-class passengers on the *Titanic* slept in two-berth cabins rather than in a shared dormitory, which was standard on most other transatlantic passenger ships.

─────────── Did You Know That? ───────────

For some third-class passengers on the *Titanic* the food they ate aboard was better than anything they had ever eaten before.

A BRIGHT SHIP

There were 10,000 light bulbs on the *Titanic*. However, the lighting was actually quite dim by modern standards. The brightest light bulb on board was no more than a 75-watt equivalent, and even the deck lamps, while providing enough light to see by, had nowhere near the illuminating power of today's floodlights.

―――――――――――― Did You Know That? ――――――――――――

Five pianos (one Grand and four upright pianos) were also lost in the disaster along with a reported four cases of opium.

TITANIC'S LITTLE BLACK BOOK

During the construction of the *Titanic* at the famous Harland & Wolff Shipyard, and indeed for many years previously, a 'Fines Book' was kept by the Time Office at the Belfast shipyard. Anyone in breach of the rules would be reported to the clerk in the Time Office by their foreman or 'Hat' and their name, board number and trade would be recorded in the Fines Book with a brief description of the offence and the fine imposed. The men building the *Titanic* could find their names in the little 'Black Book' for a range of offences with the two most common being 'Loafing' (essentially sitting around doing nothing or wandering around) and 'Boiling Can' (heating water in a can to make a cup of tea before the allotted tea-break time).

―――――――――――― Did You Know That? ――――――――――――

Some of the bathrooms in the first-class area of *Titanic* had cigar holders.

TITANIC IN THE SHADOW OF HALLEY'S COMET

On the night of 20th April 1910, Thomas Andrews brought his pregnant wife Helen down to the Harland & Wolff Shipyard so that she could see the *Titanic* under construction. It was a truly memorable moment for Thomas and Helen as Halley's Comet lit up the cold night sky above the Belfast shipyard. The 1910 sighting of Halley's Comet was the first for which photographs exist and the first for which spectroscopic data were obtained. In a strange twist of fate, the next time Halley's Comet appeared was 1986, one year after the wreck of the *Titanic* was discovered lying 2½ miles down on the bed of the Atlantic Ocean and where the body of Thomas Andrews still lies. Halley's Comet appears every 75–76 years.

BIGGER THAN THE WORLD'S TALLEST BUILDING

If the *Titanic* had been stood on end in 1912, she would have been taller than the world's tallest skyscraper at the time, New York's Metropolitan Life Tower. *Titanic* would have stretched 882 feet, 9 inches into the city's Manhattan skyline beside the 700-feet-high building. Metropolitan Life Tower was the tallest building in the world 1909–13, preceded by the Singer Building (612 feet) and succeeded by the Woolworth Building (792 feet). It was not until April 1930, 18 years after the *Titanic* disaster, that a building exceeded the size of *Titanic*. That building was the 71-storey Bank of Manhattan building at 40 Wall Street which stood 927 feet tall.

A COSTLY MISCALCULATION

Just before the last lifeboat on the *Titanic*, Collapsible D, was lowered into the water from A Deck, Miss Edith Evans, thinking that there was only room for one more person in it (there were 24 in it at the time and it could accommodate 47 people), turned to her friend Mrs John Murray Brown and said: 'You go first. You have children waiting at home.' Mrs Brown got into the lifeboat, which left at 2:05 am under the command of Quartermaster Arthur Bright. Sadly for Edith the ship sank just 15 minutes later and she went down with her.

A BRUSH WITH DEATH TOO FAR

John Kennedy from 1 Rosemary Place, Watergate, Limerick, Ireland was one of the 113 third-class passengers who boarded RMS *Titanic* at Queenstown, Ireland on Thursday 11th April 1912 (Ticket No. 368783, £7 15s). He arrived in Queenstown on the train from Limerick just in time as the paddle-steamer *America* was about to ferry the passengers boarding at Queenstown out to *Titanic*. He was celebrating his 20th birthday and hoping to begin a new life in New York along with his brother, Michael, who encouraged him to come to the 'Land of the Free' where Michael had emigrated a few years earlier. John is believed to have been rescued from the *Titanic* disaster by the *Carpathia* in Lifeboat No.15. Upon his safe arrival in New York he went to live with his brother at 29 Perry Street, Brooklyn, New York. John lodged a claim for compensation with the White Star Line for £533 ($2,665), the biggest lodged by an Irish survivor of the *Titanic* disaster. However, when the White Star Line eventually paid out on the claims they received, they only paid a paltry 3 cents for every $1 claimed.

■ THE MOVIE TRIVIA ■ ■ ■ ■ ■ ■ ■ ■ ■ ■ ■ ■ ■ ■

Reba McEntire was offered and had accepted the role of the unsinkable Molly Brown, but due to later film schedule conflicts she politely turned the offer down. Kathy Bates stepped in.

EXPLOSION ON THE *TITANIC*

At the US Senate Committee inquiry following the sinking of the *Titanic*, Senator Smith informed J, Bruce Ismay that there had been some suggestion by passengers who left the ship in lifeboats, that an explosion took place after she collided with the iceberg. Ismay replied that he had no knowledge of any such explosion.

TABLE FOR TWO

On the evening of Sunday 14th April 1912, J, Bruce Ismay went for dinner on *Titanic* along with the ship's doctor, Dr. William O'Loughlin. Contrary to popular belief, Captain Smith did not dine with the two men.

ONE PIECE OR TWO?

For a great number of years after the *Titanic* sank, many survivors disagreed on the ship's end as she plunged to the bottom of the North Atlantic. Some eyewitnesses, including 17-year old Jack Thayer, claimed that the Titanic had broken in two but many others totally disagreed with this assertion. In 1913, Titanic survivor Colonel Archibald Gracie had his book entitled *The Truth About The Titanic* published and in it he discounted the 'she broke in two' claims. Gracie believed that those who belonged to the 'broke in half' school had merely witnessed *Titanic's* forward funnel collapse into the sea. Sixty years after her demise, the maritime author John Maxtone-Graham was another who disagreed with Thayer's claim. However, when Dr Robert Ballard discovered the wreck in 1985 the great ship lay in two pieces on the bed of the Atlantic nearly ⅓ mile apart. Thayer was finally proven correct.

A HERCULEAN TASK

The *Titanic* had 5 anchors in total, 3 of the Hall's Patent stockless type and 2 kedge anchors. Two of the stockless anchors were the ship's working anchors; these were the bower anchors attached to the ship's anchor chains. A larger centre anchor sat in reserve in a well at the forward end of the forecastle deck. One kedge anchor was stored further aft on the forecastle deck and the second one on the poop deck. The large anchors at the bow were supplied and manufactured at Messrs Noah Hingley & Sons Ltd of Netherton, near Dudley, England. Harland & Wolff placed the order for *Titanic's* anchors with this Black Country family-run business in late 1910.

The centre anchor weighed 16½ tons and the two bow anchors each weighed 8½ tons. The two kedge anchors were bolted down to the decking on the forecastle and railings on the poop deck. At the time *Titanic's* centre anchor was the largest anchor ever forged by hand and remained so for many years later. It measured a staggering 18 feet and 6 inches in length. The cast steel head of the anchor was 10 feet, 9 inches wide and the anchor weighed a mammoth 15 tons, 16 cwts. However, Hingley's cannot lay claim to making every part of the anchors. The head of the anchor was cast by John Rogerson & Co in Newcastle-upon-Tyne upon the request of Hingley's and manufactured to the 1906 Hall's Patent. The steel hand and drop forged anchor shank were sub-contracted out by Hingley's to a local rival, Walter Somers Ltd. This was largely because this company had a much more powerful hydraulic drop hammer compared to the one in use at the Hingley works in 1910–11. Meanwhile, Hingley's yard manufactured the anchor shackle and pin, anchor head locking pins and retaining blocks, anchor attachment links, anchor chains (for the side anchors), mooring swivel chains and anchor chains deck stoppers. Each link for the anchor chains was of an impressive scale and made from steel which Hingley's proudly claimed 'Hingley's Best'. The largest link was situated within the anchor attachment and measured 36 inches. The others were forged at 33 inches. Each link was forged from pig-iron bars, heated up and run through a machine known as a mandrel.

After each section of chains was forged, Hingley's 'Chain Gang' had the lengthy task of checking each link, and in the region of 1,200 feet of chain was forged for the *Titanic*. Transportation for the *Titanic* anchor came from the Great Bridge (West Midlands) haulage company 'W. A. Ree'. Ree's arrived at Hingley's yard with a massive 10-ton wooden wagon and 8 fully grown Shire horses, massive animals each weighing over a ton and able to pull 3 tons each. But it took a further six horses belonging to Hingley's Yard to pull the ship's centre anchor out of the yard as an uphill incline from the Proving House to the main road had to be negotiated before arriving at the goods yard at Dudley Railway Station. The remaining group of six, which bought the total to twenty, were sent without usage from the L.N.W.R office at Dudley Station. The anchor was then transported via rail down the North West coast to Fleetwood in Lancashire. From Fleetwood, the anchor was put aboard the passenger/cargo steamer *Duke of Albany* and sent across the Irish Sea to Donegal Quay in Belfast. From there it went on to the shipyards of Harland & Wolff via the Belfast shipyard's own horses and cart, where it was painted black and then fitted aboard the liner.

--------------------- Did You Know That? ---------------------

All three of the White Star Line's Olympic Class liners had their centre anchors painted matt white while at the Hingley works. However, the *Titanic* was the only one of the three that had the name 'Hingley. Netherton' painted upon the shank. Both side anchors of the *Olympic* were painted matt white and sent that way to Belfast. Both of *Titanic's* side anchors were painted matt black and the *Britannic's* side anchors were painted matt white.

TITANIC'S WRITERS' GROUP

On board the *Titanic* a writers' group was formed by Mrs Helen Churchill Candee. Along with Mrs Candee 'Our Coterie', as they were collectively known, also included Edward Pomeroy Colley, Edward Kent, J. Clinch Smith, Mauritz Håkan Björnström-Steffansson and Hugh Woolner.

WARNING SHOTS FIRED

Hugh McElroy, a purser on the *Titanic*, reportedly fired his pistol into the air to prevent a group of men jumping into Collapsible Lifeboat D.

THE SILVER CUP

When they were being taken to New York on the *Carpathia*, some of the survivors of the *Titanic* formed a group to honour the bravery of Captain Rostron and his crew of their rescue ship. The group included Molly Brown and they later presented Captain Rostron with an inscribed silver cup and distributed medals to each one of the *Carpathia's* 320 crew members.

TITANIC'S LAST GOODBYE

On 10th April 1912, the Allan liner *Tunisian* reported running into a large ice field 887 miles east of St. John's, Newfoundland. Seven days later the *Tunisian* arrived in Liverpool from Canada and upon arrival her captain, Captain Fairfull, crew and passengers were shocked to learn the news that the *Titanic* had sunk just two days earlier quite close to the area where the *Tunisian* had reported ice. One of *Tunisian's* passengers said that at one time their ship appeared to be surrounded by mountains of ice with at least 200 icebergs visible. Approaching midnight on Saturday 13th April 1912, the Marconi wireless operator on the *Tunisian* had been in contact with the *Titanic's* wireless operators, Jack Phillips and Harold Bride, and sent a 'Good Luck' message to the White Star Line vessel for her maiden voyage. Back in Liverpool the *Tunisian's* Marconi wireless operator said that he received the message 'Many thanks. Goodbye' back from the *Titanic* but little did he know at the time that this would be *Titanic's* last Goodbye.

TITANIC'S OWN LITTLE ANGEL

In 1998, a small cherub which was recovered from the wreck of the Titanic was placed on display in Osaka, Japan. The ornate piece of *Titanic* memorabilia is believed to be from the Shelter Deck landing aft and one of a pair which were mounted on the side banisters of *Titanic's* impressive Grand Staircase.

TITANIC'S FIRST AND LAST

Miss Maria Nackid was 23 months old when she survived the *Titanic* disaster. She was just 2 years and 2 months old when she died, the first and youngest *Titanic* survivor to die. On the other hand, Mary Wilburn (née Davies) was 28 years old when she was rescued by the *Carpathia* after the *Titanic* sank and died on 29th July 1987, aged 104-years and 2 months, the longest-lived survivor of the disaster. Millvina Dean was the last *Titanic* survivor to die when she passed away on 31st May 2009; she was just 9 weeks old when she boarded the great ocean liner. Ironically, the same day that Millvina died also marked the 98th anniversary of *Titanic's* launch in Belfast.

───────────── Did You Know That? ─────────────

Marjorie Newell Robb (born 12th February 1889; died 11th June 1992) was the last remaining survivor who was a first-class passenger on *Titanic*.

───────────── Did You Know That? ─────────────

Titanic and many other ships were able to 'Morse' to each other not only via wireless, but by means of a Morse lamp – a lamp atop the ship's bridge that flashed on and off in response to a sending key operated by an officer. *Titanic's* officers attempted to Morse the ship that many thought was nearby after the collision with the iceberg (believed to have been the *Californian*).

A DAY TO REMEMBER

Belfast was a hive of activity on the morning of 31st May 1911 with tens of thousands of people from in and around the city converging on the Harland & Wolff Shipyard at Queen's Island. They came from everywhere and by any means possible including bicycle, bus, car, ferry, horse and cart, lorry, rowing boat, tram and Shanks's pony (on foot). Those in attendance witnessed two spectacular sights that day: firstly the *Olympic* was completing her sea trials whilst her younger sister, the *Titanic*, rested majestically in the shipyard's huge dry dock on Slipway No.3 with the onlookers anxiously awaiting her launch. It was a beautiful spring day in Belfast while most of Harland & Wolff's 15,000 workforce (including the 6,000 men who helped to build the *Titanic*) turned up after having received their official invitation to *Titanic's* launch by her owners, the White Star Line. It was a time for the workers to put on their best suits and treat their families to a day out that for many they would surely never forget. With so many people taking up a viewing place along the banks of the River Lagan the more adventurous opted for an alternative vantage point and climbed adjacent stacks of coal and timber to catch a view of these two magnificent leviathans. The White Star Line spared no expense on the day and chartered the steamer *Duke of Argyll* to transport the invited dignitaries and press from Fleetwood, Lancashire to Belfast to witness the launch of the *Titanic*. Three special stands were erected at Harland & Wolff to seat many of the guests with perhaps the most famous of them all being John Pierpont Morgan, the American tycoon whose International Mercantile Marine Corporation effectively owned the *Titanic*. As the 12.00 noon launch time approached the crowd had swelled to nearly 100,000 which was a third of the city's entire population at the time.

Lord William James Pirrie, the Chairman of Harland & Wolff who along with his wife was celebrating his birthday that day, and J. Bruce Ismay, Chairman and Managing Director of the White Star Line, made one final inspection of the launch equipment before 12.00 noon. Then at 12:05 pm, a red signal flag was hoisted on *Titanic's* stern to alert nearby tugboats to stay clear. Five minutes later a rocket was fired into the air, the smoke letting the eager crowd know that *Titanic's* launch was just five minutes away. A second rocket was fired at 12.14 pm and as the huge timber supports were knocked away one by one at 12.15 pm, the largest man-made object ever moved in the world at the time made her way slowly down the slipway and into Belfast Lough with thousands waving their white handkerchiefs in the air cheering 'there she goes' followed by several choruses of 'Rule Britannia!' And so began *Titanic's* short but illustrious life at sea, thought to be the first of many hundreds of voyages which the White Star Line hoped would help place their company at the pinnacle of the cut-throat battle for transatlantic passenger travel.

Did You Know That?

The Belfast Harbour Commissioners fenced off part of the Albert Quay in Belfast, a prime spot to witness *Titanic* in all her glory, and charged entrants two shillings to view the launch from the area. All proceeds were donated to the city's three hospitals.

AMERICA AND IRELAND STAND SIDE BY SIDE

The paddle steamer *America* transported 113 of *Titanic's* third-class passengers to the ship as she dropped anchor about one mile off Roche's Point lighthouse in the Ringabella estuary at Queenstown, Ireland on Thursday 11th April 1912. All 113 booked their travel to the USA with James Scott & Company, Shipping Agents, Queenstown, Ireland. The White Star Line house flag fluttered above their heads on a large flagpole at the wharf whilst the Cunard Line's lion ruffled in the light breeze on another flagpole in an adjacent wharf. James Scott & Company had invited the press along to witness the majesty of *Titanic* with a first-hand view of

proceedings that day from *Ireland* (like the *America*, a paddle-steamer owned by the Clyde Shipping Company). Meanwhile, the hundreds who stood watching from the wharf said a tearful farewell to their loved ones who had dreams in their hearts of a new and prosperous life in America. As the *America* passed the White Star wharf and out towards the *Titanic*, those aboard the paddle steamer caught a glimpse of St Colman's Cathedral, many blessing themselves one final time on Irish shores. As the *America,* commanded by Captain Tobin, approached the *Titanic*, the 113 men, women and children about to board her looked up in amazement as *Titanic's* huge black hull towered into the sky. Little did they know it at the time but a great many of the 113 emigrants that day, many following in the footsteps of relatives before them, would never reach their land of milk and honey. On 19th April 1912, four days after news reached Queenstown that the *Titanic* had sunk, the *America* and the *Ireland* were tied up at Admiralty Pier, Queenstown with their flags at half-mast as a mark of respect to the 1,523 who died in the disaster.

— Did You Know That? —

St Colman's Cathedral has a statue to Our Lady, Star of the Sea, which was placed so that the mother of Jesus Christ faced Queenstown harbour. The statue was paid for by passengers and crew members of the famous *Great Eastern* ocean liner which, one stormy night in September 1861, was forced to take shelter in Queenstown.

TITANIC'S KENTUCKIANS

Two Kentuckians sailed on *Titanic's* ill-fated maiden voyage, both boarding the ship as first-class passengers at Southampton. Firstly there was Dr. Ernest Morawick, an ophthalmologist from Louisville and secondly, Charles Hallace Rolmane, who was born in Georgetown on 11th July 1866. Rolmane was the managing director of the Throgmorton Trust Company in London for a few years and enjoyed gambling. Indeed, Rolmane was born Charles Hallace Romaine but used several aliases, perhaps to ensure that those he played cards with did not know his true identity. Rolmane survived the *Titanic* disaster but Morawick went down with the great ship. On 18th January 1922, Rolmane was accidentally killed by a taxi in New York.

TITANIC'S SAVED SOCIETY COUPLE DIVORCED

Mr William Ernest Carter, his wife Lucile Polk Carter, and their two children, William and Lucile, survived the *Titanic* disaster. However, less than two years after being rescued by the *Carpathia*, Mrs Polk Carter commenced divorce proceedings in January 1914. Mrs Carter's mother was Mrs W. Stewart Polk and a member of an old Southern family related to President James K. Polk, the 11th President of the United States of America (1845-49). The Carters were prominent members of society in Pennsylvania.

NO DANGER

Anna Katherine ('Annie Katie') Kelly boarded the *Titanic* as a third-class passenger (Ticket No. 9234, £7 15s) at Queenstown, Ireland on Thursday 11th April 1912. She was a member of the famous Addergoole Fourteen on the ship from County Mayo and only one of three from the group who survived the sinking of the *Titanic*. Later she claimed that the stewards did not waken her or any of her fellow passengers. Annie also claimed that when some passengers from the third-class area attempted to go up on to the boat deck, they were turned back by the stewards who told them there was nothing to worry about. When she arrived safely in New York on the *Carpathia* she was admitted to hospital for a short while to get over the shock of the disaster. Whilst in hospital she said that she was asked to sign what she thought was a receipt for a train ticket to Chicago when in fact it was a document releasing the White Star Line from any liability towards her.

--------------------- Did You Know That? ---------------------

Annie was rescued by the *Carpathia* from Lifeboat No.16 and said that she only managed to secure a place in the lifeboat when John Bourke's wife, Catherine, and his sister Mary Bourke, got out of it when John was not allowed to join them.

IN SAFE KEEPING

In 1806, Thomas Perry founded Thomas Perry & Sons Ltd at the Highfields Works, Bilston, West Midlands, England. By 1850 the company was well established and operated as a fully functional iron founders manufacturing items such as bedsteads, fencing, railing, gates, palisades and other wrought-iron and cast-iron work. It was during the latter part of the 19th century that they started specialising in the heavier end of the trade, producing armour plate for warships, gun batteries, along with light and heavy duty safes for companies, homes and shipping.

In early 1911, Perry's received the order to produce safes for the newly-commissioned White Star Line ship, *Olympic*. Upon receiving the safes intended for use in the purser's office and Post Office on the *Olympic*, the White Star Line then placed another order with Perry's for safes for their next Olympic class passenger liner, *Titanic*. Shortly after the *Titanic* struck an iceberg, passengers started to gather at the purser's office to retrieve valuables which they had placed in the care of the purser. The safes were emptied and *Titanic's* passengers went about their business of survival. As *Titanic* upended and tore herself apart, some of her safes left the sinking liner and ended up scattered about the ocean floor. During the discovery of the wreck of *Titanic* in September 1985 by Dr Robert Ballard, her safes were photographed lying in the debris field for later investigation. During Ballard's dive to the wreck the following year, an attempt was made to open one of the newly-discovered safes. Although the bronze handle turned, the safe refused to give up its secrets. Finally, during a recovery expedition in 1987, one of the safes (originally thought to be the purser's office safe, but later discovered to have actually been the restaurant office safe) was recovered and opened on live American television. The show was hosted by the actor Telly Savalas and witnessed by millions of viewers. When the safe was finally opened it contained a leather bag, some paperwork and some money.

Did You Know That?

Perry's advertised their safes on posters with one in particular boasting that they were 'The Nation's Safeguard' and depicted an image of one of their 'new improved' safes with the Crown Jewels inside it.

THE ITALIAN

On Day 5 of the US Senate Committee inquiry into the *Titanic* disaster, Fifth Officer Harold Lowe said that everyone he loaded into Lifeboat No.14 was either a woman or a child with the exception of one passenger whom Lowe said was Italian and sneaked into the lifeboat dressed like a woman. During his testimony he said: 'I found this Italian. He came aft, and he had a shawl over his head and I suppose he had skirts. Anyhow, I pulled this shawl off his face and saw he was a man. He was in a great hurry to get into the other boat, and I caught hold of him and pitched him in.' Lowe received criticism for his use of the word 'Italian', which many Italian-Americans considered to be a slur, implying that they were cowards. When the Italian Ambassador to New York complained about Lowe's inference, Lowe retracted his 'Italian' remark.

Did You Know That?

Edward Ryan, aged 24, from Ballinareen, County Tipperary claimed to be the man who disguised himself as a woman to get into Lifeboat No. 14. He admitted it when he wrote a letter to his mother a few weeks after he was rescued.

A DEBT OWED BY SO MANY TO SO FEW

After the *Titanic* struck an iceberg and Captain Smith was informed by the ship's designer, Thomas Andrews, that the ship described in *Shipbuilder's Magazine* as 'practically unsinkable', could not stay afloat for more than a few hours, he gave the order to launch the lifeboats.

Of the 20 lifeboats aboard the *Titanic*, 16 were wooden (including 2 wood cutters) and 4 were of the collapsible kind and manufactured from wood and canvas. The maximum capacity of the 20 lifeboats was 1,178 persons, meaning that 1,050 passengers would surely lose their battle to survive in the North Atlantic Ocean. Apart from the 4 collapsible lifeboats, the 16 wooden boats were positioned beneath davits, large metal arm-like lowering mechanisms fitted with ropes and blocks and lowered by hand. Each set of davits was designed for the *Olympic* and *Titanic* to operate three lifeboats, one after the other. The boat attached to the davit would be filled and lowered. Once the boat was cast off, the arm would be then raised back into position to be connected to the next boat.

During the early design period of the *Olympic* and the *Titanic*, the first two of three new Olympic Class vessels, the decision as to the number of lifeboats on each ship was greatly considered by Alexander Carlisle, one of the managing directors at Harland & Wolff Shipyard at the time. Initially both sisters were to be allocated 48 lifeboats based on Carlisle's recommendations, giving space in them in the event of an emergency for more passengers than the ships were able to carry. However, the numbers were reduced from 48 to 32 and then to 16. Despite Harland & Wolff's recommendation to place as many lifeboats as possible on each ship, only the 4 collapsibles were added, bringing the number for each to 20. Of the 4 collapsibles, 2 sat on the roof to the officers quarters alongside the base of the first funnel and 2 sat on deck behind the cutter lifeboats. This decision was supported by the British Board of Trade who stated that all British vessels over 10,000 tons must carry a minimum of 16 lifeboats (equating to 1,060 persons). This out of date ruling meant that the *Titanic* would have space for only 47% of her passengers and crew.

The lifeboats aboard *Titanic* were designed by Harland & Wolff's own Chief Draftsman, Roderick Chisholm, who sailed aboard the *Titanic* as one of the ship's Guarantee Group out of Belfast on the 2nd April 1912. The davits were manufactured by the West Midlands firm of 'Welin Quadrant Davit' whose head office and workshops were based in Brierley Hill, West Midlands, England, with another office in London. The orders for the davits from the White Star Line were received in early 1910 and awaited approval. On the 9th March 1910, the Welin Davit office in London responded with a blueprint of the proposed double-acting gear. The blueprint indicated that both liners were to receive 32 sets of davits in total, 16 sets per vessel. Trading under the new name of 'Welin Lambie', the company remains in business to this day supplying davits to ships, oil rigs, and even NASA. In 1997, the company revisited their archives to reproduce the davits for the film set of James Cameron's *Titanic*.

Titanic's 705 passengers and crew who were lucky enough to secure a place in a lifeboat or climb onto an overturned one, owe an eternity of gratitude to the lifeboats, small wooden crafts which must have seemed tiny in comparison to the liner they were leaving behind.

A MODEL FEATURE

The model made for the 1980 movie *Raise The Titanic* remains to this day the largest complete model of the *Titanic* ever constructed. It was an impressive 55 feet long, 12 feet in height and weighed 10 tons. The model was constructed at the CBS film studios in California, USA during the summer of 1979. It was shipped to the film studios in Malta and placed into a specially constructed deep water tank, the largest of its kind in the world. The tank had a depth of over 40 feet and span of 240 feet across. After the film's prologue was finished, the 1912 model was turned into a ship that had spent 65 years on the ocean floor. The FX crew set about covering the model in sprayable concrete. The second funnel was removed and replaced with a broken twisted stump and a solid bulkhead was fitted to the tips of the bows. Next the FX crew installed three tall cowl vents onto the forecastle. This radical alteration was to allow for onboard deck scenes to be filmed with the ex-Grace Line ocean liner *Athinai* which was used as the stand-in for the raised *Titanic*. To raise the ship, the model was connected to a hydraulic arm that was attached to the base of the constructed seafloor. The model was fitted with tanks that were hidden inside the hull. As air was pumped into the tanks, the model became buoyant, and attached to the arm it would be lifted to the surface. Special cameras were built to film the raising sequence, running at 15 times the normal speed. The model remains at the film studios in Malta.

——————— Did You Know That? ———————

Raise The Titanic was originally to open with a prologue of the ship going down using sinking footage of the huge *Titanic* model built for the movie.

BUTTON-UP

Firmin & Sons Ltd, a very well established company based in Birmingham, West Midlands, England and master button maker to naval fleets, merchant shipping and even royalty, supplied the White Star Line with the buttons used on the uniforms of the officers and crew members of the *Olympic* and the *Titanic*. The button specialists were originally founded in London in 1677, and with their origins dating back to as far as the reign of King Charles II, the company became one of the longest established companies in the United Kingdom. From their humble beginnings, Firmin & Sons Ltd were soon to become the leading manufacture of buttons in every form, including livery and badges up and down the country. This achievement was recognised when the company exhibited at the Great Exhibition in London in 1851. They were renowned internationally and during the American Civil War, both sides wore Firmin buttons on their uniforms. During the late 19th century they moved from their London base to set up a new factory in Birmingham. It was from there that they manufactured and supplied buttons with the famous insignia to the White Star Line. During recovery of artefacts from the seabed in 1987 from around the site of the *Titanic*, some of the Firmin crew buttons were salvaged.

YOU OWE US $10 MILLION

On 16th January 1913, the *Washington Post* reported that to date a mammoth $8,027274 in compensation claims had been filed by *Titanic* survivors and families of the 1,523 who lost their lives in the disaster against the White Star Line (Oceanic Steam Navigation Company) in a New York court. Mrs Irene Wallach Harris, who lost her husband Henry B Harris the theatrical manager, lodged a claim for $1,000,000; Mrs May Futrelle filed a claim for $304,791.50 after her husband, the author Jacques Futrelle, went down with the ship; Mrs Lily B. Millet, whose husband was the artist Francis D. Millet, claimed $100,000 for the loss of his life. A total of 270 compensation claims had been filed to date with Mrs Harris' claim by far the largest. The man charged with dealing with the compensation claims on behalf of the US Court, Judge Hand, issued a ruling of the Admiralty Branch of the Federal District Court that no claims would be accepted after 11th February 1913. However, claimants could appeal to the US Court of Appeals for an extension of time in which to lodge a claim against the White Star Line. By the time the closing date had passed a staggering $10,000,000 had been claimed covering loss of life, loss of property and personal injury. Attorneys for the White Star Line contended that their client, *Titanic's* owners, had limited liability of $96,000 under US law which equated to the value of recovered records and passenger fares (i.e. *Titanic* did not fulfill her contract with each passenger by transporting them from Southampton/Cherbourg/Queenstown to New York).

Did You Know That?

There are actually so many differences between *Titanic* and her sister ship, *Olympic*, that it requires a book to list them all. In 2004, noted *Titanic* researchers Bruce Beveridge and Steve Hall published *Olympic and Titanic: The Truth Behind the Conspiracy* to provide factual and photographic evidence of these differences and to prove why a switch would have been impossible.

THE CONSPIRACY THEORY

The conspiracy theory surrounding the *Titanic* begins when the two sister ships sat side-by-side at the Harland & Wolff Shipyard in Belfast on 6th March 1912. The *Titanic* was still under construction at the time while the *Olympic*, not for the first time, was back at the shipyard to have some urgent and expensive repairs carried out. On 24th February 1912, RMS *Olympic* dropped one of her port propeller blades 750 miles east of Newfoundland while enroute to Southampton. For a second time in the space of just six months she made her way back to Belfast for urgent and expensive repairs. Meanwhile, work on *Olympic's* younger sister, *Titanic*, was interrupted. On 6th March 1912, the *Titanic* was moved out of the dry dock at Harland & Wolff in order that the *Olympic* could enter to facilitate the repair work necessary. The conspiracy theorists claim that late one night the ship's names were changed so that the White Star Line could recoup the substantial outlays it had paid out on two repairs to the *Olympic*, one of which was quite costly and undertaken after her collision with HMS *Hawke*, an Admiralty vessel in September 1911. This collision is thought by some to have broken the *Olympic's* back, a term referring to permanently damaging the integral strength of the keel. And therein lies the claim that the *Olympic* became the *Titanic* and the *Titanic* assumed the mantle of the *Olympic*. The conspiracy theorists suggested that the White Star Line (principally J. Bruce Ismay and John Pierpont Morgan) would then arrange for the *Olympic* to sail as the *Titanic* on the younger sister's maiden voyage from Southampton to New York on 10th April 1912, but ensure that an accident occurred during the crossing. The latter would then fool the *Titanic's* insurers into paying out on the actual loss of the *Olympic*. It was also claimed that the White Star Line would ensure that another vessel would be in close proximity to the *Titanic* (actually the *Olympic*) when the disaster at sea occurred so that the passengers and crew aboard her could be safely rescued which in turn would look good for the company. The conspiracy theorists went on to say that on the evening of Sunday 14th April 1912, J. Bruce Ismay forced Captain Smith to increase the speed of *Titanic* despite the fact that the ship had received numerous ice warnings that day and that Captain Smith had decided to order an unscheduled course change as a result of the ice warnings; the change was to take *Titanic* a bit off course to rendezvous with the ship which the White Star Line had 'tailing' the *Titanic*. The waiting ship was, supposedly, the *Californian*. What ostensibly went wrong is that Smith had the wrong type of distress rockets fired off from the bridge, ones the *Californian's* officers did not recognise as the pre-determined signal. The conspiracy theory makes a good bedtime story, but is so filled with technical and factual errors, that it is dismissed as it should be – nothing more than an entertaining 'what if?' *Olympic* and *Titanic*, although at first glance identical twin sisters, in reality had so many differences between them – porthole and vent locations, for example, which were not easily altered – that a switch would have required extensive yard work and the unlikely silence of thousands of Harland & Wolff workers. The idea that something like this could have been pulled off in secret stretches credibility, to say the very least. Besides, as *Titanic* was under-insured by $2.5 million, a conspiracy to deliberately sink her hardly made good business sense.

Did You Know That?

At the time of the disaster the *Titanic* carried insurance of £1,000,000 ($5,000,000) with the remaining risk carried by the White Star Line's insurance fund.

WHEN ICE STRIKES

The *Titanic* was not the first ship to meet her doom after colliding with an iceberg. On 11th May 1833, the Scottish brig, *Lady of the Lake,* bound from Belfast to Quebec struck an iceberg in the North Atlantic about 250 miles off Cape St. Francis, Newfoundland, resulting in the death of 197 of the 231 people aboard her. Indeed, the *Titanic* was not even the first vessel to meet her doom following a collision with an iceberg off Newfoundland's Grand Banks. The following vessels were among those presumed lost to icebergs in that area:

March 1841	The steamer *President* crossing between New York and Liverpool, lost with 120 aboard.
March 1854	The *City of Glasgow* from Liverpool bound for Philadelphia with 480 aboard.
February 1856	The *Pacific* bound for New York from Liverpool, 185 aboard.
May 1870	The *City of Boston* from Boston bound for Liverpool, lost with 191 aboard.
February 1892	The White Star Line's *Naronic* from Liverpool bound for New York.
February 1896	The steamer *State of Georgia,* from Aberdeen for Boston.
February 1899	The steamer *Allegheny,* from New York bound for Dover.
February 1902	The steamer *Huronian,* from Liverpool bound for St. Johns.

All of these vessels were presumed lost claiming the lives of everyone aboard. Between February and May the Grand Banks are most populated with icebergs, and prior to 1901 no ships were fitted with wireless communications.

MOVING HOME

Sometime during 1906, the White Star Line decided to move the home port for its transatlantic liners involved in the mail service to New York from Liverpool down to Southampton. The southern port had much better facilities than its north-west counterpart.

TITANIC'S VICTIMS CLOSELY GUARDED

The bodies of 306 *Titanic* victims were landed by the *Mackay-Bennett* at 'Flagship Pier', North Coaling Jetty No.4, HM Dockyard, Halifax, Nova Scotia, Canada at approximately 9:30 am on Tuesday 30th April 1912. When the bodies were taken off the ship they were given armed protection by the Canadian Army and then transported by horse-drawn hearses to the temporary morgue at the Mayflower Curling Rink. A total of 330 bodies were recovered from the wreck site and brought to Halifax.

THE WHITE STAR LINE'S PLAN

It was the intention of the White Star Line to run a weekly service across the Atlantic using the *Olympic* and the *Titanic*, thereby hoping to attract passengers away from the Cunard Line's *Lusitania* and *Mauretania*. The sister ships were to depart Southampton on a Wednesday with stop-offs to collect passengers and mail at Cherbourg, France and Queenstown, Ireland and were scheduled to arrive in New York the following Wednesday. Both ships would then be re-coaled and leave New York for the return journey to Southampton on the following Saturday morning.

───────────── Did You Know That? ─────────────

The White Star Line owned a vessel named *Atlantic*. The RMS *Atlantic* was built by Harland & Wolf and launched on 26th November 1870. On 1st April 1873, she ran onto rocks and sank off the coast of Nova Scotia, Canada. When the bodies were recovered from the wreck site and prepared for burial, one of the crew members was discovered to be a woman in her early twenties. Her gender was unknown to her fellow crew members until her body was washed ashore.

HARD TO SPOT

It is well documented that the two lookouts, Frederick Fleet and Reginald Lee, on duty when the *Titanic* struck an iceberg, did not have any binoculars in the crow's nest of the foremast. However, binoculars were neither standard issue to the lookouts nor standard equipment in the crow's nest, and even if Fleet and Lee had had them they more than likely would have had a hard time spotting the iceberg much sooner than when they did with the naked eye. It was a perfectly clear night and with no moon shining and only starlight for illumination, neither the water nor indeed the iceberg was readily visible from their position high up above the ship. On that fateful Sunday evening the North Atlantic was a flat calm which was unusual for April, and so there were no waves breaking at the foot of the iceberg to warn Fleet and Lee of its presence. Up until the *Titanic* disaster, and long afterwards as well, avoidance of icebergs was dependent on visual watches from the vessel's lookouts and officers on the bridge. On a clear day they could see over 11 miles from the crow's nest which normally afforded the ship a sufficient period of time to take evasive manoeuvres. It was also standard practice for ships to halt when encountering ice fields at night and wait for daybreak before proceeding further, just as the *Californian* had done earlier that evening in the same general area that *Titanic* was heading towards.

Did You Know That?

Reginald Lee died on 6th August 1913 from complications of pneumonia whilst serving aboard the *Kenilworth Castle*. On 11th January 1965, Frederick Fleet hanged himself two weeks after his wife's death.

TITANIC'S ACME LINK

In the early 1860s, a farmer named Joseph Hudson left his home in Derbyshire and moved to Birmingham, West Midlands, England to work as a trained toolmaker. He converted the wash house attached to the side of his terraced home in St Mark's Street in the city into a workshop where he began making snuff boxes, cork screws and small portable pocket whistles. He also carried out shoe repairs. Hudson managed to overcome the problem that most whistles had by finding a distinctive sound that would carry afar. Indeed, he discovered the distinctive sound by mistake. One evening he was playing his violin and when he attempted to place it on a nearby table, it fell to the floor and smashed. Upon impact with the ground the violin made a loud screeching noise and Hudson knew instantly that this was the sound he had been searching for. His small workshop remained so until 1883 when the London Metropolitan Police advertised for a new brand of whistle to replace their cumbersome means of communication, a rattle. Hudson replied to the request by developing the Metropolitan Police Whistle. When the police tested the whistle on Clapham Common, London, their expectations were met when the whistle could be heard over a mile away. On the heels of this, Hudson decided to name his company ACME. From the early years of pocket whistles, Hudson's business grew and ACME went on to manufacture and supply whistles to many countries around the world. The ACME range included not only whistles for the police force, but also boy scouts, football clubs, sports organisations (including FIFA), mountain rescue, animal training and shipping (including lifeguards, naval and merchant shipping and sea rescue). For almost 140 years, ACME produced some 93 different types of whistles and it is said that many of today's modern whistles owe their existence to the ACME range.

ACME supplied the new White Star Lines Olympic class liners, the *Olympic* and the *Titanic*, with the crew pocket whistle now commonly known as the world famous 'Thunderer'. They also made the boatswain pipe with chain and the ACME 'Stentor' megaphone, the device used by Captain Edward John Smith to call out to passengers and crew 'Abandon ship!' as the *Titanic*'s forecastle came awash with water during the early hours of Monday 15th April 1912. It was during one of the dives to the wreck site of the *Titanic* in the mid 1990s that one of the bridge megaphones was recovered from the debris field. The ACME Company still trade from their Birmingham offices to this day, producing replica *Titanic* 'Thunderer' whistles for the general public and avid collectors of *Titanic* memorabilia.

THE ATLANTIC'S FARMER

Captain Edward John Smith of the *Titanic* captained SS *Runic* from March to April 1891 and her sister ship, the SS *Cufic* (twice: December 1888 & January 1895). Both the *Runic* and the *Cufic* were built by the Harland & Wolff Shipyard in Belfast for the White Star Line as livestock carriers, serving the Liverpool to New York route. The *Cufic* (Yard No. 210) was launched in Belfast on 10th October 1888 whilst the *Runic* (Yard No. 211) was launched on New Year's Day 1889.

--- Did You Know That? ---

On 18th December 1919, while transporting wheat from Portland to Gibraltar, the *Cufic* foundered resulting in the loss of all 40 of her crew.

THE DELAYED TURN

On the evening of Sunday 14th April 1912, Captain Smith accepted an invitation from Mr George Widener to attend a dinner party aboard the *Titanic* which Mr Widener was hosting in his honour. Just before Captain Smith left the bridge to prepare for dinner he left instructions in the Night Order Book for the turning point on *Titanic*'s outward Southern Track across the North Atlantic Ocean to be made at 5.50pm, 30 minutes later than when the turn was initially scheduled to be made. Once the turning point was made the *Titanic* then headed westward towards New York. During the subsequent inquiries into the *Titanic* disaster,

Fourth Officer Joseph Boxall testified that the turn was made just as Captain Smith had ordered and the reason for the 30-minute time alteration was due to ice warnings received by the *Titanic* earlier in the day from other vessels that had already passed the ice fields.

Did You Know That?

In 1911–12, the North Atlantic Ocean witnessed its mildest winter in 30 years, which resulted in a higher number of icebergs than normal calving from the Greenland ice shelf.

LLOYDS TESTING

Lloyds Testing was established from the ideas of Samuel Brown, who was an officer for the Royal Navy. After retiring from service, he founded his own chain-making business in 1803. As he experimented with different types of chain, it was decided that a chain-testing machine was necessary. After his death in 1852, his business had expanded to become the leading suppliers of iron cables throughout the world. With the introduction of the new regulations from *Lloyds Register Of Shipping*, it became compulsory for all anchors and cables supplied to any new vessels built from that year onwards to be supplied with a certificate that they had been properly tested. Testing houses were to be built to accommodate all means of testing of large and small scale anchors, cables and chains. This empire was to become the *Lloyds Test House*, now known as *Lloyds British Testing*. The first and largest of them all was opened in the early 1860s on Primrose Hill, Netherton, West Midlands. The Proving House, as it was named, sat directly opposite the recently established anchor and chain makers Noah Hingley & Sons Ltd who soon become the leading manufacturers and suppliers of anchor chains and anchors to all corners of the world. As the Proving House workshops were on the opposite side of the road to Hingley's, this meant that any anchors and cables could be sent a short distance for approval.

The *Titanic* anchors were sent over to Lloyds for inspection and testing. The shanks were tested and weight established. The ship's build number from the Harland & Wolff yard, No.401, was stamped onto the shank along with the date and year it was tested, the initials of the Lloyds supervisor Jack Holloway, its weight and breaking strain weight. The anchor head was also tested for its weight. If underweight, the anchor head was shot-blasted with pig-iron to counterbalance the head. Once this was achieved, the head was then, like the shank, stamp marked with the weight, breaking strain, date and supervisor initials. The next task was for Lloyds to assemble the anchor on site. Once completed, the anchor was painted white and the 'Hingley. Netherton' markings were painted onto both sides of the shank.

A highly dramatized and inaccurate illustration of *Titanic* in her final moments.
The lifeboats are shown oversize and full of passengers, and the sea is rough with ice about.
(*Illustrated London News*/ Jonathan Smith collection)

The chains, which had already been checked by the Hingley works, were put through tests by Lloyds. If a small section of chain was being tested, the chain was attached to a machine which would pull the length of chain until breaking point. The machine worked via hydraulics and sat at one end of a dugout in the floor of the Proving House. This dugout provided a channel that the chains would sit inside. One end of the chain was secured in a holding frame at one end of the test channel. The machine end would secure the opposite end of the chain. As pressure was applied to the section of chain, the machine would assert certain set tonnage to the links. When the set tonnage was reached, the chain would then be sent *past* that tonnage until the chain broke. If the chain broke *before* the set tonnage, the chains were not passed. If they broke past that set tonnage, the chain was passed. Once small sections had been tested, longer sections were then put into the testing beds. A larger machine was used and longer lengths, in fathoms, were stretched across the floor of the Proving House with the fathoms of chains being passed around drums that sat upon the floor of the test area. Each link in each set of fathoms of chain was individually checked for any signs of fracture before being passed. Each fathom was then marked with dates and Proving House initials. In the case of *Titanic*, there were 1,200 feet of chains to be tested and inspected.

After becoming the longest established of the Lloyds Proving House in the Midlands, the Netherton test house closed its doors on business in March 1990.

The workshops were then sold to C. Beech & Sons, supplier and stockist of steel who remain at those premises to this day. The buildings still retain much of their character as in the days of when the *Titanic* and her sister's huge anchors dwarfed all those who worked upon them.

LEAVING OUT THE 'C'

Of the 15 vessels captained by Captain Edward John Smith only one of them did not end with the letter 'C', the *Lizzie Fennell*.

─────────────── Did You Know That? ───────────────

On 13th January 1871, the *Lizzie Fennell* arrived in New York from Havana with one of her crew members in irons following an attempted mutiny aboard the ship which resulted in her captain, Captain A. W. Deering, and her First Officer being badly injured. The second mate was thrown overboard.

ONE SISTER FEEDING THE OTHER

Although the coal strike in Great Britain had ended on 6th April 1912, it would be at least a further 2–3 weeks before the White Star Line would be fully stocked with sufficient quantities of coal for all of the company's vessels. Consequently, the White Star Line ensured that *Titanic* had enough coal for her maiden voyage on Wednesday 10th April 1912. *Titanic* was loaded with 4,427 tons taken from 5 International Mercantile Marine Company ships as well as what was left over from her older sister, the *Olympic*. Some coal may have been taken off the *Olympic* or left over (on the coal barges) from when the *Olympic* loaded coal herself as the *Olympic* had left Southampton only hours before *Titanic's* arrival at the port on 3rd April 1912.

─────────────── Did You Know That? ───────────────

SS *Britannic* (1874) was the first of three ships to sail with the *Britannic* name. All three were members of the White Star Line fleet.

■ THE MOVIE TRIVIA ■ ■ ■ ■ ■ ■ ■ ■ ■ ■ ■ ■ ■ ■ ■

Gloria Stuart, aged 86-years old, was aged by make-up to play a 101-year old Rose.

Did You Know That?

Olympic's first year of her transatlantic passenger service was dismal from a financial perspective, with costly delays afforded by the September 1911 collision with HMS *Hawke* and the February 1912 loss of her port propeller, both incidents requiring major refit work in Belfast, which resulted in her having to cancel seven transatlantic trips.

TITANIC'S BRIDGE TELEGRAPHS

J.W. Ray & Co., 17 South Castle Street, Liverpool, lay claim to supplying *Titanic* and her sisters with the telegraphs for the navigating bridge, reciprocating engine room and docking bridge. Engine-order telegraphs on the bridge sent orders to the starting platform in the reciprocating engine room as to the stopping, starting and desired speed of the port and starboard engines. In the engine room, the telegraph would ring and the pointer on the dial would indicate the command sent; following this the engine room officer would acknowledge by moving the handles on his telegraph to match the pointer on the dial. This would, in turn, ring a bell and cause the pointer on the bridge telegraph to move to the command sent. Another engine-order telegraph on the docking bridge at the stern sent engine orders to the navigating bridge for relay to the engine room in the event the ship was being conned from the docking bridge aft, and another relayed line-handling and helm orders aft and the status of mooring lines forward. The docking bridge was a raised platform on the poop deck at the stern of the ship and extended from one side of the ship to another and slightly out over each side; it gave a raised vantage point to supervise the handling of mooring lines and any tugs assisting the ship at the stern, and also had an auxiliary wheel (helm) connected directly to the steering gear in the compartment below in the event the Telemotor system failed to the wheel on the navigating bridge. Telegraphs replaced old-fashioned speaking tubes on ships like *Titanic* when the distance between the bridge and engine room was too far for speaking tubes to work, and in addition commands sent via telegraphs could not be misinterpreted as they were clearly shown on a glass dial. J. W. Ray & Co. gave film-maker James Cameron copies of their plans for *Titanic's* telegraphs and Cameron had an identical set of telegraphs made for use in his 1997 blockbuster *Titanic*.

■ THE MOVIE TRIVIA ■■■■■■■■■■■■■■

In the scene where the water comes crashing into the Grand Staircase room, director James Cameron only had one shot at getting it right as the entire set and furnishings were going to be destroyed by the enormous inrush of water.

THE TANK TOP

The tank top of the *Titanic* formed a watertight inner bottom about 5 feet above the top of her keel.

CHIEF NAVAL ARCHITECT SACKED

Following the death of Thomas Andrews in the *Titanic* disaster, Edward Wilding succeeded Andrews as Harland & Wolff's Senior Naval Architect. Wilding had been trained by Andrews and assisted him with designing the *Titanic*. After the sinking he focused on making improvements to large vessels which would increase their safety. On 1st January 1914, Wilding was appointed a Managing Director at the shipyard but after discussing alterations and designs to ships with their owners without informing Lord Pirrie of his actions, he was forced to step down from his position.

TITANIC ALL WEIGHED-UP

Sometime in early 1912, the White Star Line placed an order with the Birmingham-based company, W & T Avery, who specialised in weighing equipment, for Avery scales to be used onboard the *Titanic*. Under the guidance of William Hipkins, the Managing Director, the company grew and branched out into a bigger and better future. With the recent introduction of larger scales, including heavy duty weighbridge scales, this meant that the company could look to develop their reputation overseas. From small household, office and work scales, came scales for most needs, including transportation. Hipkins widened the prestige of the Avery name and trademark into what was at the time described as 'the finest weighing machine factory in the world'. However, Hipkins knew that to truly dominate the world market in weighing appliances W & T Avery had to conquer America. He boarded the *Titanic* as a first-class passenger at Southampton on Wednesday 10th April 1912 for her maiden voyage to New York. The company remains in business today but under the trading name of Avery Weigh-Tronix, specialising in the making and supplying of light to heavy duty weighing scales to businesses all over the world.

———— Did You Know That? ————

During the war years, W & T Avery went on to produce 25-pounder field guns, 17-pounder anti-tank guns, along with mine sinkers and shell fuses. Because of their involvement with the supply of materials for the war, the factory became a target for enemy bombing raids. In 1940 and 1942, the factory was badly damaged by parachute mines.

MEAL TIMES

Meals were served aboard the *Titanic* as follows:

First Class	
Breakfast	8 am westbound, 8:30 eastbound
Luncheon	1 pm
Tea	4 pm
Dinner	7pm–11 pm
Second Class	
Breakfast (if one sitting, but if numbers of passengers did not permit everyone to be served in one sitting, two sittings at 7:30 and 8:30 am)	8–10am
Luncheon	12:30 if one sitting, 12 noon and 1pm (if two sittings)
Tea	4 pm
Dinner (if one sitting, 6 pm and 7 pm if two sittings)	6:30 pm
Third Class	
Breakfast two sittings	8 am and 9 am
Dinner two sittings	12 and 1 pm
Tea two sittings	5 pm and 6 pm

TITANIC'S EXHAUSTS

Very little is known about the company *Thomas Piggott & Co.*, a long and well established engineering company that once traded from the Atlas Works, Birmingham, West Midlands. The company was first founded in 1822, but between the years of 1845 and 1936, it was well known for production of boiler steam pipes for many of the 'Black Country' foundries. There large production shops also manufactured pipes for steam engines, gas works, steel-rolling mills along with pipe supporting bridges, water tanks, steel chimneys, gas holder tanks and boilers. Sometime during 1910 the Thomas Piggott works received the order to produce both the main steam and exhaust pipes for the three sisters, *Olympic*, *Titanic* and *Britannic*. The company ceased trading during the late 1930s.

BE ON TIME OR GO HOME WITH NO PAY

During the construction of the *Olympic* and the *Titanic* at the Harland & Wolff Shipyard in Belfast between 1908–11, if a worker turned up after the gates had been closed, he could not get in and had to return home losing a day's pay.

SISTERS CROSS PATHS

On 3rd April 1912, the *Olympic* commenced her 7th transatlantic trip from Southampton to New York, just 12 hours before her younger sister, the *Titanic*, arrived in Southampton to prepare for her maiden voyage to New York. The *Olympic* left New York on Saturday 13th April 1912 for the return leg of her journey and was 750 nautical miles from New York when she received her sister's call for help in the early hours of Sunday 15th April 1912.

Did You Know That?

The letters of the ship's name on the bows of *Olympic* and the *Titanic* were cut into the steel, and then painted in yellow chromate – the same colour as the sheer stripe running the length of the ship between the black and white sections of the hull.

FROM WHITE STAR TO ROYAL MAIL

When she set sail on her maiden voyage, the *Titanic* was one of 13 transatlantic steamers which carried the Royal and US Mail.

Did You Know That?

Masters of Royal Mail ships were required to consider the safety of the mail secondary only to that of the passengers themselves.

SERVING HER COUNTRY

During the First World War (1914–18), 10 of the 35 White Star Line's steamers were lost in combat. When the war ended, the company was given several German liners as reparations.

NO RETURN

When the White Star Line ran its transatlantic passenger service, Queenstown was an emigrant loading point, only frequented on outbound legs.

BIG PAYOUTS

Not long after the *Titanic* sank, the periodical *Insurance Press* ran an article in which it claimed that life and accident insurance companies lost $3,464,111 (almost £693,000) as a result of the disaster. The article stated that the life insurance companies had to pay $1,881,111 of the $3,464,111 to the beneficiaries of policy-holders who lost their lives, while the accident companies were liable for $1,583,000.

Did You Know That?

Herbert Fuller Chaffee from Amenia, Cass County, North Dakota, USA, who went down with the ship, held the largest amount of life insurance – $146,750. Emil Brandeis from Omaha, Nebraska, USA held the largest amount of accident insurance cover – $175,000.

TITANIC'S FIRST CLAIM SETTLED

On 20th April 1912, just five days after the *Titanic* disaster, the *Washington Herald* printed a story in which it claimed that the first payout for the loss of a life in the *Titanic* disaster was made by the Metropolitan Life Insurance Company to a brother of Henry Sutehill who lost his life when the *Titanic* sank. The company was said to have paid out the sum of $1,000.

BELGIAN CONSUL SUES THE WHITE STAR LINE

In early September 1913, Pierre Mali, the Belgian Consul in New York, lodged a claim at New York's Federal District Court against the White Star Line requesting the sum of $46,250 as compensation for the 'lost natives of his country'. Mali was acting as the administrator of the estates of Edmond Van Melkebeke, Alphonse de Pelsmaeker, Rosalie Govert Van Impe and Catherine Van Impe, all of whom lost their lives in the *Titanic* disaster.

Did You Know That?

The *New York Times* printed a story stating that Mali's claim for $46,250 had brought the total of claims lodged against the White Star Line up to a whopping $16,850,362.

TITANIC'S LORD MAYOR

Christopher Head, aged 42, a former Lord Mayor of Chelsea, London, boarded the *Titanic* as a first-class passenger at Southampton (Ticket No. 113038, £42 10s, Cabin B-11). At the time Head was a Director of Henry Head and Co. (Limited), Insurance Brokers and Underwriters. He lost his life in the *Titanic* disaster and his body, if ever recovered, was never identified.

MEMENTOES FROM THE *TITANIC*

On 23rd April 1912, just four days after arriving safely in New York onboard the Carpathia, *Titanic* survivor John Borak, gave an interview to the *Newark Star* newspaper sensationally claiming that he was shot at by officers on the *Titanic* when he attempted to climb into a lifeboat. To substantiate his claim Borak showed the reporter his overcoat which had six holes in it, holes he claimed were bullet holes. Borak said that he secured a place in the last lifeboat to be lowered from the sinking White Star liner. However, upon inspection of *Titanic's* passenger list, a John Borak does not appear to have sailed on *Titanic's* maiden voyage.

MOTHER AND BABY REUNITED

On 23rd April 1912, just four days after arriving safely in New York onboard the Carpathia, *Titanic* survivor Mrs Alexander Thomas gave an interview to the *Newark Star* in which she told how she was separated from her 6-month-old child as the call for women and children to enter the lifeboats was made. When pressed to enter a lifeboat by one of the ship's officers she initially refused not wishing to leave the sinking vessel without her baby. However, she said that when she was informed by one of the officers that a female passenger had taken her baby safely into one of the other boats she reluctantly entered the lifeboat. Mother and child were reunited aboard their rescue ship, RMS *Carpathia*.

THE *TITANIC* SETS SAIL AGAIN

In January 2010, a 1:150 scale replica model of RMS *Titanic* was put up for sale online by the New York-based Hammacher Schlemmer, a company which sells curios and gadgets. The model is 6-feet long, comprises in excess of 300 handcrafted pieces, possesses a cruising speed of 5mph and costs £1,500. The replica *Titanic* can be steered from as far as 75-feet away and uses rechargeable batteries, which drive the three propellers.

WHEN IT ALL WENT WRONG FOR MR WRIGHT

Mr George Wright, a self-made millionaire businessman from Halifax, Nova Scotia, Canada decided to visit Europe in the autumn of 1911 and booked his passage across the Atlantic on the *Empress of Ireland*. Wright had made a fortune following the publication of *Wright's World Business Directories*. The story goes that he was in Paris when he learned of *Titanic's* maiden voyage and decided he wished to travel aboard the world's most luxurious ocean liner. He boarded the *Titanic* at Cherbourg on Thursday 11th April 1912. None of *Titanic's* survivors could recollect seeing Wright on the ship and his body, if ever recovered, was never identified.

─────────── Did You Know That? ───────────

George Wright bequeathed his ornate home to the Local Council of Women who still maintain it to this day and on occasion open it to the public.

SKILLED WORKMEN

The average pay for the riveting squad which worked on the *Titanic* was as follows (averaged out per week based on the number of rivets they applied to the ship, their pay actually being based on the number of rivets applied and not an hourly wage):

Riveter	£2 per week
Holder-on	£1 per week
Runner boy	12–14 shillings (depending on length of time served)
Heater boy	10–14 shillings (depending on length of time served)

─────────── Did You Know That? ───────────

In April 1912, the miners in Great Britain were on strike demanding a pay rise. At the time they were being paid £1 per week.

AS SIMPLE AS 1, 2, 3, 4

The three famous sisters, *Olympic*, *Titanic* and *Britannic* were given the Harland & Wolff Yard Numbers 400, 401 and 433 respectively. When these three Yard Numbers are added together they total 1,234.

A LADDER TO HEAVEN

Most of *Titanic's* 705 survivors climbed aboard the *Carpathia* using the ship's Jacob's Ladders which were lowered down to the lifeboats. However, many of the young children were hoisted aboard in ash bags and some of the women were assisted aboard by other means. In the Bible (Genesis), Jacob's Ladder is a ladder to heaven which Jacob, the third patriarch of the Jewish people, envisioned during his flight from his brother Esau. A Jacob's Ladder consists of vertical ropes or chains supporting horizontal wooden or metal rungs.

EXPANDING THE FLEET

The following table lists the costs of construction of several of the first White Star Line ships ordered by the company from the Harland & Wolff Shipyard in Belfast (excludes *Baltic* and *Cedric*).

Name	Year	Cost
Oceanic	1899	£1,000,000
Celtic	1901	£556,442
Adriatic	1907	£632,464
Megantic	1909	£377,599
Olympic	1911	£1,764,659*
Titanic	1912	£1,564,606

* It is believed that this figure also includes the cost of the *Olympic's* refit in 1913.

The above table is reproduced with the kind permission of Mark Chirnside from his presentation entitled *The 'Olympic' Class Ships: A Business Perspective*. All figures are taken from a valuation list covering the White Star Line's fleet at the end of December 1916, except that:

■ *Oceanic's* cost is taken from a newspaper report;

■ *Titanic's* cost is taken from the research of Mark Warren;

■ *Britannic's* cost is taken from a valuation prepared following her loss and verified by consulting insurance documentation.

FINE DINING

The White Star Line stocked their fleet of vessels with products made by Elkington & Co., manufactures from the late Victorian to the early Edwardian eras, of electro-plated goods such as cutlery, kettles and tableware and many smaller household items including table lamps. With electro-plated ware gracing the tables of such fine examples of shipping as *Oceanic*, *Adriatic* and *Majestic*, Elkington went on to supply to the White Star Line's Olympic Class sisters *Olympic*, *Titanic* and *Britannic*. From the luxury of first class, passengers could be pampered, dine and relax in the knowledge that an established company who supplied all the great restaurants and stately homes in the United Kingdom graced their tables and cabins while at sea. However, the Elkington wares were not only prominent in first class; both second class and third class had the privilege of using Elkington knives, forks, spoons and ashtrays. Founded in 1836, Elkington & Co. of Newhall Street, Birmingham (also with sales offices in London) first started as a company of silver-smiths. They soon devised a system of being able to electro-plate quality items and, between 1838 and 1885, they had successfully patented a new way to electro-plate one metal onto the surface of another. They achieved great success at the Great Exhibition in London in 1851. From their catalogue they sold items including tea services, sugar bowls, claret jugs, kettles, cruet stands, baskets, tureens, tankards, dressing tableware, kitchenware, knives, forks, spoons and many other fine serving and decorative utensils, all being sent to many of the high-end restaurants, homes, hotels and the shipping industry throughout the world.

■ THE MOVIE TRIVIA ■■■■■■■■■■■■■■■

20th Century Fox purchased 40 acres of waterfront south of Playas de Rosarito in Mexico and started building a brand new studio on 31st May 1996. A 17 million gallon tank was built for the exterior of the reconstructed ship, built to full scale, providing 270 degrees of ocean view.

——— Did You Know That? ———

During dives to the debris field that surrounds the wreck of *Titanic*, a number of items of silverware have been recovered, including tableware, light fittings and ashtrays, and all bearing the Elkington initials.
In 1997, James Cameron approached the company while making his movie *Titanic* and using their archived patterns, Elkington once again created the finery that was to grace the tables of Cameron's version.
The company still trade today, but under the auspices of British Silverware Ltd.

BOND TO THE RESCUE

Contrary to popular belief, John Pierpont Morgan did not write personal cheques to finance the construction of the *Olympic* and the *Titanic* and neither did his company (International Mercantile Marine Company). The White Star Line financed the cost of the two sister ships by means of a bond issue in October 1908. Each bond was worth £100 with an issue price of 97 pounds, 10 shillings. A total of £2,500,000 was authorised and the first issue consisted of £1,250,000 in 4½% bonds with each bond to be fully redeemed by 30th June 1922. In July 1914, the White Star Line issued a prospectus for a second bond. Each bond was worth £100 with an issue price of £95. The authorised total of £2,500,000 was increased to £3,375,000 and the second issue consisted of £1,500,000 in 4½% bonds. All of the second issue was to be redeemed in full by 30th June 1943, but due to financial difficulties experienced by the White Star Line during the late 1920s the holders of the second issue bonds were never repaid. A total of £473,700 remained outstanding as at 31st December 1930.

Did You Know That?

The *Germanic* served the White Star Line for more years (76) than any other vessel and set a record for the second-longest in maritime history that a vessel has been engaged in active sea duty (1874 to 1950).

TITANIC'S REPLACEMENT

In their 1913 annual report International Mercantile Marine Company (IMMC) informed the company's shareholders about a new vessel which would replace the *Titanic*: a steamer of approximately 33,600 tons with a top speed of 19 knots for the New York-Liverpool service. The ship was to be named *Germanic* and was to enter service in 1916. *Germanic* would be bigger than the *Adriatic* but smaller than the *Olympic*. Work was suspended on the *Germanic* when the First World War began in 1914 and when the war ended in 1918 *Germanic* was renamed *Homeric* and redesigned as a 40,000 gross tons passenger liner. It was IMMC's intention to build the *Homeric* as a direct replacement for the *Britannic* which was lost during the war. However, on 17th June 1920, Harold A. Sanderson who had replaced J. Bruce Ismay as the President of IMCC, informed Lord Pirrie, Chairman of Harland & Wolff, at a dinner party held aboard the *Olympic* that, owing to an economic downturn, the costs of constructing the *Homeric* could not be justified.

─── Did You Know That? ───

Harland & Wolff Shipyard built a ship named *Germanic* for the Oceanic Steam Navigation Company in 1874. Meanwhile, the *Columbus* built by the F. Schichau Shipyard in Danzig, Germany for the Norddeutscher Lloyd Line was given to the White Star Line as part of the war reparations and was renamed the RMS *Homeric*.

ROCKING THE FOUNDATIONS

Approximately 3,000 people worked at Messrs Noah Hingley & Sons Ltd of Netherton, near Dudley, England in 1910 when Harland & Wolff placed the order for *Titanic's* anchors. The large anchors at the bow were supplied and manufactured at Hingley's yard. Hingley's had a housing estate built for the company's workforce which sat right on the doorstep of the main Hingley works. Hingley's also built a church for the company's employees which was situated adjacent to the main anchor shops. However, the pounding of the 800 ton steam hammers resulted in damage to the church, breaking brickwork, windows and door frames and also caused some damage to nearby homes.

THE LAST FAMILY MEMBER

The last ship built by Harland & Wolff for the White Star Line was the *Georgic* (Yard No. 896). She was launched in Belfast on 12th November 1931 and delivered to the Oceanic Steam Navigation Company on 10th June 1932. She operated the Liverpool to New York route. On 10th May 1934, *Georgic* became part of the fleet of the newly amalgamated Cunard-White Star Line and she joined the *Britannic* (the third ship belonging to the White Star Line bearing this name) on the London, Southampton, New York route. In August 1939, the *Georgic* returned to the Liverpool to New York route and made five round trips before being called upon to transport troops during World War II. The *Georgic* completed her service in 1960 and was scrapped a year later at Inverkeithing, Fife, Scotland.

─── Did You Know That? ───

The *Georgic* replaced the *Olympic* on the Southampton to New York route for a brief time when *Titanic's* big sister was undergoing a major overhaul.

A PROFITABLE COMPANY – 1

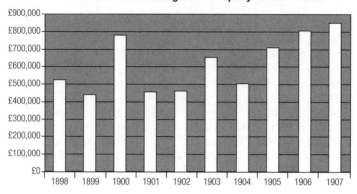

A PROFITABLE COMPANY – 2

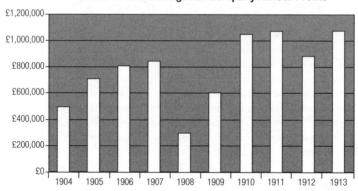

The above tables are reproduced with the kind permission of Mark Chirnside from his presentation entitled *The 'Olympic' Class Ships: A Business Perspective.*

THE RMS TITANIC MISCELLANY

THE END OF THE LINE FOR THE FAMOUS WHITE STAR BURGEE

The last original White Star Line ship in service was the third *Britannic* (Yard No. 807). Like her two relatives before her she was built at the Harland & Wolff Shipyard in Belfast. The third *Britannic* was launched on 6th August 1929 and delivered to the Oceanic Steam Navigation Company on 21st June 1930. She was a motor vessel (M/V) powered by diesel engines and was rated 26,943 gross registered tons and was 712 feet long (217m). She made her maiden voyage from Liverpool-Belfast-Glasgow-New York on 28th June 1930. On 10th May 1934, *Britannic* became part of the fleet of the newly amalgamated Cunard-White Star Line and in 1935 she serviced the London-New York route and remained there until the Second World War began. During the war she served as a troopship before resuming the Liverpool-New York route in 1948. When the Cunard-White Star Line reverted to being the Cunard Line in 1954, the *Britannic* and her younger sister *Georgic* became the last White Star Line vessels in service. She made her final transatlantic voyage on 25th November 1960 marking the last ever transatlantic crossing by a White Star Line ship and then made her way to the shipbreakers the following month.

CRYSTAL CLEAR

With a product commonly known today as 'Stuart Crystal' or 'Waterford Crystal', the company of Stuart & Sons started at the Red House Glass Works in Stourbridge, West Midlands in 1827. In an area nicknamed the Crystal Mile due largely to the amount of crystal ware factories in that region, Stuart & Sons soon gained world renown for their pioneering advances of early Victorian glass colouring and continuous glass melting technology. Employing some of the finest craftsmen in the area, Stuarts specialised in cut glass table wares, including drinking glasses, decanters, bowls and vases, sending out their products not only to homes, but hotels, restaurants, shipping and even royalty. The White Star Line proudly kitted out many of their ships with the finery that was Stuarts, including *Olympic* and *Titanic*.

--- Did You Know That? ---

One other well established crystal ware company within the Crystal Mile is 'Tudor Crystal'. The company, founded in 1788 and still in business today, reproduced some of the White Star Line tableware in 1997 for use in James Cameron's movie *Titanic*.

■ THE MOVIE TRIVIA ■■■■■■■■■■■■■■

The detached stern section of the full-size set was relocated onto a separate tilting platform which then permitted it to be rapidly turned vertical in order to shoot the final phase of *Titanic's* sinking. This sinking scene took 10 takes, with each take requiring 100 stunt actors to fall from or along the set while 1,000 extras were attached to the railings by safety harnesses.

■ THE MOVIE TRIVIA ■■■■■■■■■■■■■■

Titanic is the biggest box-office draw in movie history, grossing more than $1.8 billion worldwide. It overtook *Star Wars* (1977) as the highest grossing movie of all time.

SILENT NIGHT

Hoskins & Sewell of Bordesley, Birmingham, founded in 1845, were one of the United Kingdom's leading bed suppliers to home and trade. The firm specialised in brass beds, mattresses, wooden cabin beds, bedsteads, bed tubes, bed cabinets and bedding. At their main store and showroom in London, Hoskins & Sewell took a huge number of orders for the various items in their catalogue and sent these orders to their Birmingham factory to be filled. In 1911, a Hoskins & Sewell trade advertisement indicated that the White Star Line's new Olympic-Class vessels, the *Olympic* and the *Titanic*, had the ship's first-class rooms fitted out with the company's brass cot berths. The advertisement also stated that each ship's second-class and third-class accommodation areas and the crew's accommodation were also supplied with their bedding products. Hoskins & Sewell remained in business until the mid-1960s when they ceased trading.

Titanic berthed at Southampton on the 8 April 1912
(Jonathan Smith postcard collection)

TITANIC'S CARGO MANIFEST

It is claimed that the contents of *Titanic's* hull, her cargo, was worth in the region of £85,000 when she left Southampton harbour on 10th April 1912.

Shipper	Item(s)
Wakem & McLaughlin	43 cases of wine 25 cases of biscuits
Thorer & Praetorius	1 bale of skins
Carter, W.E.	1 case (a Renault car)
Fuchs & Lang Manufacturing	4 cases of printers blank
Spalding & Brothers	34 cases of athletic goods
Park & Tilford	1 case of toothpaste 5 cases of drug sundries 1 case of brushware
Maltus & Ware	8 cases of orchids
Spencerian Pen Company	4 cases of pens
Sherman Sons & Company	7 cases of cotton
Claflin, H.B. & Company	12 cases of cotton lace
Muser Brothers	3 cases of tissues
Isler & Guve	4 bales of straw
Rydeman & Lassner	1 case of tulle (veil and scarf netting)
Petry, P.H. & Company	1 case of tulle
Metzger, A.S.	2 cases of tulle
Mills & Gibb	20 cases of cottons 1 case of gloves
Field, Marshall & Company	1 case of gloves
NY Motion Pic. Co.	1 case of film
Thorburn, J.M. & Company	3 cases of bulbs

Shipper	Item(s)
Rawstick Trading Company	28 bags of sticks
Dujardin & Ladnick	10 boxes of melons
American Express Company	25 cases of merchandise
Tiffany & Company	1 cask of china
Lustig Bros.	4 cases of straw hats
Kuyper, P.C. & Company	1 case of elastic cords 1 case of leather
Cohen, M. Bros	5 packages of skins
Gross, Engle Co	61 cases of tulle
Gallia Textile Company	1 case of lace goods
Calhoun, Robbins & Company	1 case of cotton laces ½ case of brushware
Victor & Achiles	1 case of brushware
Baumgarten, Wm & Co	3 cases of furniture
Spielman Company	3 cases of silk crepe
Nottingham Lace Works	2 cases of cotton
Naday & Fleisher	1 case of laces
Rosenthal, Leo J. & Company	4 cases of cotton
Leeming, T. & Company	7 cases of biscuits
Crown Perfume Company	3 cases of soap perfume
Meadows, T. & Company	5 cases of books 3 boxes of samples 1 cases of parchment
Thomas & Pierson	2 cases of hardware 2 cases of books 2 cases of furniture

Shipper	Item(s)
American Express Company	1 case of elastics 1 case of Edison gramophones 4 cases of hosiery 5 cases of books 1 case of canvas 1 case of rubber goods 3 cases of prints 6 cases of film 1 case of tweed 1 case of fittings 1 oak beam 1 case of plants 1 case of speedometers 1 package (effects) 2 cases of samples 8 cases of paste 3 cases of cameras and stands 4 cases of books
Sheldon, G.W. & Company	1 case of machinery
Maltus & Ware	15 cases of alarm apparatus 11 cases of orchids
Hempstead & Sons	30 cases of plants
Brasch & Rothenstein	2 cases of lace collars 2 cases of books
Isler & Guve	53 packages of straw
Baring Bros. & Company	63 cases of rubber 100 bagged gutta (percha)
Altman, B. & Company	1 case of cotton
Stern, S.	60 cases of salt powders
Arnold, F.R. & Company	6 cases of soap
Shieffelin & Company	17 packages of wool fat
American Motor Company	1 package of candles
Strohmeyer & Arpe	75 bales of fish
National City Bank of New York	11 bales of rubber
Kronfeld, Saunders & Company	5 cases of shells

Shipper	Item(s)
Richard, C.B.	1 case of films
Corbett, M.J. & Company	2 cases of hat leather
Snow's Express Company	3 cases of books
Van Engen E.H. & Company	1 case of various woollen garments
Lippincott, J.B. & Company	10 cases of books
Lazard Freres	1 bale of skins
Aero Club of America	1 case of machinery 1 case of printed material
Witcombe, McGrachlin & Company	856 rolls of linoleum
Wright & Grahm Company	437 casks of tea
Gillman J.	4 bales of skins
Arnold & Zeiss	134 cases of rubber
Brown Brothers & Company	76 cases of dragon's blood 3 cases of gum
American Shipping Company	5 cases of books
Adams Express	35 cases of books
Lasker & Bernstein	117 cases of sponges
Oelrichs & Company	2 cases of pictures
Stechert, G.E. & Company	12 packages of periodicals
Milbank, Leaman & Company	2 cases of woollen garments
Vandegrift, F.B. & Company	63 cases of champagne
Downing, R.F. & Company	1 case of felt 1 case of metal 2 cases of tennis balls 1 case of engine packing
Dublin, Morris & Kornbluth	2 packages of skins
International Trading Company	1 case of surgical instruments 1 case of ironware

Shipper	Item(s)
Pitt & Scott	4 cases of printed material 1 case of machinery 1 case of pictures 1 case of books 1 case of merchandise 1 case of lotions 1 case of photos
Sheldon, G.W. & Company	1 case of elastics 2 cases of books 1 box of golf balls 5 cases of instruments
American Express Company	2 parcels - merchandise
Vandegrift, F.B.	1 case of merchandise
Budd, S.	1 parcel - merchandise
Lemke & Buechner	1 parcel - merchandise
Nicholas, G.S. & Company	1 case of merchandise
Adams Express Company	4 rolls of linoleum 3 bales of leather 1 case of hats 6 cases of confectionery 5 cases of books 1 case of tin tubes 2 cases of soap 2 cases of boots
Wells Fargo & Company	3 cases of books 2 cases of furniture 1 case of pamphlets 1 case of plants 1 case of eggs 1 case of whiskey
International News Company	10 packages of periodicals
Van Ingen, E.H. & Company	1 parcel
Sterns, R.H. & Company	1 case of cretonne (silk)
Downing, R.F. & Company	1 case of iron jacks 1 case of bulbs 1 case of hosiery

Shipper	Item(s)
Carbon Machinery Equip. Company	1 case of clothing
Sanger, R. & Company	3 cases of hair nets
Flietman & Company	1 case of various silk goods
Rush & Company	1 case of hair nets
Blum, J.A.	3 cases of various silk goods
Tiedeman, T. & Sons	2 cases of various silk goods
Costa, F.	1 case of various silk goods
Tolson, A.M. & Company	1 case of gloves
Mathews, G.T. & Company	2 cases of books and lace
Tice & Lynch	5 cases of books 1 bag of frames 1 case of cotton 2 cases of stationery
US Export Company	1 case of scientific instruments 2 cases of sundries 3 cases of test cords 1 case of briar pipes 2 cases of printed material
Pape, Chas. & Company	1,196 bags of potatoes
Sauer, J.P. & Company	318 bags of potatoes
Rusch & Company	1 case of velvets
Mallouk, H.	1 case of laces
Bardwill Bros	8 cases of laces
Heyliger, A.V.	1 case of velvet
Peabody, H.W. & Company	13 bales of straw goods
Simon, A.I. & Company	1 case of raw feathers
Wilson, P.K. & Sons	2 cases of linens
Manhattan Shirt Company	3 cases of tissues
Broadway Trust Company	3 cases of coney (rabbit) skins
Prost. G.	1 case of car parts
Young Bros.	1 case of feathers
Wimpfheimer, A. & Company	3 cases of leather

Shipper	Item(s)
Brown Bros. & Company	15 cases of rabbit hair
Goldster, Morris	11 cases of feathers
Cobb. G.H.	1 case of lace tissue
Anderson Refridg, Mach. Company	11 cases of refrigeration equipment
Suter, Alfred	18 cases of machinery
American Express Company	1 case of packed packages 3 cases of tissues 2 barrels of mercury 1 barrel of earth 2 barrels of glassware 3 cases of printed material 1 case of straw braids 3 cases of straw hats 1 case of cheese
Meadows, Thomas & Company	3 cases of hosiery
Uchs & Hegnoer	3 cases of silk goods
Cauvigny Brush Company	1 case of brushware
Johnson, J.G. Company	2 cases of ribbons
Judkins & McCormick	2 cases of flowers
Spielman Company	1 case of gloves
American Express Company	18 cases - merchandise
Wakem & McLaughlin	6 bales of cork
Acker, Merrall & Condit	75 cases of anchovies 225 cases of mussels 1 case of liquor
Engs. P.W. & Sons	190 cases of liquor 25 cases of syrups
Schall & Company	25 cases of preserves
NY & Cuba SS Company	12 cases of butter 18 cases of oil 2 hogsheads of vinegar 19 cases of vinegar 6 cases of preserves 8 cases of dried fruit 2 cases of wine

Shipper	Item(s)
Du Bois, Geo. C.	16 hogshead wine
Hollander, H.	185 cases of wine 110 cases of brandy
Van Renssaller, C.A.	10 hogshead wine 15 cases of cognac
Brown Brothers & Company	100 cases of shelled walnuts
Bernard, Judas & Company	70 bundles of cheese
American Express Company	30 bundles of cheese 2 cases of cognac
Moquin Wine Company	1 cases of liquor 38 cases of oil
Knauth, Nachod & Kuhne	107 cases of mushrooms 1 case of pamphlets
Lazard Freres	25 cases of sardines 3 cases of preserves
Acker, Merrall & Condit	50 cases of wine
Dubois, Geo. F.	6 cases of vermouth 4 cases of wine
Heidelbach, Ickelheimer & Company	11 cases of shelled walnuts
First National Bank of Chicago	300 cases of shelled walnuts
Blechoff, H. & Company	35 bags of rough wood
Baumert, F.X. & Company	50 bundles of cheese
Rathenberger & Company	190 bundles of cheese
Haupt & Burgi	50 bundles of cheese
Sheldon & Company	40 bundles of cheese
Percival, C.	50 bundles of cheese
Stone, C.D. & Company	50 bundles of cheese
Phoenix Cheese Company	30 bundles of cheese
Petry, P.H. & Company	10 bundles of cheese
Reynolds & Dronig	15 bundles of cheese
Fouger, E.	41 cases of filter paper

Shipper	Item(s)
Munro, J. & Company	22 cases of mushrooms
	15 cases of peas
	3 cases of beans
	10 cases of mixed vegetables
	10 cases of peas
	25 cases of olives
	12 bundles of capers
	10 bundles of fish
	20 bundles - merchandise
Austin, Nichols	25 cases of olive oil
	14 cases of mushrooms
On Order	14 cases of factice
	13 cases of gum
	14 casks of gum
	285 casks of tea
	8 bales skins
	4 cases of opium
	3 cases of window frames
	8 bales of skins
	8 packages of skins
	1 case of skins
	2 cases of horse hair
	2 cases of silk
	8 bales of raw silk
	4 packages of hair nets
	200 packages of tea
	246 cases of sardines
	30 rolls of jute bagging
	1.963 bags of potatoes
	7 cases of raw feathers
	10 cases of hatters' fur
	3 cases of tissues
	1 case of rabbit hair
	31 packages of crude rubber
	7 cases of vegetables
	5 cases of fish
	10 cases of syrups
	2 cases of liquors
	150 cases of shelled walnuts
	15 bundles of cheese
	8 bales of buchu

Shipper	Item(s)
On Order (continued)	2 cases of grandfather clocks
	2 cases of leather
Holders of original bills of lading	79 goat's skins
	16 cases of calabashes
	5 bales of buchu
	4 cases of embroidery
	3 barrels of wine
	12 cases of ostrich feathers
	4 cases of feathers
	3 bales of skins
	33 bags of argols
	3 bales of sheep skins

One of the last photographs taken of the *Titanic* as she steams away from Ireland
after departing Queenstown at 1.40pm on 11 April 1912.
(Jonathan Smith collection)

A BANQUET FIT FOR A KING

First-class passengers aboard the *Titanic* dined on the finest of foods available, whilst many third-class passengers had the best, and for a great many of them the last, meal of their life.

First Class *April 14th 1912*

BREAKFAST

Baked apples – Fruit – Steamed Prunes

Quaker Oats – Broiled Hominy – Puffed Rice

Fresh Herring

Findon Haddock – Smoked Salmon

Grilled Mutton – Kidneys & Bacon

Grilled Ham – Grilled Sausage

Lamb Callops – Vegetable Stew

Fried, Shirred, Poached & Boiled Eggs

Plain & Tomato Omelettes to Order

Sirloin Steak & Mutton Chops to Order

Mashed, Saute & Jacket Potatoes

Cold Meat

Vienna & Graham Rolls

Soda & Sultana Scones – Corn Bread

Buckwheat Cakes

Blackcurrant Preserve – Narbonne Honey

Oxford Marmalade

Watercress

LUNCHEON

Consomme Fermier – Cockie Leekie

Fillets of Brill

Eggs A l'Araeneuil

Chicken a la Maryland

Corned Beef, Vegetables, Dumplings

FROM THE GRILL
Grilled Mutton Chops

Mashed, Fried and Baked Jacket Potatoes

Custard Pudding

Apple Meringue – Pastry

BUFFET
Salmon Mayonnaise – Potted Shrimps

Norwegian Anchovies – Souse Herrings

Plain & Smoked Sardines

Roast Beef

Round of Spiced Beef

Veal & ham Pie

Virginia & Cumberland Ham

Bologna Sausage – Brawn

Galantine of Chicken

Corned Ox Tongue

Lettuce – Beetroot – Tomatoes

CHEESE
Cheshire, Stilton, Gorgonzola, Edam, Camembert,

Roquefort, St. Ivel, Cheddar

Ice draught Munich Lager Beer: 3d (7c) & 6d (13c) a Tankard

Second Class
April 14th 1912

LUNCHEON

Consomme a la Julienne

Tripe with Calves' Feet

Roast Ribs Beef

Baked, Jacket & Mashed Potatoes

Cold

Roast Beef

Roast Pork

Ormskirk Brawn

Corned Beef

Salad

Ground Rice Pudding

Small Pastry

Biscuits, Cheese

Dessert, Coffee

Third Class
April 10th 1912

BREAKFAST

Quaker Oats and Milk

Smoked Herrings

Beefsteak and Onions

Jacket Potatoes

Fresh Bread & Butter

Marmalade, Swedish Bread

Tea, Coffee

NB: Menus reproduced with the kind permission of Becky Grice, Editor of the *East Cork Journal.*

——————— Did You Know That? ———————

In *Titanic's* refrigerated stores area were two rooms for chilled beef; one
named *Eastbound Beef* and the other *Westbound Beef.* The latter was
much larger than the former as not many immigrants would be carried
on the return trip.

HALIFAX, NOVA SCOTIA
THE *TITANIC* GRAVES

The listing below, constructed electronically from the *Disposition of Bodies ex Titanic* list, shows the 306 bodies recovered by the Canadian Steamship *Mackay-Bennett* and what became of them. The original printed list is titled *Record of Bodies and Effects (Passengers and Crew S.S. 'Titanic') Recovered by Cable Streamer 'Mackay-Bennett' including bodies delivered at morgue in Halifax* with two additional typed pages listing bodies recovered by the vessels CS *Minia*, CGS *Montmagny* and SS *Algerine* (nos. 307–330); it is held by Nova Scotia Archives and Records Management (Halifax, NS).

The Canadian Steamship *Mackay-Bennett*

Name	No. on List	How Disposed of	Remarks
Van Billiard, W.	1	Forwarded, May 4th, to North Wales Depot, Pa.	Later identified from effects. Instructions N.Y. Office, wire, May 2nd. Listed as Walter Van Billiard, third class. Embarked Southampton.
Marriott, W.	2	Buried at Fairview Cemetery, Halifax, N.S.	On crew list as J.W. Marriott-Vict. Dept.
Unidentified, Female	3	Buried at Fairview Cemetery, Halifax, N.S.	Wore chemise marked 'J.H.' in red. Other clothing: Gray cloth jacket, red jersey jacket, blue alpaca blouse, blue serge skirt, woolen combinations, black stockings, black boots, gray cholera belt.
Paulsson, Baby	4	Buried at Fairview Cemetery, Halifax, N.S.	Buried by crew of C.S. 'Mackay-Bennett', by special request.
Unidentified, Female	5	Buried at Mount Olivet Cemetery, Halifax, N.S.	Effects include: Crucifix, snuff box and medallion, two silver rings and one turquoise ring.

Name	No. on List	How Disposed of	Remarks
Unidentified, Male	6	Buried at sea.	Blue tattoo mark, and wore copper wire ring on thumb of right hand. Nothing else to identify.
Robins, Mrs. A.	7	Forwarded, May 4th, to Yonkers, N.Y.	Request of Mrs. Curtin (daughter), 24 Garfield Street, Yonkers, N.Y. Third class. Embarked Southampton.
Unidentified, Female	8	Buried at Fairview Cemetery, Halifax, N.S.	Wore chemise marked 'B.H.' in red on front. Wore boots, size No 8. Sum of 150 Finnish marks sewed in clothing.
Schedid, Nihl	9	Forwarded, May 4th, to Mrs. Schedid, Mt. Carmel, Pa.	Instructions, N.Y. Office, wire, May 2nd. Listed as Daher Shedid, third class. Embarked Cherbourg.
Butt, R.	10	Buried at Fairview Cemetery, Halifax, N.S.	On crew list-Vict. Dept.
Shea, Mr.	11	Buried at Fairview Cemetery, Halifax, N.S.	On crew list as J. Shea-Vict. Dept.
Unidentified, Female	12	Buried at Mount Olivet Cemetery, Halifax, N.S.	Shoes marked 'Parsons Sons, Athlone'; medallion round neck marked 'B.V.M.'; wore wedding ring, keeper and another gold ring; locket and photo; one jet and one bead necklace.
Unidentified, Female	13	Buried at Mount Olivet Cemetery, Halifax, N.S.	Probably an Italian; wore two green cotton blouses, green cotton skirt, striped petticoat; nothing else to identify.
Williams, Leslie	14	Buried at sea.	Listed as third class. Embarked Southampton.
Hoffman, Louis M.	15	Buried at Hebrew Cemetery, Halifax, N.S.	Listed as Mr. Hoffman, second class.

Name	No. on List	How Disposed of	Remarks
Rosenshine, George	16	Delivered to A.A. Rosenshine, for forwarding to New York.	First Class.
Chapman, John H.	17	Buried at Fairview Cemetery, Halifax, N.S.	Listed as second class passenger.
Carbines, W.M.	18	Forwarded, May 10th, to St. Ives, England, via New York, at request of brothers.	Claimed by brothers from Calumet, Michigan. Second class.
Greenberg, S.	19	Forwarded, May 3rd, to Mrs. Greenberg, Bronx, New York City.	Instructions, N.Y. Office, wire, May 2nd. Second class.
Unidentified, Male	20	Buried at sea.	Wore badge of Sailors' and Firemen's Union; blue coat and blue White Star jersey. No aids to identification. Probably sailor.
Unidentified, Male	21	Buried at sea.	Had paper reading 'Dec. to Jan. 1911; First Saloon waiter S.S. Majestic', also keys marked 'locker 7 E. Deck.' Wore steward's jacket, vest and trousers; laundry mark 'E'.
Artagaveytia, Ramon	22	Claimed by Alfred Metz Green, Uruguayan Consul, to be forwarded to South America, via New York.	Instructions, N.Y. Office, letter, April 23rd. First-class passenger.
Barkworth, A.H.	23	Buried at sea.	Probably L. Turner, steward, from effects. (A.H. Barkworth listed as first-class passenger rescued.)
Turner, L.	23		(See also A.H. Barkworth) If L. Turner, on crew list-Vict. Dept.
Unidentified, Male	24	Buried at sea.	Blue jersey; blue and red flannel shirt; green trousers; black boots. Probably a sailor.

Name	No. on List	How Disposed of	Remarks
Hayter, A.	25	Buried at sea.	Identified from effects. On crew list-Vict. Dept.
Unidentified, Male	26	Buried at sea.	Addresses found on body: 'Mr. Freyer Lawrence Villa, Stephenson Road, Cowes'; also 'G. R. Barnes, 22 Sidney St., Cambridge'. Wore blue serge jacket and steward's white coat. Probably an Italian cook.
Monros, Jean	27	Buried at sea.	On crew list as J. Monoros-Vict. Dept.
Unidentified, Male	28	Buried at sea.	No effects but address of Shakin Bros., 155 Broad St., Ottawa, on body.
Unidentified, Male	29	Buried at Fairview Cemetery, Halifax, N.S.	Nothing to aid in identification.
Unidentified, Male	30	Buried at sea.	Wore badge of Sailors' and Firemen's Union. Nothing to aid in identification. Possibly a fireman.
Evans, Mr.	31	Buried at sea.	Identified from effects. On crew list as W. Evans-Engine Dept.
Sather, Simon	32	Buried at Fairview Cemetery, Halifax, N.S.	Listed as third class. Embarked Southampton.
Unidentified, Male	33	Buried at sea.	Nothing to aid in identification. Clothes indicated oiler.
Ashe, H.W.	34	Buried at Fairview Cemetery, Halifax, N.S.	On crew list as H. Ashe-Vict. Dept.
Harbeck, W.H.	35	Forwarded, May 4th, to Mrs. Harbeck, 733 Michigan Street, Toledo, O.	Instructions, N. Y. Office, wire, May 2nd. Second class.
Unidentified, Male	36	Buried at sea.	Steward's uniform. Left arm tattooed all over; right arm, clasped hands and heart, breast, Japanese fans. Gold ring engraved 'Madge'.

Name	No. on List	How Disposed of	Remarks
Johnson, Malkolm Joakim	37	Buried at Fairview Cemetery, Halifax, N.S.	Listed as Malkolm Johnsson, third class. Emb. Southampton.
Holverson, A.O.	38	Delivered to H. T. Holverson, of Alexandria, Minn., and forwarded May 1st to New York.	First class.
Unidentified, Male	39	Buried at sea.	Wore evening dress; trousers; black double-breasted overcoat; brown jacket and vest. Silver watch and a sovereign case. Nothing else to aid indentification.
Unidentified, Male	40	Buried at sea.	Nothing to aid in identification. Probably sailor.
Stone, E.J.	41	Buried at sea.	On crew list as E. Stone-Vict. Dept.
Unidentified, Male	42	Buried at sea.	Lining torn from clothing, marked 'Kinos Successors, 322–323 High Holborn, W.C. City Branch, 14 Cheapside, No. 4058. A 217/5/10. Name, Mr. Mayer.'
Nasser, Naser, Nasrallah, Nicholas, Nicola, Niqula	43	Forwarded, May 3rd, to J. J. Cronin, undertaker Brooklyn	Instructions, N.Y. Office, wire, April 29th. Second class.
Unidentified, Male	44	Buried at sea.	Steward's coat and trousers; white shirt marked 'F.W.I.', keys marked 'C Deck'; linen locker.
Keeping, Edwin	45	Buried at sea.	Valet of Mr. G. D. Wildener.
Sutton, Fred	46	Buried at sea.	Listed as first-class passenger.
Gilinski, Leslie	47	Buried at sea.	Listed as third class. Embarked Southampton.
Unidentified, Male	48	Buried at sea.	Steward's coat, vest and trousers; flannel shirt. Nothing to aid identification.

Name	No. on List	How Disposed of	Remarks
Gill, J.S.	49	Buried at sea.	On crew list as S. Gill-Vict. Dept.
Tomlin, Ernest Portage	50	Buried at sea.	Listed as Ernest Tomlin, third class. Embarked Southampton.
Drazenire, Yosip	51	Buried at sea.	Listed as Josef Drazenovic, third class. Embarked Cherbourg.
Mack, Mrs.	52	Buried at sea.	Listed as second-class passenger.
McNamee, Mrs. N.	53	Buried at sea.	Third class. Embarked Southampton.
Unidentified, Female	54	Buried at sea.	Wore wedding ring and keeper. Had one gold upper tooth.
Unidentified, Female	55	Buried at sea.	Had among effects, gold watch marked on back 'C.K.S.', pinned on left breast. Opal and pearl rings, also garnet ring, engraved 'H.N. to D.S.' Wedding ring engraved 'A.L. to C.S., April 21st, '09.' (All rings left on fingers.)
Unidentified, Male	56	Buried at sea.	Wore half hunter gold watch No. 5,119 English make, and gold chain. False teeth, upper jaw.
Unidentified, Male	57	Buried at sea.	Wore vest marked 'H.L.' Letter in pocket to 'Dear Humph', from 'Dick', possibly a steward.
Vassilios, Catavelas	58	Buried at sea.	Listed as third class. Embarked Cherbourg.
Veal, W.	59	Buried at sea.	On list as W. Vear-Engine Dept.
Unidentified, Male	60	Buried at sea.	Wore company's uniform; probably steward for rooms 82, etc.; no other marks to aid to identification.
Mangan, Mary	61	Buried at sea.	Third class. Embarked Queenstown.
Douglas, Walter D.	62	Forwarded, May 1st to G.C. Douglas (Son), Minneapolis, Minnesota.	Listed as first class.

Name	No. on List	How Disposed of	Remarks
Unidentified, Female	63	Buried at sea.	Had purse with miniature photo of young man and a photo locket. No other aid to identification.
Rice, J.R.	64	Buried at Fairview Cemetery, Halifax, N.S.	On crew list-Vict. Dept.
Unidentified, Male	65	Buried at sea.	Tattoo on right forearm; three dots.
Hinckley, G.	66	Buried at sea.	On crew list-Vict. Dept.
Sage, Will	67	Buried at sea.	Listed as third class. Embarked Southampton.
Farrell, James	68	Buried at sea.	Listed as third class. Embarked Queenstown.
Damgaard, Henry	69	Buried at sea.	Probably Henry Hansen, 3rd class. Embarked Southampton.
Kelly, James	70	Buried at sea.	Third class. Embarked Queenstown.
Unidentified, Male	71	Buried at sea.	Coat marked 'Hospital Attendant'; trousers marked 'M.O.' key ring with address Mrs. Van Push, 732 E. 15th St., New York City.
Adahl, Mauritz	72	Buried at sea.	Listed as third-class passenger. Embarked Southampton.
Unidentified, Male	73	Buried at sea.	Handkerchief marked 'H.J.'; silver watch; engineer's uniform. Nothing else to aid in identification.
Unidentified, Male	74	Buried at sea.	Nothing to aid in identification.
Hale, Reg.	75	Buried at sea.	Listed as second class passenger.
Unidentified, Female	76	Buried at sea.	Possibly Italian; name 'Ethel' inside of watch; garnet ring on watch chain, originally two stones, one missing.
Butt, W.	77	Buried at sea.	On crew list-Engine Dept.

Name	No. on List	How Disposed of	Remarks
Unidentified, Male	78	Buried at Hebrew Cemetery, Halifax, N.S.	Tattoo marks on left arm, 'E.G., anchor, clasped hands and heart and sailor'; on right arm, 'anchor and woman'.
Ale or Ala, Wm	79	Buried at Mount Olivet Cemetery, Halifax, N.S.	Listed as Wm Ali, third class. Embarked Southampton.
Jones, C.C.	80	Delivered to Dr. James H. Donnelly, May 1st, for forwarding to Bennington, Vt.	First class.
Stokes, Philip Joseph	81	Buried at sea.	Listed as second-class passenger.
Petty, J. Edwin Henry	82	Buried at sea.	On crew list as E. Petty-Vict. Dept.
Dashwood, Will G.	83	Buried at Fairview Cemetery, Halifax, N.S.	On crew list as W. Dashwood-Vict. Dept.
Unidentified, Male	84	Buried at sea.	Wore dungaree coat and trousers, and gray flannel shirt. Nothing to aid identification.
Hinton, W.	85	Buried at sea.	On crew list-Engine Dept.
Unidentified, Male	86	Buried at sea.	Had keys marked 'Engineers' Storekeeper'. Nothing else to identify.
Unidentified, Male	87	Buried at sea.	Wore badge, 'Riverside and Dock Workers' Union'. No other aid to identification, possibly a fireman.
Unidentified, Male	88	Buried at sea.	No aids to identification; probably a fireman.
Anderson, Thos	89	Buried at sea.	Listed as Thor. Anderson, third class. Emb. Southampton.
Laurance, A.	90	Forwarded, May 4th, to Liverpool via Boston, per S.S Arabic, May 7th.	Instructions, N.Y. Office, wire, May 4th. On crew list, A. Lawrence-Vict. Dept.
Smillie, J.	91	Buried at sea.	Identified from effects. On crew list-Vict. Dept.

Name	No. on List	How Disposed of	Remarks
Unidentified, Male	92	Buried at Fairview Cemetery, Halifax, N.S.	No aids to identification; probably a fireman.
Roberts, H.H.	93	Buried at sea.	Identified from effects. On crew list as H. Roberts-Vict. Dept.
Unidentified, Male	94	Buried at Fairview Cemetery, Halifax, N.S.	No aids to identification; probably a fireman.
Unidentified, Male	95	Buried at sea.	Tattooed right arm: woman, butterfly and anchor; left arm: butterfly, knight's head, and lady. Probably a fireman.
Straus, Isador	96	Delivered to Mr. M. Rothschild and forwarded May 1st, to New York.	Instructions of Mr. P. S. Straus, N.Y. First class.
Butler, Reginald	97	Buried at Fairview Cemetery, Halifax, N.S.	Listed as second-class passenger.
Gustafsson, Anders Wilhelm	98	Buried at sea.	Listed as Anders Gustafson, third class.
Unidentified, Male	99	Buried at sea.	Tattooed right arm: clasped hands and heart, American flag and lady; left arm: 'Dieu et mon droit'. No other aid to identification. Probably a fireman.
Ricks, Cyril G.	100	Buried at sea.	On crew list as C. Ricks-Vict. Dept.
Nicholls, J.C.	101	Buried at sea.	Listed as second-class passenger. Later identified from effects by Carbines Brothers of Calumet, Michigan.
Unidentified, Male	102	Buried at sea.	Wore uniform, vest and white jacket. No other aid to identification.
Adams, John	103	Buried at sea.	Listed as J. Adams third class. Embarked Southampton.
Ale, Pedro	104	Buried at sea.	

Name	No. on List	How Disposed of	Remarks
Unidentified, Male	104	Buried at sea.	Wore gray suit, also plain ring, left on finger. Effects include gold engraved ring and memo book. No further aids to identification.
Unidentified, Male	105	Buried at sea.	Wore blue serge suit and striped shirt marked 'B.D.' No other aids to identification.
Unidentified, Male	106	Buried at sea.	Tattooed: right arm, 'Aggie'; left arm, crossed hands and heart. No other aids to identification. Possibly a sailor.
Boothby, W.	107	Buried at sea.	On crew list-Vict. Dept.
Leyson, Robert W. Norman	108	Buried at sea.	Listed as second-class passenger.
Rowe, Alfred	109	Forwarded, May 4th, from Halifax via 'Empress of Britain' to Liverpool	Instructions, N.Y. Office, wire, May 3rd. First class.
Harrison, W.H.	110	Buried at Fairview Cemetery, Halifax, N.S.	First class.
Chisnell, G.	111	Buried at sea.	Identified from effects. On crew list-Engine Dept.
Unidentified, Male	112	Buried at sea.	Steward's uniform and ship's badge No. 42. No other aids to identification.
Unidentified, Male	113	Buried at sea.	Tattooed: right arm, angel of love with thistle below; left arm, girl's head in centre of anchor, a ship, and flower with 'Flo', in centre. No other aids to identification. Probably a fireman.
Unidentified, Male	114	Buried at sea.	No aid to identification. Possibly a fireman.
Rigozri, Abele	115	Buried at sea.	On crew list as A. Rigozzi-Vict. Dept.
Butterworth, J.	116	Buried at sea.	On crew list-Vict. Dept.

Name	No. on List	How Disposed of	Remarks
Unidentified, Male	117	Buried at sea.	Effects included silver watch and chain, and purse of French gold. No marks to aid in identification.
Unidentified, Male	118	Buried at sea.	No aids to identification. Possibly an oiler.
Robins, A.	119	Forwarded, May 4th, to Yonkers, N.Y.	
Humblen, Adolph	120	Buried at sea.	Listed as Adolf Hundbleu, third class. Emb. Southampton.
Louch, Chas	121	Buried at sea.	Listed as second-class passenger.
Newell, A.W.	122	Forwarded to Boston, May 1st, according to wire from Mrs. Mary A. Newell.	Listed as first-class passenger.
Tamlyn, Fred	123	Buried at sea.	On crew list a F. Tamlyn-Deck Dept.
Astor, J.J.	124	Delivered to Mr. N. Biddle, and forwarded to New York, May 1st.	First Class.
Unidentified, Male	125	Buried at sea.	Steward's uniform, washing mark 'G.V.N.' Wore company's badge, No. 37.
Long, Milton C.	126	Forwarded to Springfield, Mass., April 30th, care of J.H. Shepherd.	Letters from C. L. Long April 23rd and 24th. Father's instructions. First class.
Roberton, G.	127	Buried at sea.	Identified from effects. On crew list as G. Robertson-Vict. Dept.
Unidentified, Male	128	Buried at Fairview Cemetery, Halifax, N.S.	Ship's uniform. Carried open-face watch, made by Thomas Howard, 157 Kirkdale Road and 200 Rice Lane, Liverpool; stamped 'German make'. Had postcard with picture of 4 little girls on reverse side. Also 1×2 instantaneous snapshot of boy or young man.

Name	No. on List	How Disposed of	Remarks
Unidentified, Male	129	Buried at Fairview Cemetery, Halifax, N.S.	Tattooed right arm: girl's bust; 'Cissie' below. No other aids to identification.
Chapman, Chas H.	130	Forwarded, May 2nd, care of J. J. Griffin, 2282 7th Avenue, New York.	Instructions, N.Y. Office, wire, May 1st. Second class.
Wirz, Albert	131	Forwarded, May 8th, to Mrs. T. M. Brown, Beloit, Wisconsin.	Instructions, N.Y. Office, wire, May 7th. Third class. Embarked Southampton.
Unidentified, Female	132	Buried at sea.	No other aids to identification. Probably third-class passenger list.
Dulles, W.C.	133	Forwarded to R.R. Bringhurst, Phila., Pa., May 1st.	Instructions, N.Y. Office, wire, April 29th. First class.
Unidentified, Male	134	Buried at Fairview Cemetery, Halifax, N.S.	Jacket marked 'A.' No other aids to identification. Possibly a steward.
Allison, HJ	135	Forwarded to Montreal, May 1st, care of G. E. Clark.	Listed as a first-class passenger.
Unidentified, Male	136	Buried at Hebrew Cemetery, Halifax, N.S.	No aids to identification. Possibly a fireman.
Unidentified, Male	137	Buried at Fairview Cemetery, Halifax, N.S.	Tattooed: right arm, British and American flags. No other aids to identification. Possibly a fireman.
Fellows, Alf	138	Buried at Fairview Cemetery, Halifax, N.S.	On crew list as A. Fellows-Vict. Dept.
Unidentified, Male	139	Buried at Fairview Cemetery, Halifax, N.S.	Wore boiler suit and jacket. No other aids to identification. Possibly an engineer.
Wailens, Achille	140	Buried at Fairview Cemetery, Halifax, N.S.	Probably second class.

Name	No. on List	How Disposed of	Remarks
Unidentified, Male	141	Buried at Fairview Cemetery, Halifax, N.S.	Wore white coat marked 'A. May'. Carried keys marked 'Butcher.': Effects include picture post card, addressed Mrs. Kempsey, 83 Antrim Place, Antrim Road, Belfast.
Asplund, Carl	142	Forwarded to Mrs. Selma Asplund at Worcester, Mass., May 3rd.	Instructions, N.Y. Office, letter, April 30th. Listed as third class. Embarked Southampton.
Johanssen, Jacob Alfred	143	Buried at Fairview Cemetery, Halifax, N.S.	Listed as Jakob Johnson, third class. Embarked Southampton.
Wormald, F.	144	Buried at Hebrew Cemetery, Halifax, N.S.	Identified from effects. On crew list as T. Wormald-Vict. Dept.
Allen, Henry	145	Buried at Fairview Cemetery, Halifax, N.S.	On crew list as H. Allen-Engine Dept.
Anderson, W.Y.	146	Buried at sea.	On crew list as W. Anderson-Vict. Dept.
Graham, Geo. E.	147	Forwarded, April 30th to Toronto, care of T. Eaton & Co.; Matthews, undertaker, escort	Listed as Mr. Graham, first class.
Birnbaum, Jacob	148	Forwarded May 3rd, to Joachim Birnbaum, Red Star Line Pier 60, New York City.	Instructions, N.Y. Office, wire, May 2nd. First class.
Hodges, Henry P.	149	Buried at Fairview Cemetery, Halifax, N.S.	Listed as second-class passenger.
Talbot, George	150	Buried at Fairview Cemetery, Halifax, N.S.	On crew list as G.F.C. Talbot-Vict. Dept.
Robinson, J.M.	151	Buried at sea.	On crew list as J. Robinson-Vict. Dept.
Hell, J.C.	152	Buried at sea.	Probably J. Hill on crew list-Vict. Dept.

Name	No. on List	How Disposed of	Remarks
Lockyer, Edward	153	Buried at sea.	Third class. Embarked Southampton.
Unidentified, Male	154	Buried at sea.	Wore blue jacket, gray vest and black trousers. No other aids to identifcation.
Gill, John W.	155	Buried at sea.	Listed as John Gill, second-class passenger.
Johansson, Eric	156	Buried at sea.	Listed as third-class passenger. Embarked Southampton.
Unidentified, Male	157	Buried at sea.	Wore ship's uniform. Key, tagged linen locker No. I C Deck. Address found in effects: Miss McElroy, Layton, Spottisbury, Dorset.
Watson, W.	158	Buried at sea.	On crew list-Engine Dept.
Barker, E.T.	159	Buried at sea.	On crew list as E. Barker-Vict. Dept.
Unidentified, Male	160	Buried at sea.	Wore bracelet. No other aids to identification. Possibly a sailor.
Bailley, G.F.	161	Buried at Fairview Cemetery, Halifax, N.S.	On crew list as G. Bailey-Vict Dept.
Unidentified, Male	162	Buried at sea.	No aids to identification. Possibly a fireman.
Woodford, F.	163	Buried at Fairview Cemetery, Halifax, N.S.	On crew list as H. Woodford-Engine Dept.
Unidentified, Male	164	Buried at sea.	No aids to identification. Possibly a fireman.
Kvillner, Henrik	165	Buried at Fairview Cemetery, Halifax, N.S.	Listed as second-class passenger. (John Henrik Kvillner)
Partner, Austin	166	Forwarded to New York, May 7th, for shipment per S. S Minnehaha, sailing May 11th.	Instructions, N.Y. Office, wire, May 1st. First class.

Name	No. on List	How Disposed of	Remarks
Woody, O.S.	167	Buried at sea.	Not on crew list-Probably mail clerk.
Hewett, T.	168	Buried at sea.	On crew list-Vict. Dept.
White, R. Fraser	169	Delivered to F. A. Smith, and forwarded, April 30th, to Boston, Mass.	Listed as Richard F. White, first class. Instructions from mother.
Unidentified, Male	170	Buried at sea.	Carried key No. 73, marked 'Carpenter's Locker'. Silver watch and chain; memo book. No other aids to identification. Possibly carpenter's mate.
Connors, Patrick	171	Buried at sea.	Listed as third class. Embarked Queenstown.
Cavendish, Tyrell, W.	172	Forwarded, May 3rd, care of Simpson, Crawford & Co., to Mrs. T. W. Cavendish.	Instructions, N.Y. Office, wire, May 1st. First class.
Olsen, Henry	173	Buried at sea.	Listed as third class. Embarked Southampton.
Bateman, R.J. Rev	174	Forwarded May 6th to Mrs. R. J. Bateman, Jacksonville, Florida.	Accordance wire from Mrs. Bateman, May 2nd.
McCarthy, Timothy J.	175	Delivered to Mr. J. V. Finn, April 30th, for forwarding to Boston.	First class.
Theobold, Thomas	176	Buried at sea.	Listed as Thomas Theobald, third class. Embarked Southampton.
Mayo, W.	177	Buried at sea.	On crew list-Engine Dept.

Name	No. on List	How Disposed of	Remarks
Unidentified, Male	178	Buried at sea.	Tattooed, right arm: 'anchor and rose', wife's name 'Madge'. Six pawn tickets in possession, and following addresses: Henry Murray, Sailor's Home, Southampton, and 45 Fir Grove Road, Southampton; Sidney Sedunary, 47 Fir Grove Road and 98 N'land Road, Southampton; John Sedunary, 47 Fir Grove Road, Southampton.
Unidentified, Male	179	Buried at Fairview Cemetery, Halifax, N.S.	No aids to identification. Possibly a fireman.
Unidentified, Male	180	Buried at sea.	Wore steward's white coat; black coat and dungaree trousers. No other aids to identification.
Novel, Mansor	181	Buried at sea.	Listed as Mansouer Norel, third class. Embarked Cherbourg.
Unidentified, Male	182	Buried at sea.	No aids to identification. Possibly a fireman.
McQuillan, William	183	Buried at Fairview Cemetery, Halifax, N.S.	On crew list-Engine Dept.
Saunders, W.	184	Buried at sea.	Possibly one of the two W. Saunders' on crew list-Engine Dept.
Unidentified, Male	185	Buried at sea.	Wore blue coat with brass buttons; trousers; steward's white coat; green singlet; green jersey with white bands. Probably second-class steward.
Price, Ernest	186	Buried at Fairview Cemetery, Halifax, N.S.	On crew list-Vict. Dept.
Everett, Thos. James	187	Buried at Fairview Cemetery, Halifax, N.S.	Listed as Thos. Everett, third class. Embarked Southampton.

Name	No. on List	How Disposed of	Remarks
Hanna, Merne	188	Buried at Mount Olivet Cemetery, Halifax, N.S.	Listed as Mansour Hanna, third class. Embarked Cherbourg.
Ovies, Servando	189	Buried at Mount Olivet Cemetery, Halifax, N.S.	Listed as first-class passenger. Identified by J.A. Rodriguez of Rodriguez & Co., Havana, Cuba.
Abbott, Rossmore	190	Buried at sea.	Listed as third-class passenger. Embarked Southampton.
Davis, R.J.	191	Buried at Fairview Cemetery, Halifax, N.S.	Identified from effects. On crew list-Vict. Dept.
Matherson, D.	192	Buried at Fairview Cemetery, Halifax, N.S.	Identified from effects. On crew list-Deck Dept.
Unidentified, Male	193	Buried at Fairview Cemetery, Halifax, N.S.	Wore light rain coat; uniform jacket with green facing and vest; purple muffler; carried cigarette case; silver watch; knife with carved pearl handle, and brass button marked 'African Royal Mail'; also English lever watch.
Unidentified, Male	194	Buried at sea.	Gray overcoat Artex singlet; nightshirt; dress trousers. Wore gold ring marked 'H.B.' or 'B.H.'
Shillabeer, Charles	195	Buried at Fairview Cemetery, Halifax, N.S.	On crew list as C. Shillaber-Engine Dept.
Semperopolis, Petril	196	Buried at Mount Olivet Cemetery, Halifax, N.S.	Listed as Peter Lemberopoulos, third class. Emb. Cherbourg.
Danbom, E. Gilbert	197	Forwarded to Alfred Danbom, Stanton, Ia.,May 3rd.	Instructions, N.Y. Office, letter, April 30th. Third class. Embarked Southampton.
Unidentified, Male	198	Buried at Fairview Cemetery, Halifax, N.S.	No aids to identification. Possibly a fireman.

Name	No. on List	How Disposed of	Remarks
Davies, John James	200	Buried at sea.	On crew list as J. Davies-Vict. Dept.
Martino, A. Meo	201	Buried at Fairview Cemetery, Halifax, N.S.	(shown on list as Alphonso Meo, closer examination of effects indicates as above.) Listed as Alfonso Meo, third class. Embarked Southampton.
Clarke, J.F.P.	202	Buried at Mount Olivet Cemetery, Halifax, N.S.	Probably Bandman.
Unidentified, Male	203	Buried at Fairview Cemetery, Halifax, N.S.	Wore blue serge suit, union cable belt and striped flannel shirt. Tattooed right arm: snake around cocoanut palm, hand with bouquet of roses; left arm, woman's bust over wreath and dagger. Probably a fireman.
Ingram, C.	204	Buried at Fairview Cemetery, Halifax, N.S.	On crew list-Engine Dept.
Ackerman, J	205	Buried at Fairview Cemetery, Halifax, N.S.	On crew list as J. Akerman-Vict. Dept.
Paulsson, Alma Cornelia	206	Buried at Fairview Cemetery, Halifax, N.S.	Listed as Alma Paulsson, third class. Emb. Southampton.
Porter, Walter Chamberlain	207	Delivered to Mr. E. Sessions, April 30th, for forwarding to Worcester, Mass.	Instructions of widow. First class.
Brandeis, Emil	208	Forwarded to Mrs Brandeis, Omaha, Neb., May 2nd.	Instructions, N.Y. Office, wire, April 29. First class pass.
McCrae, Arthur Gordon	209	Buried at Fairview Cemetery, Halifax, N.S.	Listed as second class passenger. Wire from E.D. Upham, Denver, May 10.
Unidentified, Female	210	Buried at Mount Olivet Cemetery, Halifax, N.S.	Wore long green overcoat; purple jacket; skirt; no corsets; brown shoes; black stockings.

Name	No. on List	How Disposed of	Remarks
Lefevre, George	211	Buried at Fairview Cemetery, Halifax, N.S.	On crew list-Vict. Dept.
Unidentified, Male	212	Buried at Fairview Cemetery, Halifax, N.S.	Steward's uniform; first saloon steward's badge, No. 73.
Unidentified, Male	213	Buried at Fairview Cemetery, Halifax, N.S.	Wore mixture suit; green shirt; no coat. Effects include keys, pocket scissors, knife and about $45.00 money in American and Canadian bills.
Unidentified, Male	214	Buried at Hebrew Cemetery, Halifax, N.S.	Wore steward's badge No. 41. Nothing else to aid in identification.
Bernardi, Baptiste	215	Buried at Mount Olivet Cemetery, Halifax, N.S.	On crew list-Vict. Dept. In book as Bernardi Batiste.
Unidentified, Male	216	Buried at Fairview Cemetery, Halifax, N.S.	Wore steward's uniform; truss, and black boots. Nothing to aid in identification.
Samuel, O.W.	217	Buried at Fairview Cemetery, Halifax, N.S.	Possibly W. Samuels. On crew list-Vict. Dept.
Cave, H.	218	Buried at Fairview Cemetery, Halifax, N.S.	On crew list-Vict. Dept.
Rame, M.	219	Buried at Fairview Cemetery, Halifax, N.S.	Later identified from effects. Not on crew list. Probably mail clerk.
Unidentified, Male	220	Buried at Fairview Cemetery, Halifax, N.S.	Wore black coat; flannel singlet and dungaree trousers.
Goree, F.	222	Buried at Fairview Cemetery, Halifax, N.S.	On crew list-Engine Dept.
Unidentified, Male	223	Buried at Fairview Cemetery, Halifax, N.S.	Wore steward's uniform. Nothing to aid in identification.

Name	No. on List	How Disposed of	Remarks
Hartley, Wallace H.	224	Forwarded, May 4th, to Boston for shipment to Liverpool.	(Shown on the list as Hotley) Instructions, N.Y. Office, wire, May 2nd. Bandmaster.
March, John S.	225	Forwarded to Newark, N.J., May 3rd, care of Smith & Smith, undertakers.	Instructions, N.Y. Office, letter, April 30th. Mail clerk.
Teuton, Thomas	226	Buried at Fairview Cemetery, Halifax, N.S.	(Shown on list as Tenton) Not on crew list.
Dawson, J.	227	Buried at Fairview Cemetery, Halifax, N.S.	On crew list-Engine Dept.
Unidentified, Male	228	Buried at Fairview Cemetery, Halifax, N.S.	Wore dungaree coat and trousers; grey shirt and drawers; body belt. No other aids to identification.
Unidentified, Male	229	Buried at Fairview Cemetery, Halifax, N.S.	Nothing to aid in identification.
Minahan, Dr. W.E.	230	Delivered, May 2nd, to V.J. Minahan, Green Bay, Wisconsin.	Instructions, N.Y. Office, wire, April 29th, and V.J. Minahan's wire, same date. First class.
Roberts, F.	231	Buried at Fairview Cemetery, Halifax, N.S.	On crew list-Vict. Dept.
Righini, Sante	232	Forwarded to New York, May 11th, escort, F. W. Wender, for widow.	Request of Mrs. J. Stuart White, N.Y. (Mrs. White's manservant).
Unidentified, Male	233	Buried at Fairview Cemetery, Halifax, N.S.	No aids to identification.
Ostby, Engelhart C.	234	Delivered to David Sutherland, for forwarding to Providence, R. I.	Letter of H.W. Ostby, April 24th. First class.

Name	No. on List	How Disposed of	Remarks
Baxter, T.F.	235	Buried at Mount Olivet Cemetery, Halifax, N.S.	On crew list as F. Baxter-Vict. Dept.
Fox, Stanley H.	236	Forwarded, May 3rd, to Rochester, N.Y., to widow.	Order of Mrs. Emma Fox. Second class.
Unidentified, Male	237	Buried at Fairview Cemetery, Halifax, N.S.	Wore dark gray suit; letters 'F.H.' on shirt. Effects included openface nickel watch and silver chain with match box attached; tortoise-shell tobacco pouch; two little pictures-one of town hall, Portsmouth, and one of Portsmouth coat of arms.
King, Alfred	238	Buried at Fairview Cemetery, Halifax, N.S.	On crew list, A. King-Vict. Dept.
Freeman, E.	239	Buried at Fairview Cemetery, Halifax, N.S.	On crew list-Vict. Dept.
Unidentified, Male	240	Buried at Fairview Cemetery, Halifax, N.S.	Wore gray overcoat; blue serge suit and white sweater. Effects included nickel or silver box purse for coins; silver maltese cross of coronation of Edward VII, 1902, attached to watch chain; silver watch with three photos (enclosed in back thereof), of two women and a boy with cap on; maker of watch, J.B. Yabsley, 72 Ludgate Hill, London; watch key attached to chain engraved 'Panny', 2 Richmond Street, Brighton.
Blackwell, Stephen W.	241	Buried at Fairview Cemetery, Halifax, N.S.	Listed as first-class passenger.
Hosgood, R.	242	Buried at Fairview Cemetery, Halifax, N.S.	On crew list-Engine Dept.

Name	No. on List	How Disposed of	Remarks
Unidentified, Male	243	Buried at Fairview Cemetery, Halifax, N.S.	Wore black cloth overcoat; steward's vest and trousers marked 'Stone'. Effects included gold double-headed snake ring; ship's keys marked second staterooms E 99–107. Tattooed on left arm: Chinese dragon; on right arm: American flag and clasped hands.
Debreucq, Morris E.	244	Buried at Mount Olivet Cemetery, Halifax, N.S.	On crew list as M. DeBreucq-Vict. Dept.
Van Der Hoef, Wyckoff	245	Delivered to Mr. D. C. Chauncey, for forwarding to New York.	Instructions, N.Y. Office, letter, April 26th. Listed as Wychoff Vanderhoef, first class.
Wareham, R.A.	246	Buried at Fairview Cemetery, Halifax, N.S.	On crew list as R. Wareham-Vict. Dept.
White, Arthur	247	Buried at Fairview Cemetery, Halifax, N.S.	Identified from effects. On crew list as A. White-Vict Dept.
Unidentified, Male	248	Buried at Hebrew Cemetery, Halifax, N.S.	Wore dungaree trousers and gray striped jacket. Nothing to aid in identification. Probably member of cook's department.
Millet, Frank D.	249	Delivered, May 1st, to Mr. Lovering Hill, for forwarding to Boston.	First class.
Hutchinson, J.	250	Buried at Fairview Cemetery, Halifax, N.S.	On crew list-Vict. Dept.
Carney, W.M.	251	Buried at Fairview Cemetery, Halifax, N.S.	On crew list as W. Carney-Vict. Dept.
Dean, Mr.	252	Buried at Fairview Cemetery, Halifax, N.S.	On crew list as G. Dean-Vict. Dept.

Name	No. on List	How Disposed of	Remarks
Couch, F.	253	Buried at Fairview Cemetery, Halifax, N.S.	On crew list-Deck Dept.
Gough, W.	253	Buried at Fairview Cemetery, Halifax, N.S.	Identified from effects. Not on crew list.
Unidentified, Male	254	Buried at Fairview Cemetery, Halifax, N.S.	Tattooed on left arm: woman's bust and Union Jack; also woman in kilts, and on right arm: man's head (cowboy); clasped hands and heart (true love), and flower. Nothing else to aid identification. Probably a sailor.
Van Billiard, Austin	255	Forwarded, May 4th, to North Wales Depot, Pa.	Instructions, N.Y. Office, wire, May 2nd. Listed as A. Van Billiard, third class. Embarked Southampton.
Hickman, Leonard	256	Forwarded, May 4th to Honeyman, care of Simpson, undertaker, Neepawa, Manitoba.	Instructions, N.Y. Office, wire, May 2nd. Second class.
Unidentified, Male	257	Buried at Fairview Cemetery, Halifax, N.S.	Wore boiler suit; uniform jacket (double-breasted); green striped flannel shirt. Nothing found to aid identification. Possibly an engineer.
Kent, Edward A.	258	Delivered, May 1st, to H.K. White of Boston, for shipment to Buffalo, N.Y.	First class.
Allum, Owen G.	259	Forwarded May 4th to Boston, to connect with Arabic for Liverpool, May 7th.	Instructions, N.Y. Office, wire, May 2nd.
Andersen, Mr.	260	Buried at Fairview Cemetery, Halifax, N.S.	Listed as Albert Anderson, third class. Embarked Southampton. Later identified from effects.

Name	No. on List	How Disposed of	Remarks
Storey, Thomas	261	Buried at Fairview Cemetery, Halifax, N.S.	Listed as T. Storey, third class. Embarked Southampton.
Unidentified, Male	262	Buried at Fairview Cemetery, Halifax, N.S.	Wore steward's coat, vest, trousers, green overcoat, with tag 'Miller & Son, Southampton'; shirt marked 'A. Franklin'. Effects included nickel watch stamped 'Joe Meyer's Special' on face. Bunch of keys, including key of stateroom 38; wire spring belt with anchor buckle, stamped inside with a wreath surmounted by a crown; small card printed 'Mr. W. Harris', with 'Jun.' added in writing.
Nicholson, A.S.	263	Forwarded, May 6th, to F.E. Campbell, 214 West 23rd Street, New York.	Instructions, N.Y. Office, wire, May 4th. First class.
Unidentified, Male	264	Buried at Hebrew Cemetery, Halifax, N.S.	Wore steward's white coat; blue coat and trousers; uniform vest; blue jersey; black boots; drawers were marked 'H. Lyon'. Effects included brass watch stamped on face 'Evening Times'; gold-rimmed spectacles, and tickets for 'second stateroom D 51 to D 89'.
Unidentified, Male	265	Buried at Fairview Cemetery, Halifax, N.S.	Wore steward's uniform. Effects included silver watch; keys marked Nos. 7 and 9. Nothing further to aid identification. Probably a steward.
Piazza, Pompeo	266	Buried at Mount Olivet Cemetery, Halifax, N.S.	On crew list-Vict. Dept.
Brown, J.	267	Buried at Fairview Cemetery, Halifax, N.S.	On crew list-Engines Dept.

Name	No. on List	How Disposed of	Remarks
Marsh, F.	268	Buried at Fairview Cemetery, Halifax, N.S.	On crew list-Engine Dept.
Crosby, E.G.	269	Delivered to Howard G. Kelley, V.P., G.T. Ry., for shipment to Milwaukee, May 3rd.	First class.
Deeble, A.	270	Buried at Fairview Cemetery, Halifax, N.S.	Indentified from effects. On crew list-Vict. Dept.
Milling, F.C. or J.C.	271	Forwarded, May 6th, to Boston, for cremation.	Instructions, N.Y. Office, wire, May 4th. Ashes to be ultimately sent to Clausen, Copenhagen. Listed as second class.
White, J.	272	Buried at Fairview Cemetery, Halifax, N.S.	On crew list-Vict. Dept.
Holloway, Sidney	273	Buried at Fairview Cemetery, Halifax, N.S.	On crew list-Vict. Dept.
Unidentified, Male	274	Buried at Fairview Cemetery, Halifax, N.S.	Wore blue suit; pajamas and drawers marked 'L. B.' Effects included key with tag marked 'second staterooms F1 to F14'. No further aid to identification. Possibly a steward.
Gee, Arthur	275	Forwarded to New York, May 9th, to be sent to Liverpool, per S.S. Baltic.	Instructions, N.Y. Office, wire, May 6th. First class.
Gradiage, E.	276	Buried at Fairview Cemetery, Halifax, N.S.	Identified from effects. On crew list as E. Grodidge-Engine Dept.
Jaillet, H.	277	Buried at Mount Olivet Cemetery, Halifax, N.S.	On crew list-Vict. Dept.

Name	No. on List	How Disposed of	Remarks
Unidentified, Male	278	Buried at Hebrew Cemetery, Halifax, N.S.	Wore dungaree coat and trousers; gray flannel drawers. No aids to identification. Possibly a fireman.
Unidentified, Male	279	Buried at Fairview Cemetery, Halifax, N.S.	Wore blue serge suit; white shirt; underclothes marked 'B.C.' Tattooed on right arm, a monument (a cross in memory to my dear mother), and on left arm 'B.C.' Clothing made by Wolf Bros., 50 East Street, Southampton. Possibly a steward.
Reeves, R.	280	Buried at Fairview Cemetery, Halifax, N.S.	On crew list-Engines Dept.
Unidentified, Female	281	Buried at Fairview Cemetery, Halifax, N.S.	Wore black coat; blue shirt; red jersey; green blouse; wollen singlet; gray underskirt; black boots and stockings. No other aids of identification.
Rogers, Edward J.W.	282	Buried at Fairview Cemetery, Halifax, N.S.	On crew list as E.J. Rogers-Vict. Dept.
Kantor, Cenai	283	Forwarded to 1735 Madison Ave., New York, care of Spieler.	Instructions, N.Y. Office, wire, April 29th. Listed as second-class passenger, S. Kantor.
Sawyer, Frederick	284	Buried at Fairview Cemetery, Halifax, N.S.	Listed as third class. Embarked Southampton.
Johansson, Gustaf Joel	285	Buried at Fairview Cemetery, Halifax, N.S.	Listed as Gustav Johansson, third class. Emb. Southampton.
Faunthorpe, Harry	286	Forwarded to Mrs. Faunthorpe; care of Mr. William Stringfield, Philadelphia, Pa.	Instructions, N.Y. Office, wire, May 3rd. Second class.

Name	No. on List	How Disposed of	Remarks
Norman, Robert D.	287	Buried at Fairview Cemetery, Halifax, N.S.	Listed as second-class passenger.
Unidentified, Male	288	Buried at Mount Olivet Cemetery, Halifax, N.S.	Wore two gold rings, one a chain ring; white shirt with fancy front. Carried gun-metal watch. No other aids to identification. Probably a Greek.
Unidentified, Male	289	Buried at Hebrew Cemetery, Halifax, N.S.	Wore steward's uniform, and gold ring with green stone; ship's key, No. 37. Tattooed: left arm, anchor, cross and heart (all in one).
Bristow, R.C.	290	Buried at Fairview Cemetery, Halifax, N.S.	On crew list as R. Bristow-Vict. Dept.
Unidentified, Male	291	Buried at Hebrew Cemetery, Halifax, N.S.	Wore two pairs pants; pajamas; blue suit; dark overcoat; uniform buttons on vest; blue striped woolen vest; wrist watch. No other aids to identification.
McCaffry, Thomas	292	Delivered to E. E. Code, May 2nd, for forwarding to Montreal.	First class.
Weisz, Leopold	293	Forwarded to E. Armstrong & Co., Montreal.	Instructions Montreal Office, wire, April 30th. Listed as second-class passenger.
Swane, George	294	Buried at Fairview Cemetery, Halifax, N.S.	Listed as second-class passenger.
Del Carlo, Sabastiano	295	Forwarded to Boston, April 30th, for shipment to Italy by Cretic May 18th.	Request of widow. Listed as second class.
Unidentified, Male	296	Buried at Fairview Cemetery, Halifax, N.S.	Tattooed: Right arm, ship on back of hand; girl and snake on arm, left arm, girl's bust. No other aids to identification. Possibly a fireman.

Name	No. on List	How Disposed of	Remarks
Giles, Ralph	297	Buried at Fairview Cemetery, Halifax, N.S.	Listed as second-class passenger.
Linhart, H. Wenzel	298	Buried at Mount Olivet Cemetery, Halifax, N.S.	Wire from Rud Linhart May 6th, and N.Y. Office May 2nd. Listed as Wenzel Zinhard, third class. Embarked Southampton.
Buckley, Katherine	299	Forwarded to Boston, May 3rd.	Request of sister Margaret, 71 Montview St., Roxbury, Mass. Boston Office, letter, April 29th. Third class. Embarked Queenstown.
Cox, H. Denton	300	Buried at Fairview Cemetery, Halifax, N.S.	On crew list as W. Cox-Vict. Dept.
Poggi, Emilio	301	Buried at Fairview Cemetery, Halifax, N.S.	On crew list as E. Poggi-Vict. Dept.
Morgan, Thomas	302	Buried at Mount Olivet Cemetery, Halifax, N.S.	On crew list as T. Morgan-Engine Dept.
Unidentified, Male	303	Buried at Fairview Cemetery, Halifax, N.S.	Tattooed: Right arm, clasped hands across heart, girl's bust with wreath beneath. Left arm, life belt with 'Good Hope' ship in centre.
Der Zacarian, Maurpre	304	Buried at Fairview Cemetery, Halifax, N.S.	Listed as third-class passenger. Buried in Halifax at request of brother.
Givard, Hans Christensen	305	Buried at Fairview Cemetery, Halifax, N.S.	Listed as second-class passenger.
Henderkovic, Tozni	306	Buried at Mount Olivet Cemetery, Halifax, N.S.	Listed as Ignaz Hendekovic, third class. Emb. Southampton.

Source: http://www.gov.ns.ca/nsarm/virtual/titanic/ships.asp?Ship=Mackay-Bennett

--------------------------------- Did You Know That? ---------------------------------

The Cable Ship (CS) *Mackay-Bennett was* launched in 1884 and was named for two founders of the Commercial Cable Company, John W. MacKay and James G. Bennett. The vessel arrived in Halifax in March 1885, based there to facilitate the at-sea repairs of underwater telegraph cables in the North Atlantic. The CS *Mackay-Bennett* set sail for the Titanic disaster area on 17th April 1912.

The Canadian Steamship *Minia*

Name	No. on List	How Disposed of	Remarks
Hays, Charles M.	307	Delivered to Mr. Howard G. Kelley, V.P., G.T. Ry., and taken to Montreal.	First class.
Unidentified, Male	308	Buried at Fairview Cemetery, Halifax, N.S.	Handkerchief marked 'A.H.F.' No other aids to identification.
Moen, Sigurd H.	309	Forwarded to New York, May 10th, for shipment to Norway by Scandinavian American Line.	Instructions, N.Y. Office, May 10th. Third class. Embarked Southampton.
Unidentified, Male	310	Buried at sea.	No aids to identification. Probably a fireman.
Donate, Italo	311	Buried at Fairview Cemetery, Halifax, N.S.	On crew list as Italio Donati-Vict. Dept.
Gerios, Youssef	312	Buried at Mount Olivet Cemetery, Halifax, N.S.	Listed as third class. Embarked Cherbourg.
Gatti, L.	313	Buried at Fairview Cemetery, Halifax, N.S.	On crew list-Vict. Dept. (Restaurant manager)
Wiklund, Jacob Alfred	314	Buried at Fairview Cemetery, Halifax, N.S.	Listed as Jacob Wiklund, third class. Emb. Southampton.

Name	No. on List	How Disposed of	Remarks
Whitnam or Wiltnham or Wilthnarn,	315	Buried at Fairview Cemetery, Halifax, N.S.	Possibly H. Wittman. On crew list-Vict. Dept.
Stanbrook, A.	316	Buried at Fairview Cemetery, Halifax, N.S.	On crew list-Engine Dept.
Elliott, Edw	317	Buried at Fairview Cemetery, Halifax, N.S.	On crew list as E. Elliott-Engine Dept.
Unidentified, Male	318	Buried at sea.	Wore brass watch and chain. No other aids to identification. Probably a fireman.
Howell, C.	319	Buried at Fairview Cemetery, Halifax, N.S.	On crew list as A Howell-Vict. Dept.
Carlwright, L.A.	320	Buried at Fairview Cemetery, Halifax, N.S.	Not on crew list.
King, T.W.	321	Buried at Fairview Cemetery, Halifax, N.S.	On crew list E.W. King-Vict. Dept.
Fynney, Joseph J.	322	Delivered to Mr. Hoseason, C.N.S.S Co., to be taken to Montreal.	Listed as second class.
Mullin, Thomas A.	323	Buried at Fairview Cemetery, Halifax, N.S.	On crew list as T. Mullen-Vict. Dept.

Source: http://www.gov.ns.ca/nsarm/virtual/titanic/ships.asp?Ship=Minia

———————— Did You Know That? ————————

The Anglo-American Telegraph Company's CS *Minia* was chartered by
the White Star Line on 21st April 1912 and went to sea the following
day under the command of W.E.S. DeCarteret, with undertaker
H.W. Snow and the Rev. H.W. Cunningham (rector, Anglican Parish of
St. George, Brunswick Street, Halifax) on board.

The Canadian Government Ship *Montmagny*

Name	No. on List	How Disposed of	Remarks
Unidentified, Male	326	Buried at sea.	Wore steward's white coat; light check overalls; coatmaker's mark. 'Baker & Co., Southampton'. No further aids to identification. Possibly a steward.
Reynolds, Harold	327	Buried at Fairview Cemetery, Halifax, N.S.	On 'Montmagny'. Listed as third class. Embarked Southampton.
Unidentified, Female	328	Buried at Mount Olivet Cemetery, Halifax, N.S.	Wore lace trimmed red and black overdress; black under dress; green striped underskirt; black woolen shawl and black slippers. No further aids to identification. Probably a third-class passenger.
Smith, C.	329	Buried at Fairview Cemetery, Halifax, N.S.	On Montmagny. Probably one of the C. Smiths. On crew list-Vict. Dept.

Source: http://www.gov.ns.ca/nsarm/virtual/titanic/ships.asp?Ship=Montmagny

— Did You Know That? —

The Canadian Government Ship (CGS) *Montmagny* was a lighthouse-supply and buoy-tender vessel owned by the Federal Department of Marine and Fisheries. She sailed from her home-port of Quebec City on 13th May 1912 for routine activities in the Gulf of St. Lawrence and northern New Brunswick waters. As she cruised towards Halifax, she was asked to search for bodies and wreckage from the *Titanic*.

■ THE MOVIE TRIVIA ■■■■■■■■■■■■■

During filming Leonardo DiCaprio's pet lizard was run over by a truck, but thankfully recovered.

The Steam Ship *Algerine*

Name	No. on List	How Disposed of	Remarks
McGrady, James	330	Buried at Fairview Cemetery, Halifax, N.S.	Body picked up by SS *Florizel*

Source: http://www.gov.ns.ca/nsarm/virtual/titanic/ships.asp?Ship=Algerine

Titanic's massive 15½ ton centre anchor sitting on W. A. Ree's 20 ton haulage dray and photographed outside the Lloyds Proving House, Netherton after being lowered onto the dray (Jonathan Smith collection).

———————— Did You Know That? ————————

The SS *Algerine* was reputedly a vessel owned by Bowring Brothers of St. John's, Newfoundland, and was contracted by the White Star Line to search for bodies.

THE END OF A JOURNEY

Titanic's journey came to an end not in New York to a tumultuous welcome from crowds of thousands, but on a cold dark night in the mid-Atlantic thanks to a brush with fate and a nearby iceberg. One thing that I have discovered is that in almost a century since the *Titanic* plunged to her watery grave, there is much misunderstanding and misinformation being perpetuated about the circumstances surrounding the disaster. Some 'experts' claim that her rudder was her 'Achilles Heel'; a great many claim that the ship was going too fast through the ice field in an attempt to make a record transatlantic crossing; the inferior quality of her rivets has been suggested by some; others point to a criminal lack of lifeboats aboard *Titanic*; some even cite a conspiracy theory claiming that the *Olympic* and the *Titanic* were switched as part of some huge insurance fraud. Then there is the mystery of the locked gates in third class and of course no disaster story would be complete without an urban legend or two thrown in for good measure.

I do not regard myself as an expert on the *Titanic* but in the year I have spent compiling my work I have had the pleasure of dealing with many people who in my opinion are most certainly experts in different areas of the ship from her design to her construction, to her exterior and interior, to her colouring, to her hull, to her flags and many other aspects of this magnificent ship. This book has been a journey for me as well, one in which I've not only learned much more than I expected but have been surprised at times at the facts and survivors' testimony that lies behind some of the legends of popular history. I hope you have enjoyed my book and I hope that I have helped to dispel some misconceptions you may have had about the most famous ocean liner the world has ever known.

Titanic was the largest man-made object ever moved when she was launched at the Harland & Wolff Shipyard in Belfast on 31st May 1911, a magnificent example of Edwardian craftsmanship and engineering. The *Titanic* was not just some ship which was hurriedly cobbled together by some slapdash shipbuilding firm. Indeed, she was built by 3,000 men at Harland & Wolff which at the time was the biggest and most prestigious shipbuilders in the world, and ships like the *Olympic*-Class liners were the end result of decades of tried and true experience combined with conservative, well-thought-out innovation. I was born and bred in Belfast; my late father worked all of his life at the yard; my late uncle worked aboard the *Canberra* (a ship my Dad helped to build), and I am proud that the city of my birth also gave birth to the *Titanic*. Many people all over the world are intrigued with the *Titanic* story but only the people of Belfast can

claim her as one of their own. When she sank the city felt sadness and pain and collectively mourned the loss of the 1,523 poor souls who went down with her. However, these lives were not lost in vain as the *Titanic* disaster culminated in significant and enduring contributions to maritime safety.

Finally, I have nothing but the utmost respect for those men who built the *Titanic*, and in many ways I would like to think that my book pays tribute to Harland & Wolff's most memorable ship.

John

BIOGRAPHIES

Thomas Andrews – The Master Shipbuilder

Thomas Andrews Jnr. was born on 7th February 1873 at the Andrews family home, Ardara House, Comber, County Down, Northern Ireland. Thomas Andrews Snr. was the managing director and head of the draughting department for the Harland & Wolff Shipyard in Belfast. His mother was Eliza Pirrie. In 1884, aged 11, he attended Royal Belfast Academical Institute and studied there until he was 16 when he left to take-up an apprenticeship at the Harland & Wolff Shipyard in Belfast. His uncle, Viscount Pirrie, was part-owner of the shipyard. He spent his first three months in the joiner's shop, then one month in the cabinetmaker's shop followed by two months working on ships at the yard. Three and a half years into his five-year apprenticeship he joined the drawing office and slowly worked his way up the company, becoming manager of the construction works in 1901.

In 1907 Andrews, a member of the Institution of Naval Architects, followed in his father's footsteps and was appointed the managing director and head of the draughting department at Harland & Wolff. That same year Andrews was in charge of the plans to build a new Olympic-Class passenger liner for the White Star Line: RMS *Olympic,* the older sister ship to RMS *Titanic.* On 24th June 1908, Thomas married Helen Reilly Barbour and the couple had one child, a daughter Elizabeth Law Barbour Andrews, born on 27th November 1910. It was also in June 1908 that Thomas began overseeing the plans to build the *Titanic* which he helped design with William Pirrie and Alexander Carlisle. As the head of the draughting department at the yard, one of Andrews' main roles was to sail on the maiden voyage of every ship built at the Belfast shipyard. This was so as he and a few members of his team could observe at first hand how the ship performed and note any potential improvements. So when *Titanic* left Belfast for Southampton on 10th April 1912 Andrews was aboard and was still on the ship when she set sail for New York via Cherbourg, France and Queenstown, Ireland.

When *Titanic* struck the iceberg, Andrews was asleep in his stateroom. Captain Smith summoned Andrews to the deck and asked him to inspect the damage. When Andrews discovered that six of the ship's forward watertight compartments were filled with water he informed Captain Smith that *Titanic* was going to sink within the next few hours. The ship was designed to stay afloat with up to four watertight compartments being breached. Andrews then searched many of the staterooms and informed passengers to put on their lifebelts and go up on deck to

wait for a seat in a lifeboat. Andrews, aged 39 at the time, stayed on the doomed vessel to the very end and was last seen in the first-class smoking room. His body, if ever recovered, was never identified. Four days after *Titanic* sank his father received a telegram from his mother's cousin who had questioned survivors as to his whereabouts. The telegram read: '*INTERVIEW TITANIC'S OFFICERS. ALL UNANIMOUS THAT ANDREWS HEROIC UNTO DEATH, THINKING ONLY SAFETY OTHERS. EXTEND HEARTFELT SYMPATHY TO ALL.*'

--- Did You Know That? ---

His older brother, John, was the second Prime Minister of Northern Ireland (1940–43).

Sir Edward James Harland – 1st Baronet

Edward James Harland was born on 15th 1831 in Scarborough, North Yorkshire, England, the seventh child of ten (fourth boy of six). The young Edward was educated at Edinburgh Academy and when he turned 15 years old he began an apprenticeship at the engineering works of Robert Stephenson and Company in Newcastle-upon-Tyne. During the apprenticeship, Harland met Gustav Christian Schwabe who was a partner in John Bibby & Sons, a shipping company based in Liverpool. When Harland completed his apprenticeship Schwabe got him a job in Glasgow working for J. and G. Thomson Marine Engineers who were shipbuilding for John Bibby & Sons. Harland worked hard and became head draughtsman before leaving Glasgow in 1853 to return to Newcastle, as the manager of the Thomas Toward Shipyard. The following year the 23-year old Harland decided to move to Belfast upon accepting an invitation to become the manager of Robert Hickson's shipyard at Queen's Island, Belfast. In 1857 Harland hired Schwabe's nephew, Gustav Wilhelm Wolff, as his personal assistant and decided it was time he had his own shipyard. However, his attempts to open a new yard in Liverpool failed. Then on 21st September 1858, Hickson wrote to him offering to sell him his Queen's Island yard for the sum of £5,000. With Schwabe's financial backing Harland accepted Hickson's offer and on 1st November 1858 purchased the shipyard to create his own company, Edward James Harland & Company. John Bibby & Sons ordered three ships from Harland, the *Venetian, Sicilian* and *Syrian* and, impressed with the quality of the ships, Bibby ordered six more boats from Harland in 1860. On 26th January 1860, Harland married Miss Rosa Wann, of Vermont, Belfast and a year later formed another partnership, this time with Wolff who he made a partner in his company which was renamed Harland & Wolff.

In 1874, Harland invited William James Pirrie, a former apprentice at the Queen's Island yard, to become a partner in the business although the Harland & Wolff name remained. The trio enjoyed much business success with the White Star

Line placing many orders for ocean liners. The famous White Star liners built by Harland & Wolff Shipyard were first designed by Harland on the model of a fish swimming through the water. The three men were so successful that Harland was once asked the nature of the three men's business relationship and he replied: 'Well, Wolff designs the ships, Pirrie sells them and I smoke the firm's cigars.' In 1889, Harland retired leaving Wolff and Pirrie to carry on.

Sir Edward Harland served as the Chairman of the Belfast Harbour Board from 1875 to the mid-1880s and was twice Lord Mayor of Belfast, (1885 and again in 1886). In the year he retired he was elected without opposition Member of Parliament for the Northern Division of Belfast on the death of Sir William Ewart and moved to London. He was re-elected unopposed twice, in 1892 and 1895, and served as a Member of Parliament for his constituency until he died suddenly on 24th December 1895 without leaving an heir to his baronetcy.

Did You Know That?

Harland's father was a doctor and an amateur engineer; he invented a patented steam-powered carriage in 1827.

Joseph Phillippe Lemercier Laroche

On 26th May 1886, Joseph Laroche was born in Cap Haitien in the northern part of Haiti. The young Laroche grew up in the city and in 1901, aged 15, he decided that he wanted to become an engineer. As there was no school in his native land which taught engineering he moved to France with a teacher, Monsignor Kersuzan, the Lord Bishop of Haiti. Laroche settled in Beauvais, home of the engineering school, and lived with Monsignor Kersuzan, although on occasion he also travelled to Lille for some lessons. One day the Monsignor told Joseph that he had to visit a friend in Paris and invited him to accompany him. The pair visited the home of Monsieur Lafargue, a wine seller who lived in Villejuif. During this visit Joseph fell in love with Monsieur Lafargue's daughter, her, and after he graduated from school and received his engineering certificate, he married Juliette in March 1908. The Lafargues were an upper-middle-class family. Joseph hoped to quickly secure employment as an engineer working in Paris but unfortunately for him, despite his excellent qualification and skills, racial prejudice existed in France at that time. When he eventually did find employment, his employers used the colour of his skin against him and paid him very little, wrongly claiming that Joseph was too young and inexperienced. In 1911, he and his family decided to return to Haiti the following year where he believed there would be a need for qualified young engineers. When Joseph learned in March 1912 that his wife was pregnant they decided that it was best to travel to Haiti as soon as possible rather than wait for the baby to be born and then travel such a long distance with a newborn child.

Joseph's mother bought the tickets as a welcome present for the new family on CGT's (French Line) newest steamship *France,* a four-funnelled liner whose maiden voyage was scheduled for 20th April 1912, bound for New York from Le Havre, France. CGT's policy at that time required children to stay in the nursery during the day, which angered Joseph and Juliette. Consequently the couple, not wishing to be separated from their two daughters, Simone and Louise, changed their tickets and booked second-class tickets for *Titanic's* maiden voyage from Southampton to New York with stop-offs in Cherbourg, France and Queenstown, Ireland, leaving ten days earlier on 10th April 1912.

When *Titanic* struck the iceberg. Joseph led his pregnant wife and his two girls safely to a lifeboat and watched as they were lowered down into the sea. This was the last time he ever saw them as he lost his life in the *Titanic* disaster. The lifeboat in which Juliette, Simone and Louise were afloat was rescued by the Cunard Line's RMS *Carpathia* and taken to New York, arriving there on 18th April 1912. However, the loss of her husband and personal belongings frightened Juliette and she decided to immediately return to France. They arrived back in Le Havre in May and she moved in with her father. Joseph Jnr. was born shortly after his father's death. The Laroches lived in poverty throughout the First World War and in 1918 Juliette received a settlement of 150,000 francs from Alexandre Millerand, the White Star Line's advocate. She used the monies to open a fabric-dyeing business in her home. Simone died aged on 8th August 1973 and Louise died in January 1998. Juliette died on 10th January 1980 aged 91 and on her grave a plaque is engraved: 'Juliette Laroche 1889-1980, wife of Joseph Laroche, lost at sea on RMS Titanic, April 15th 1912.'

Did You Know That?

Alexandre Millerand became the President of France in 1920.

SS *Californian*

SS *Californian* was a steamship of Frederick Leyland & Company Ltd. (part of J.P. Morgan's International Mercantile Marine Company) launched on 26th November 1901 with her maiden voyage commencing on 31st January 1902. The ship was constructed by the Caledon Shipbuilding & Engineering Company in Dundee, Scotland. The ship, captained by Stanley Lord, will forever be remembered as the ship which might have saved *Titanic's* passengers, had it answered her distress signals. The *Californian* had left Liverpool on 5th April 1912 for Boston, Massachusetts carrying a mixed cargo but no passengers. On the evening of 14th April 1912, she received several ice warnings and at 6.30 pm Captain Lord ordered Cyril Evans, the wireless operator, to send an ice warning to the nearby *Antillian*, a message which was overheard by Harold Bride, the wireless operator on *Titanic.*

The message stated that three large icebergs had been sighted 15 miles (24 km) north of the course *Titanic* was on. Bride delivered the message to the bridge.

At 10.21 pm Lord took the decision to go no further after the *Californian* encountered a large ice field south of the Grand Banks of Newfoundland and ordered the engines to be stopped. At approximately 11:20 pm Lord saw what he thought was a steamship passing to the east of the *Californian's* position and instructed Evans to notify the ship – believed to be *Titanic* - that the *Californian* was stopped and surrounded by ice. Evans' call was rebuffed by Jack Phillips, the wireless operator on *Titanic*, as he was too busy dealing with messages sent and received by passengers. Around 11:28 pm Evans turned off his radio and went to bed. Third Officer Charles Victor Groves on the *Californian* attempted to raise the ship by Morse lamp at 11:30 pm but had no luck. It was about this time – 11:40 pm – that *Titanic* struck the iceberg. Shortly after midnight Second Officer Herbert Stone took over the watch on the *Californian* from Groves. At 00:45 am Stone observed what he thought was a shooting star over the ship, but when he saw four more he realised they were rockets. He reported this to Lord, who by this time was resting in the Chart Room. Lord asked if they were private company signals. Stone replied that he did not know but that they appeared to be white rockets. Lord ordered him to attempt contact again via the Morse lamp, but no reply was received. Meanwhile, Stone and Third Officer Gibson, who had returned to the bridge, observed three more rockets, making a total of eight. Stone directed Gibson to wake Lord and inform him that they had seen eight rockets and that the steamer appeared to be disappearing to the southwest. Lord's only reply was to ask if there were colours in the rockets. He did not wake Evans, the wireless operator; had he done so, Evans would have immediately heard *Titanic's* calls of distress.

A great deal of debate, often heated, exists to this day owing to some information suggesting that the *Californian* could not possibly have seen the *Titanic* from her position. However, the fact is inescapable that *Titanic* fired eight white rockets, and eight white rockets were observed by the *Californian* during the time *Titanic* was signalling for help. Lord was condemned for his inaction and tried for years to clear his name, but without success. Indeed, both the American and British official inquiries into the *Titanic* disaster reached the decision that the *Californian* was most likely to be the '*Mystery Ship*' in close proximity to the *Titanic* when she was sending distress signals. In July 1912 the Leyland Line asked Captain Lord to resign his commission, which he reluctantly did. However, Lord was back at sea less than seven months later when John Latta, the owner of the Nitrate Producers Steamship Co. (Lawther/Latta), offered him a commission. Lord commenced employment with Lawther/Latta in February 1913.

Did You Know That?

Captain Stanley Lord was forced to retire in March 1927 as a result of his failing eyesight. He was 49 years old at the time.

William James Pirrie – 1st Viscount Pirrie

William James Pirrie was born on 31st May 1847 in Quebec, Canada. His parents were both Irish and when he was just 2 years old the family noved to Ireland and lived in Conlig, County Down. He attended Royal Belfast Academical Institute and studied there until he was 15, when he left to take up a position as a gentleman apprentice at Harland & Wolff in 1862. In 1874 he was made a partner in the Belfast shipyard and when Sir Edward Harland died in 1895 he was appointed Chairman of Harland & Wolff, a position he was to hold until his death.

His sister, Eliza, was the mother of Thomas Andrews Jnr. whom Pirrie and Alexander Carlisle worked alongside in drawing up the plans to build RMS *Titanic*. In early January 1912 it was widely reported in Belfast that Lord William James Pirrie, the Chairman of Harland & Wolff Shipyard, had booked the Ulster Hall, Bedford Street, for the evening of 8th February 1912 for a meeting which would be attended by Winston Churchill, First Lord of the Admiralty, and John Redmond, leader of the Irish Nationalist Party. Tensions were running high in the city at the time with the Unionists, led by Edward Carson, strongly opposing a proposed 'Home Rule Bill' Pirrie, like Churchill a Liberal, was anxious to divorce himself from the political furore and bigoted attitude of the Unionists against the Nationalists. However, the Unionists then booked the Ulster Hall for the same date with the intention of not vacating the building when it came to the time for Lord Pirrie's meeting to take place. Rather than risk the chance of confrontation with the Unionists, Lord Pirrie moved his meeting to a marquee in Celtic Park, Belfast, a predominantly Nationalist area. No major incidents took place at the Celtic Park meeting but just four days later, 12th February 1912, Lord Pirrie was covered in eggs and flour as he attempted to embark on his luxury steam yacht, *The Valiant*, docked at Larne Harbour. The crowd was enraged with Lord Pirrie's comment during his meeting that the Unionists were bigoted towards the Nationalists. On 19th February 1912, with *Titanic's* maiden voyage just over seven weeks away, Lord Pirrie was lying in a London hospital bed suffering from an enlarged prostate gland. Indeed, the voyage took place while the 65-year-old recuperated on his yacht in the Baltic Ocean.

Lord Pirrie died of pneumonia on 6th June 1924 while at sea on a business trip to South America. His body was brought back on the White Star Line's RMS *Olympic*, the older sister of the *Titanic*, and he was buried in Belfast City Cemetery. A memorial to Lord William James Pirrie was unveiled in the grounds of Belfast City Hall in 2006.

Did You Know That?

William James Pirrie was elected Lord Mayor of Belfast in 1896 and became Belfast's inaugural Freeman of the City in 1898.

Benjamin Guggenheim

Benjamin Guggenheim, the fifth of seven sons of the wealthy mining magnate Meyer Guggenheim, was a passenger onboard RMS *Titanic*. He was joined by his mistress, a French singer named Madame Léontine Aubart, his valet, Victor Giglio, his chauffeur, René Pernot and Madame Aubart's maid, Emma Sägesser. When *Titanic* struck the iceberg, Guggenheim and Giglio were asleep in their first-class cabin while Pernot was in his cabin in second class. Madame Aubart and Emma Sägesser were placed in Lifeboat No.9 while Guggenheim and Giglio returned to their cabin and changed into their evening wear. It is claimed that Guggenheim told a survivor: 'We've dressed up in our best and are prepared to go down like gentlemen. If anything should happen to me, tell my wife I've done my best in doing my duty.' All three men lost their lives in the disaster and their bodies, if even recovered, were never identified. Both Madame Aubart and Emma Sägesser survived and died in the same year, 1964.

Did You Know That?

In James Cameron's 1997 movie *Titanic,* Guggenheim was played by Michael Ensign.

Colonel John Jacob Astor IV

Colonel John Jacob Astor IV was an American millionaire who died in the sinking of the *Titanic*. Astor was an astute businessman, real estate builder, inventor and writer. In 1897, he built the Astoria Hotel in New York which at the time was dubbed 'the world's most luxurious hotel'. His inventions included a brake for a bicycle, a pneumatic road-improver, a 'vibratory disintegrator' which helped produce gas from peat moss, and a turbine engine. In 1894, his book entitled *A Journey in Other Worlds* was published, a science fiction novel set in the year 2000. Four years later he was made a lieutenant colonel of a US volunteer battalion which he self-financed in Cuba during the Spanish-American War. Astor, aged 47, married for a second time in 1911 and when he discovered that his 18-year old wife, Madeline Talmadge Force, became pregnant when they were touring Europe and Egypt, he decided to return to the USA where the baby would be born. Astor booked a first-class suite on *Titanic's* maiden voyage from Southampton to New York on 10th April with the Astors joining the ship when it stopped off at

Cherbourg, France. When *Titanic* struck the iceberg Astor put Madeline in a lifeboat and when he asked if he could accompany her, he was politely refused permission. He lost his life in the disaster and his body was recovered by the *Mackay-Bennett* one week after *Titanic* sank, 22nd April 1912. He was identified by the initials 'JJA' which had been sewn on the label of his jacket. When his body was dragged from the sea a gold watch, cufflinks (gold with diamonds), a diamond ring with three stones, £225, $2,440, £5 in gold, 7s. in silver, 5 ten-franc pieces, a gold pencil and a pocketbook were found on him. According to members of the crew of the *Mackay-Bennett*, Astor's body was covered in blood and soot leading them to think that he was killed by the first funnel after it collapsed. He was buried in Trinity Church Cemetery, New York.

--- Did You Know That? ---

John Jacob Astor IV was the richest person on RMS *Titanic*, worth an estimated $100 million.

SS *Mount Temple*

Mount Temple was one of the ships that responded to the distress signals issued by RMS *Titanic* after she struck an iceberg. *Mount Temple*, under the command of Captain James Henry Moore, reached the location from which *Titanic* sent her SOS around 04.30 am but was separated from the scene of the wreck by an ice field and therefore was unable to assist in the rescue operations. The ship was built by Armstrong, Whitworth & Co., Newcastle, England and launched on 18th June 1901. She made her maiden voyage, Newcastle-upon-Tyne to New Orleans, USA on 19th September 1901. In September 1914, shortly after the outbreak of the First World War, she was commissioned by the British government as a troop carrier but returned to commercial service the following year. On 6th December 1916, she was captured approximately 455 miles north west of the Azores islands and scuttled by the German surface raider SS *Moewe*, resulting in the loss of four lives. The remaining 107 aboard were interned by the Germans. The *Mount Temple* was the fourth of 18 vessels that Canadian Pacific Lines lost during World War I.

--- Did You Know That? ---

The *Mount Temple* was carrying a varied cargo when she was captured, including 22 wooden crates of dinosaur fossils, collected in the Badlands of Alberta, Canada by Charles H. Sternberg and his son, Levi. The fossils were en route to Sir Arthur Smith-Woodward, keeper of the British Museum's Natural History Department.

The Major

Arthur Godfrey Peuchen was born on 18th April 1859 in Montreal, Quebec, Canada. He was the son of Godfrey Peuchen of Westphalia, Prussia and Eliza Eleanor Clark of Hull, England. His father was a railroad contractor in South America (his grandfather had managed the London, Brighton, and Midlands Railway). He attended a private school in Montreal, Canada and moved to Toronto in 1871. In Toronto he signed up for the Queen's Own Rifles becoming a lieutenant in 1888, captain in 1894 and in 1904, a major. Aged 52, he was the Vice-Commodore of the Royal Canadian Yacht Club and decided that he wished to go on *Titanic's* maiden voyage. However, it is reported that when he learned that Captain Edward Smith was in charge of the great ship, he said: 'Surely not that man!' Peuchen's crossing on the *Titanic* was to be his fortieth transatlantic voyage. When Lifeboat No.6 was lowered down, Robert Hichens, who was already in the lifeboat called for help. *Titanic's* Second Officer Charles Lightoller then asked Peuchen to help them and he agreed, sliding down 25 feet of rope to reach the lifeboat. It is said that he left behind $200,000 in bonds and $100,000 in stocks in his cabin. Whereas many of the men who survived the disaster, none more so than J. Bruce Ismay, became social outcasts and accused of cowardice, Peuchen sought out Lightoller aboard the rescue ship, *Carpathia*, and asked him to sign an affidavit which stated Peuchen had been ordered by the officer to man Lifeboat No.6. He died on 7th December 1929 aged 69 in Toronto and was buried at Mount Pleasant Cemetery, Toronto.

————————— Did You Know That? —————————

Some of the survivors in Lifeboat No.6 stated that Peuchen had complained that he was tired and stopped rowing. However, unlucky for Peuchen the 'Unsinkable' Molly Brown was in the lifeboat and reportedly made him start rowing again.

Canadian Steamship *Mackay-Bennett*

The Canadian steamship *Mackay-Bennett* was a cable repair ship registered in London (but working out of Halifax, Nova Scotia) and owned by the Commercial Cable Company. The ship was built by John Elder & Co., Glasgow, Scotland and was launched from the Fairfield Shipyard in September 1884. The *Mackay-Bennett* was christened by Mrs Mackay, wife of the popular millionaire president of the company. The ship was used to repair undersea cables in the North Atlantic but following the sinking of *Titanic* the White Star Line hired the vessel at an agreed rate of $550 per day to carry out the difficult task of recovering dead bodies which were floating in the North Atlantic. The ship sailed under the command of Captain Frederick Harold Larnder from the wharf at 155–157 Upper Water Street, Halifax,

Nova Scotia at 12:28 pm on Wednesday 17th April 1912. Also on board were Canon Kenneth Cameron Hind of All Saints Cathedral, Halifax, and John R. Snow, Jr., the chief embalmer with the firm of John Snow & Co., the province of Nova Scotia's largest undertaking firm, which the White Star Line hired to oversee the arrangements. The *Mackay-Bennett* found 306 of the 1,523 *Titanic* victims, more than any other ship (328 bodies were recovered in total). Of the 306 bodies recovered by the *Mackay-Bennett*, 116 were buried at sea (only 56 of the 116 were identified), 190 bodies remained on board. The ship arrived at 'Flagship Pier' at North Coaling Jetty No. 4, HM Dockyard, Nova Scotia, Canada at approximately 9:30 am on Tuesday 30th April 1912. The ship was retired (storage hulk) in May 1922.

——————— Did You Know That? ———————

During 'The Blitz' on Britain in World War II, the *Mackay-Bennett* was sunk during a German bombing raid but later refloated. The ship was scrapped in 1963.

Eleanor Ilene Johnson Shuman

Eleanor Ilene Johnson was born on 23rd August 1910 in St. Charles, Illinois, USA. She was the daughter of the newspaper editor Oskar Walter Johnson and his wife, Alice Wilhelmina Backberg. In early 1912, Eleanor's mother took her and her older brother, Harold (born in 1908), to the family home in Finland to visit Alice's father who was dying. When they ended their visit they travelled to England to catch their ship back to the USA. However, when they arrived in England they learned that there was a national coal strike and their ship had cancelled its transatlantic crossing due to a shortage of coal. They discovered that RMS *Titanic* had sufficient fuel stocks put aside to make its maiden voyage to New York leaving Southampton on 10th April 1912, and Alice managed to book three of the last places available in third class. Eleanor was just 18 months old when she boarded *Titanic*. Alice and her two children shared a cabin with Elin Braf and Helmina Nilsson. After *Titanic* struck the iceberg, Eleanor and her two children were placed in lifeboat No. 15 and survived the sinking after they were picked up by the RMS *Carpathia*. They arrived safely in New York on 18th April 1912. It is claimed that Alice got into the lifeboat with Eleanor in her arms while Harold was tossed into the boat from the ship by a member of the crew. In 1934, Eleanor married Delbert Shuman, an International Harvester engineer. Eleanor worked for the Elgin Watch Company, Illinois and later as a telephone operator until her retirement in 1962. She died on 7th March 1998 in Elgin, Illinois aged 87.

Did You Know That?

In 1958, Eleanor and her brother attended the New York premiere
of the movie *A Night To Remember*.

The *Titanic*'s Orphans

Michel Marcel Navratil, and his brother Edmond Roger Navratil, were aboard
Titanic with their father, Michel, when she struck the iceberg and were two of the
last living survivors of the sinking. Michel Snr. was attempting to emigrate to the
USA with his two sons after his wife, Marcelle, had been awarded full custody of
the boys on their divorce. After *Titanic* struck the iceberg their father placed them
in Collapsible D, the last lifeboat launched. When the two young boys were in the
lifeboat they were fed biscuits by Hugh Woolner, a first-class passenger. Their
lifeboat was picked up by the RMS *Carpathia* and they arrived safely in New York
on 18th April 1912, three days after *Titanic* went down. On their arrival in New
York they could not identify themselves as they did not speak English. However, a
French-speaking first-class passenger named Margaret Hays took responsibility for
the boys and lovingly cared for them at her home until their mother could be
located. As a result of many newspaper articles featuring a photograph of the
brothers, their mother sailed to New York and was reunited with her sons on 16th
May 1912. She returned to France with Michel and Edmond on the RMS *Oceanic*.
Michel, aged just 3 when *Titanic* sank, later claimed to remember his father telling
him: 'My child, when your mother comes for you, as she surely will, tell her that
I loved her dearly and still do. Tell her I expected her to follow us, so that we might
all live happily together in the peace and freedom of the New World.'

Did You Know That?

Michel and Edmond were known as the 'Titanic Orphans' as they were
the only children rescued without a parent or guardian (until their
mother was reunited with them).

Mary Davies

Mary Wilburn (née Davies) was 29 years old when she boarded RMS *Titanic* at
Southampton. She was going to visit her sister who lived on Staten Island, New
York. Mary survived the sinking of the ship and a few months after the disaster she
returned home to England, courtesy of the White Star Line. However, the following
year she returned to the USA where she worked as a cook and then in 1915, she
married John A. Wilburn. Mary, born on 17th May 1883 in London, died on 29th
July 1987 in Syracuse, New York. When she died, aged 104, she became, and still
remains, the oldest living survivor of the disaster.

Ernst Axel Martin Welin

Ernst Axel Martin Welin, 1862–1951, was a Swedish inventor and industrialist. In 1889, he started his own engineering company, Welin Davit & Engineering Company Limited. Welin invented a new and improved davit for lowering boats from aboard ships, the Welin davit. RMS *Titanic* was equipped with Welin davits and after the sinking his sales of the Welin davit increased significantly.

Did You Know That?

Between 1886 and 1888, Welin worked as a weapons designer for Thorsten Nordenfelt in London.

Major Butt – The Forgotten Hero

Major Archibald Willingham Butt was born on 26th September 1865 in Augusta, Georgia, USA. In 1888, he commenced a career in journalism following his graduation from the University of the South in Tennessee. His first job was with the Louisville *Courier Journal* and he later was employed as a reporter in Washington for a group of Southern-based newspapers. It was during his time in the capital that he was appointed Secretary of the Mexican Embassy. On 2nd January 1900, he was appointed Assistant Quartermaster, United States Volunteers, and served his country during the Spanish-American War. Archibald Butt then served as a Quartermaster in the Philippines from March 1900 – June 1903 and after a brief period in Cuba (September 1906 – August 1908) he was made military aide to President Theodore Roosevelt. When William Howard Taft succeeded Roosevelt as the President of the USA on 4th March 1909 he retained the services of Archibald Butt and the two men became close friends. In early 1912, Taft was becoming increasingly unpopular with the American public and Roosevelt began to make overtures about running for office again in March 1913. Finding himself caught between his two friends Archibald Butt's health began to deteriorate and he requested a six weeks' leave of absence from his White House duties. Butt sailed for Europe with his friend Francis Millet, who was en route to Rome on business at the American Academy, which he directed. Both men were booked to return to the USA on RMS *Titanic*'s maiden voyage with Major Butt boarding the ship at Southampton as a first-class passenger (ticket number 113050, £26 11s), Cabin B-38. On the night *Titanic* struck the iceberg, Major Butt was dining with the ship's Captain at the Widener Dinner Party in the À La Carte Restaurant. After dinner the Major and his friends retired to the Café Parisien, a popular meeting place for the vessel's first-class passengers. When *Titanic* struck the iceberg, Captain Smith is said to have informed Major Butt that the ship was doomed and that the lifeboats were being readied. Many eyewitness reports state that upon hearing this Butt immediately offered his services, giving words of comfort to many women who

were crying whilst also barking out orders to members of the crew whom he felt needed to provide more assistance to the passengers.

A *Titanic* survivor, Mrs. Henry B. Harris, made the following statement: 'I saw Major Butt just before they put me into a collapsible raft with ever so many women from the steerage. The man's conduct will remain in my memory forever. He showed some of the other men how to behave when women and children were suffering that awful mental fear that came when we had to be huddled into those boats. Major Butt was near me, and I know very nearly everything he did. When the order to take to the boats came he became as one in supreme command. You would have thought he was at a White House Reception, so cool and calm was he. A dozen or so women became hysterical all at once as something connected with a lifeboat went wrong. Major Butt stepped to them and said: "Really you must not act like that; we are all going to see you through this thing." He helped the sailors re-arrange the rope or chain that had gone wrong and lifted some of the women in with gallantry. His was the manner we associate with the word aristocrat.'

When *Titanic* sank on 15th April 1912, President Taft knew nothing about it as he visited Poll's Theatre, Washington to watch a play entitled *Nobody's Widow*. The President had read in the papers that the ship had struck an iceberg but was under the impression that all aboard, including Major Butt, had been picked up and taken to safety at Halifax, Nova Scotia. However, when the news was given to him that lives were lost the President immediately went to the telegraph room at the White House where he told the operator to keep him fully informed throughout the night in relation to any news reports about the doomed liner. Shortly after midnight on 15th April 1912 the White Star Line received the following message: 'Have you any information concerning Major Butt? If you communicate at once I will greatly appreciate. William Howard Taft.' When the President was later told that his close friend and influential military aide, had perished in the disaster he was visibly shocked. At the memorial service held at Butt's home in Augusta on 2nd May 1912 in front of 1,500 mourners, President Taft called his former aide affectionately by his first name and choked with tears as he paid a personal tribute: 'If Archie could have selected a time to die he would have chosen the one God gave him. His life was spent in self-sacrifice, serving others. His forgetfulness of self had become a part of his nature. Everybody who knew him called him Archie. I couldn't prepare anything in advance to say here. I tried, but couldn't. He was too near me. He was loyal to my predecessor, Mr. Roosevelt, who selected him to be military aide, and to me he had become as a son or a brother.' Very few books or movies about *Titanic* mention the heroics of Major Butt but without question he was a calming influence for many on board a slowly sinking vessel while many of those whom he helped to safety certainly never forgot what he did for them that fateful night.

---------------------------- Did You Know That? ----------------------------

Major Butt accompanied President Taft to Washington Senators' opening
home game of the 1910 Major League Baseball (MLB) season.
It was the first time in history that a US President opened a game of
professional baseball, a tradition that remains in place today for the start
of an MLB season.

Three Quick Ladies

Winnifred Vera Quick was just 8 years old when *Titanic* sank. She was born on
23rd January 1904 in Plymouth, England. In 1910, her father, Frederick Charles
Quick, emigrated to Detroit, USA where he worked as a plasterer and when he
had enough money saved up he paid for his wife, Jane Richards Quick, and two
daughters (Winnifred and Phyllis May) to join him in the United States. Shortly
after his wife booked their passage. She was notified that her ship's sailing had been
cancelled as a result of the coal strike in England at the time and that they would
be transferred to the RMS *Titanic* which was setting sail for New York on its'
maiden voyage on 10th April 1912. The Quicks boarded *Titanic* at Southampton
as second-class passengers and Winnifred was seasick for most of the time. When
Titanic struck the iceberg, the Quicks were fast asleep in their beds and had to be
awakened by a steward who directed them up to A-Deck. Mrs Quick placed
Winnifred and Phyllis in Lifeboat No. 11 but she was at first refused permission
to join her children when one of the deckhands informed her that only children
were allowed in the lifeboat. However, after arguing with the deckhand she was
allowed to join her daughters. They were safely picked up by the RMS *Carpathia*
and a wireless message was sent to Mr Quick in New York that his family was safe
and well. When *Carpathia* docked in New York on 18th April 1912, the Quicks
were reunited. In 1918, Winnifred met Alois Van Tongerloo, a master carpenter,
and five years later they were married, going on to have five children. On 4th July
2002, Winnifred died in East Lansing, Michigan, USA, aged 98. Her sister died
in 1954 and her mother died in 1965.

---------------------------- Did You Know That? ----------------------------

Winnifred never returned to England after the *Titanic* disaster and never
participated in any of the events organised by survivors.

The CGS *Montmagny*

CGS *Montmagny*, a Canadian Government Steamship, was the third of four ships commissioned by the White Star Line to search for bodies in the aftermath of the sinking of *Titanic*. The ship sailed from Sorel, Quebec to Halifax, Nova Scotia to collect supplies. On Monday 6th May 1912, *Montmagny* left Halifax under the command of Captain Peter Crerar Johnson and Capitaine François-Xavier Pouliot. On board was Father Patrick McQuillan from St. Mary's Basilica, Halifax, Reverend Samuel Henry Prince from St. Paul's Church, Halifax, plus Cecil E. Zink, an undertaker from Dartmouth, and John R. Snow, Jr., the undertaker who had been on the *CS Mackay-Bennett*. *Montmagny* replaced the *Minia* to continue the search for bodies lost at sea. However, as with the previous attempts, the weather made conditions difficult and the *Montmagny* recovered only four bodies (body numbers 326 to 329), one of which was buried at sea. On Monday 13th May 1912, the remaining three bodies were brought to Louisbourg, Nova Scotia and shipped to Halifax via the Sydney & Louisbourg and Canadian National Railways. After a brief re-bunkering period during which more supplies were brought on board, *Montmagny* returned to the wreckage scene. Despite sailing as far as the Gulf Stream the search for additional bodies proved a fruitless task with only small pieces of wood lying on the surface of the water. On 23rd May 1912, *Montmagny* returned to Halifax and resumed her normal duties with the Canadian Government as a lighthouse supply and buoy tender. During the search for the bodies a crew member salvaged a chair which he then used for many years on his front porch. In 1969, the Russell family donated the chair to the Dartmouth Museum along with a life-jacket from *Titanic*. However, neither item was of any great interest to the museum whose theme was the story of Dartmouth and so they were placed in storage. The life-jacket was traded off some years later to a collector of *Titanic* memorabilia. On 30th July 1980, Edward Kamuda the President and founder of the *Titanic* Historical Society, attended the world premiere of the movie *Raise the Titanic* in Boston, Massachusetts, as a guest of the Copley Plaza Hotel and ICPR Public Relations of New York. During the post-premiere activities this original, authentic deck-type chair that had been obtained from the Dartmouth Heritage Museum by the Copley Plaza was donated to the *Titanic* Historical Society.

Did You Know That?

The wooden chairs on White Star Line ships were standard, some made with split cane seats while others had slats.

Helen Churchill Candee

Helen Churchill Candee (born Helen Churchill Hungerford), an American author, feminist, geographer, interior designer and journalist, was travelling in Europe in the spring of 1912, completing research for her new book entitled *The Tapestry Book*. However, when she received a telegram from her daughter, Edith, informing her that her son Harold had been hurt in a car accident she quickly made plans to return home on *Titanic*. After *Titanic* struck the iceberg she was rescued in Lifeboat 6. Helen Churchill Candee was a supporting character in Danielle Steele's novel *No Greater Love* which is based on the sinking of the *Titanic*. In 2003, she was portrayed in cameo in *Ghosts of the Abyss*, a Walt Disney 3-D documentary outlining James Cameron's (director of the 1997 movie *Titanic*) expedition to the wreck of the famous ocean liner. Candee was played by the actress Adriana Valdez with one scene depicting her character visiting the bow of *Titanic* on the evening before it sank, a similar scene to Jack and Rose's in Cameron's movie. She died aged 90 on 23rd August 1949 at her summer cottage at York Harbour, Maine, USA.

Did You Know That?

During the First World War (1914–18) Candee worked as a nurse in Milan and Rome for the Italian Red Cross and was decorated for her service. One of her patients in Milan was the American journalist and writer, Ernest Hemingway.

Jacques Futrelle

The American journalist, mystery crime writer and theatre manager, Jacques Futrelle, and his wife were returning to New York as first-class passengers on *Titanic* when the ship left Southampton on 10th April 1912. Futrelle's most famous detective character was Professor Augustus S.F.X. Van Dusen, known as 'The Thinking Machine', who managed to solve extremely difficult crimes. Futrelle's *The Problem of Cell 13,* is considered to be one of the most famous detective stories ever written. After *Titanic* struck the iceberg Futrelle ensured that his wife had a safe place on a lifeboat, helping her into Lifeboat No.9. Futrelle died in the disaster and several of his stories, which he had written during his stay in England, went down with the ship.

The Van Billiards

In early 1900, Austin Blyler van Billiard emigrated from the USA to Europe to work as an electrician at the Universal Exposition that was opening in Paris, France in April 1900. Whilst working at the Universal Exposition, he met an English lady named Maude Murray whom he married on 3rd November 1900. They had two children, James William (born on 20th August 1901) and Walter John (born on 28th February 1903). In 1906 they moved to Central Africa where Austin worked as a diamond merchant and two more children were born there. In 1912, Austin and his wife decided to travel to the USA where Austin hoped to find employment as a diamond merchant. The family made their way to England on a French steamer and stayed with Maude's parents in London. Austin booked himself and his two oldest children on *Titanic* with the intention of sending enough money for his wife and remaining two children to join them later. They boarded *Titanic* at Southampton as third-class passengers and all three lost their lives. Austin's body and Walter's body were recovered from the Atlantic by the SS *Mackay-Bennett* but James's body, if found, was never identified. Maude was awarded £640 compensation for the loss of her husband and sons, £100 of which was contributed by the Red Cross.

--------------------- Did You Know That? ---------------------

The 1900 Universal Expedition began in Paris on 15th April 1900, exactly 12 years to the day before the three van Billiards' bodies were prematurely claimed by the North Atlantic.

The Newells

Marjorie Newell was on board *Titanic* for the ship's maiden voyage along with her father, Arthur, a successful banker and her older sister, Madeline. The Newells boarded *Titanic* at Cherbourg as first-class passengers and were making their way back to Lexington, Massachusetts after a trip to Egypt and Palestine. Mr Newell occupied Cabin No. D-48 while his daughters were in D-36. Shortly after *Titanic* struck the iceberg at 11.40 pm on Sunday, Arthur awoke his two girls and ushered them up to the boat deck where he placed them in Lifeboat No.6. The two girls survived the disaster but Arthur lost his life. His body was recovered by the SS *Mackay-Bennett*. Marjorie recalled the moment their rescue ship, the RMS *Carpathia*, docked in New York on 18th April 1912 and how her mother, Mary, almost fainted with shock upon the sight of her two girls minus her husband. Mrs Newell would not permit *Titanic* to be discussed at the family home and slept with her late husband's watch tucked under her pillow. Marjorie died peacefully in her sleep on 11th June 1992, aged 103.

--------------------- Did You Know That? ---------------------

When she died Marjorie was the last remaining survivor who was a first-class passenger on *Titanic*.

Captain Sir Arthur Henry Rostron

Arthur Henry Rostron was born in Astley Bridge, Bolton, Lancashire on 14th May 1869. In 1886, aged 17, he joined the Royal Navy's training vessel HMS *Conway* as a cadet. Two years later he was sent on an apprenticeship to the Waverley Line of Messrs, Williamson, Milligan and Co., Liverpool and served on *Cedric the Saxon*, an iron clipper ship. Over the course of the next five years he gained valuable experience whilst serving on various vessels which took him all around the world. After successfully passing his extra master's certificate he joined the Cunard Line in January 1895 and served on the RMS *Umbria* as Fourth Officer. Spells on other Cunard vessels (*Aurania, Cherbourg, Etruria, Saxonia, Servia* and *Ultonia*) followed before he was given the commission of First Officer on the RMS *Lusitania* in 1907. On 6th September 1907, the day before RMS *Lusitania*'s maiden voyage, he was appointed Captain of the *Bresica*, a cargo ship. Four years later Rostron took command of his first passenger ship, the *Pennonia*, on the New York to Mediterranean route (he also commanded the *Ivernia*, the *Pavonia* and the *Saxonia* 1907–11). He was a Royal Navy Reserve during the Russo-Japanese War. On 12th January 1912, he was presented with his sixth command, Captain of the Cunard liner RMS *Carpathia*. Four months later, 11th April 1912, the RMS *Carpathia* left New York for a voyage to the Mediterranean with scheduled stops at Fiume, Genoa, Gibraltar, Naples and Trieste. Rostron will forever be remembered as the saviour of 705 of *Titanic*'s passengers and crew. Captain Rostron was in his cabin when his First Officer, H. Dean, and his Radio Operator, Harold Cottam, knocked on his door in the early hours of Monday 15th April 1912 to inform him that *Titanic* was sending distress signals. He asked Cottam if he was positive that the distress calls were from *Titanic* and when told that they were, he immediately ordered his ship to be turned around and to steam to her assistance. Captain Rostron received worldwide praise for his humane efforts to reach the ill-fated liner before she sank, and for his efficient preparations for and conduct of the rescue of the survivors. Whilst en route to assist *Titanic*, Captain Rostron, nicknamed 'The Electric Spark', because of his efficiency and masterful planning, made plans for *Titanic*'s survivors and gave various orders to his officers and crew including: recall all off-duty crew members to re-commence duty, turn off the ship's steam heating system to give the ship more speed, set up first aid rooms in the ship's dining rooms, gather all spare blankets, prepare drinks for the survivors (coffee, tea and brandy), allocate crew members to draw up a list of survivors rescued and at the same time ensure that the passengers on *Carpathia* were not alarmed at the ship's decision to turn back towards New York.

In 1913, he was appointed captain of the *Caronia* before being given the command of the Carmania, *Campania* and the *Lusitania*. During World War I he commanded the *Aulania* which was converted into a troopship and in 1915, he was involved in the Gallipoli campaign. In September 1915, he left the *Aulania* to take control of the RMS Mauretania before being made Captain of the *Ivernia* in April

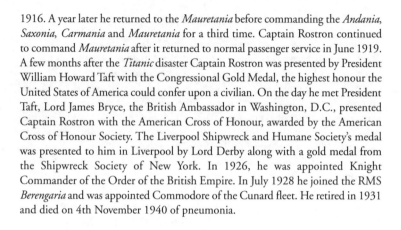

1916. A year later he returned to the *Mauretania* before commanding the *Andania*, *Saxonia*, *Carmania* and *Mauretania* for a third time. Captain Rostron continued to command *Mauretania* after it returned to normal passenger service in June 1919. A few months after the *Titanic* disaster Captain Rostron was presented by President William Howard Taft with the Congressional Gold Medal, the highest honour the United States of America could confer upon a civilian. On the day he met President Taft, Lord James Bryce, the British Ambassador in Washington, D.C., presented Captain Rostron with the American Cross of Honour, awarded by the American Cross of Honour Society. The Liverpool Shipwreck and Humane Society's medal was presented to him in Liverpool by Lord Derby along with a gold medal from the Shipwreck Society of New York. In 1926, he was appointed Knight Commander of the Order of the British Empire. In July 1928 he joined the RMS *Berengaria* and was appointed Commodore of the Cunard fleet. He retired in 1931 and died on 4th November 1940 of pneumonia.

Did You Know That?

When Cunard took the decision to scrap Captain Rostron's beloved RMS *Mauretania* in 1935, he was invited to sail on her for her last voyage, a trip to a ship breaker's yard in Scotland. However, when the moment came for him to board the ship he was so overcome with emotion that he could not force himself to go aboard and instead wiped the tears away from his eyes as he waved her off from the quay side.

■ THE MOVIE TRIVIA ■■■■■■■■■■■■■■■

James Cameron forfeited his $8 million director's salary and his percentage of the gross earnings from the movie when the studio raised concerns at how much over budget the movie was running.

Titanic's Big Sister –RMS *Olympic*

On 20th October 1910, Ship No.400 built by the Harland & Wolff Shipyard eased her way down the slipway in Belfast (her keel had been laid on 16th December 1908). The ship launched that day was RMS *Olympic*, *Titanic*'s older sister. The 45,324 ton Olympic Class ocean liner was delivered to her owners, the White Star Line, on 31st May 1911, the first of three similar ships which J. Bruce Ismay hoped would surpass the vessels owned by the White Star Line's principal rival, Cunard. Up to the launch of the *Olympic* the Cunard Line's RMS *Lusitania* and RMS *Mauretania* dominated transatlantic passenger travel.

As many as 100,000 people were gathered in and around the Belfast shipyard to see her launched with her hull painted grey to make her stand out more in the black and white photographs taken of her by the newspaper men in attendance (she was later repainted black). RMS *Olympic* set sail on her maiden voyage on 14th June 1911 from Southampton to New York, the same route RMS *Titanic* would start on 10 months later. On board the leviathan for her maiden voyage were her designer, Thomas Andrews, and a 'Guarantee Group' from Harland & Wolff who would look for ways to improve the vessel. She was a commanding sight as she made her way out of the White Star Dock at Southampton harbour with thousands waving her off at the quay side. Like *Titanic* she had a dummy fourth funnel which was solely for ventilation purposes. However, although the *Olympic* surpassed the *Lusitania* and the *Mauretania* for luxury, she could not match the speed of her rivals, which were both winners of the coveted blue riband for the fastest Atlantic crossing. On 20th September 1911, under the command of Captain Edward Smith (later to captain *Titanic* on her maiden voyage), she collided with the Royal Navy cruiser HMS *Hawke* under the command of Commander W.F. Blunt in the Spithead Channel. It is reported that Captain Smith's subordinate stated that the Commander of the *Hawke* was entirely to blame for the accident with Captain Smith commenting: 'Anyhow, the *Olympic* is unsinkable, and the *Titanic* will be the same when she is put in commission.' The ships were sailing through the channel when *Hawke* veered into the starboard side of *Olympic* which was travelling at a speed of about 19 knots. The collision destroyed *Hawke's* bow and resulted in two large holes in the *Olympic's* hull, one above the waterline and another below it. Fortunately, no one was killed, and the two ships were able to make it back to port under their own steam. *Olympic* made her way back to Belfast where she was repaired at the Harland & Wolff Shipyard, resulting in a delay to work on *Titanic*. At the subsequent Admiralty Court investigation into the collision the *Hawke* and her crew were exonerated from any blame, and it was thought that the large amount of water displaced by the *Olympic* had generated a suction that had drawn *Hawke* off her course, causing her to veer into *Titanic's* big sister. The repair work to the *Olympic* resulted in the White Star Line placing an announcement in *The Times* on 11th October 1911, stating that the date for *Titanic's* maiden voyage had been put back from 20th March 1912 to 10th April 1912.

In February 1912, *Olympic* lost a propeller blade out in the North Atlantic and once again she had to return to Harland & Wolff for repairs. On 9th October 1912, less than six months after her younger sister sank, the *Olympic* was withdrawn from service and went back to her place of birth to be refitted with new safety measures and devices after valuable lessons were learned following *Titanic's* demise. The refitting included an increased number of wooden lifeboats being installed along her boat deck, taking the total up to 64; an inner watertight skin was constructed in the boiler and engine rooms; several of the watertight bulkheads were extended up to B-Deck. Another major piece of work carried out on her was the outward extension of the Café Parisien and À La Carte restaurant. She returned

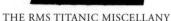
to normal service in 1913 and remained the largest ocean liner in the world until the Hamburg America Line's SS *Imperator* entered passenger service in June 1913.

On 27th October 1914, less than three months after the outbreak of the First World War, the *Olympic* went to the help of HMS *Audacious* which had struck a mine off the north coast of Donegal, Ireland laid by the German auxiliary mine layer *Berlin*. Captain Haddock of the *Olympic* took aboard all non-essential crew from the *Audacious* and along with the destroyer *Fury* attempted to tow the battleship towards Lough Swilly. However, this proved fruitless when the towlines parted and she sank. In early September 1915, the White Star Line received notification from the British Government that the *Olympic* would be required for Government service throughout the duration of the war. She was converted into a troopship and fitted out with 12-pound and 4.7-inch guns. The *Olympic* transported British troops to Mudros, Greece to fight in the Gallipoli campaign and on 1st October 1915, she picked up survivors from the French ship *Provincia* which had been sunk by a German U-Boat off Cape Matapan, Greece. The Canadian government secured her services 1916–17 to transport its troops from Halifax, Nova Scotia to Britain. During her period serving the Canadians she was given more weapons (6-inch guns) and was painted with a dazzle camouflage scheme in 1917. When the United States of America entered the war, *Olympic* transported thousands of US troops to Europe but still served Canada's war needs. On 12th May 1918, the *Olympic* spotted and attacked a German U-Boat (U103) while en route to Southampton with US troops onboard. The U-Boat dived after coming under fire from *Olympic* but before she could dive deep enough to be safe, *Olympic*, under the command of Captain Bertram Fox Hayes, rammed her, hitting her conning tower and ripping through her hull with her portside propeller. The U-Boat's crew blew her ballast tanks and scuttled and abandoned the submarine. However, the incident resulted in *Olympic* having to return to Southampton with two hull plates dented and her stern twisted to one side.

In February 1919, three months after the First World War ended, *Old Reliable*, the nickname given to *Olympic* in recognition of her efforts during the war, was in Liverpool when a dent was discovered below the waterline of her hull. It is believed that the dent was caused by a torpedo from a German U-Boat which had failed to detonate. At the end of the summer of 1919, she returned to Belfast to be restored as a passenger liner. She was given a new luxurious interior and converted to burn oil and recommenced her transatlantic passenger service in 1920. The *Olympic* was given further refits in 1927–28, 1928–29 and 1932. On 15th May 1934, *Olympic* struck the Nantucket lightship as she was making her way into a fog-bound New York. *Olympic* knew that there were other vessels close by and homed in on the radio of the Nantucket lightship but ended up striking her, resulting in her sinking with the loss of 7 of her 11 crew, four going down with the ship and three dying later of their injuries.

In December 1933, the Oceanic Steam Navigation Company (the White Star Line) agreed to merge with the Cunard Line following years of discussions and

buy-out/merger schemes from as early as 1930–31. The new Cunard White Star Line Limited was formed in May 1934. It received a government loan to build the *Queen Mary* and set about retiring the oldest ships in its fleet including the *Olympic*. In 1935, the *Olympic* was sold to Sir John Jarvis for £100,000 to be partially demolished at the Jarrow Shipyard which would bring much needed employment to the North East of England. In 1937, *Olympic's* hull was towed to Inverkeithing, Fife, Scotland to TW Ward's yard for final demolition. However, before she was broken up her fittings were sold at auction with some purchased by the White Swan Hotel in Alnwick, England. Some of *Olympic's* panelling, bathrooms, electrical light fittings, flooring and furniture was bought by Douglas Smith of Smith & Walton to fit out his company's new paint factory in Haltwhistle, Northumberland. In early 2000, 'Celebrity Cruises' purchased the original wooden panels from *Olympic's* À La Carte restaurant and created Olympic's restaurant onboard their latest cruise ship, *Millennium,* which was launched in July 2000.

Did You Know That?

Olympic's ramming of the German U-Boat is the only known incident of the First World War in which a passenger liner sank an enemy warship.

Annie Clemmer Funk – *Titanic's* Heroine

Annie Clemmer Funk was born on 12th April 1874 in Bally, Pennsylvania, USA to German parents who were devout Mennonites and consequently she was born to piety and God. She studied the Bible at Moody Bible College and in 1906 she decided to become the first Mennonite woman missionary. Annie served as a missionary in Janjgir in the Central Province of India from November 1906 to April 1912. Whilst in India she learned to speak the Hindi language and in 1908 opened the first school for girls in Janjgir.

In the spring of 1912 Annie received a telegram at the school advising her that her mother was ill and requesting her to return home to Pennsylvania. Annie made her way to Liverpool where she booked a place on the American Line's *SS Haverford* which was bound for Philadelphia, USA. However, a coal strike in Britain resulted in the SS Haverford's sailing being cancelled. Unluckily for Annie as it later transpired, she managed to book a second-class place on *Titanic's* maiden voyage to New York from Southampton and transferred her ticket at a cost of £13.00.

She spent her 38th and last birthday aboard *Titanic*, the most luxurious ocean liner in the world at the time. Thirty minutes or so after *Titanic* struck an iceberg, Annie was awoken by a steward and told to put on her life-jacket and go up on to the boat deck where she was later loaded into a lifeboat. However, when Annie saw a crying mother standing on the boat deck with her two children waiting to be placed in a lifeboat, she got out of her already full lifeboat and gave her place to the thankful mother and her children. When *Titanic* sank, the extremely brave and righteous Annie went down with the ship. Her body, if ever recovered, was never identified. Two memorials were erected in her honour: one in her home town in Pennsylvania at the Hereford Mennonite Church Cemetery and one in India at the *Annie C. Funk Memorial School* in Janjgir. The inscription on the Memorial in Pennsylvania reads:

Erected by
The Eastern District Conference
of the Mennonite Church
in Memory of

ANNIE C. FUNK
Missionary in India 1906-1912

Daughter of
James B. And Susan Funk
Born April 12, 1874. Died April 15, 1912
Aged 38 Years And 3 Days.

She was coming home on her first furlough,
when death overtook her in the wreck of the steamship titanic
off the coast of newfoundland.
Her life was one of service in the spirit of the master –
not to be ministered unto but to minister.

Did You Know That?

The children of the Quakertown and Philadelphia Mennonite congregations raised enough money to purchase Annie a bicycle which she rode in India along with her Bible and a portable organ.

The Real 'Jack' Dawson

Just as we saw in James Cameron's 1997 blockbuster movie '*Titanic*', a man who signed his name J. Dawson did board the RMS *Titanic* at Southampton on Wednesday 10th April 1912 for the famous leviathan's doomed maiden voyage. However, the J. stood for Joseph, not Jack as in Cameron's epic and he was born in the slums of Dublin in September 1888. In March 1909, following the death of his mother to breast cancer, Joseph's father, Patrick, asked his brother Thomas, a Priest living in Birkenhead, Liverpool to help his son Joseph and his daughter Catherine commence a better life for themselves. All three of Joseph's uncles on his father's side became priests: Bernard, Thomas and William. So Joseph and his sister Catherine made their way by boat to their Uncle Tom's home.

Not long after arriving in England the 21-year old Dawson enlisted in the Royal Army Medical Corps, just as his half-brother Timothy had done at the turn of the 20th century. Shortly after entering the Army he took-up boxing and was soon posted to a large military hospital in Netley, situated just three miles away from Southampton. However he became disillusioned with army life and set his ambitions on a life at sea after reading about the world's great ocean liners, many of which were close by at Southampton harbour. After receiving a temporary certificate of discharge from his army service on 30th June 1911, he visited Southampton where he met John Priest, a ship's fireman. The pair became very friendly and Joseph started dating John's sister, Nellie, while at the same time dreaming about life on a luxury liner having listened to numerous tales from John. His dreams came true when he found work as a coal trimmer on the RMS *Majestic* and then, aged 23, he secured work as a old coal trimmer alongside John on *Titanic*. As a member of the ship's famous Black Gang, it was his job to even out the piles of coal that were shovelled into the ship's huge furnaces.

Joseph froze to death in the icy cold waters of the North Atlantic not long after the great ship sank. His body was fished out of the sea by the Canadian Steamship *Mackay-Bennett* (Body No. 227 recovered) and brought back to Halifax Nova Scotia, Canada where he was laid to rest at Fairview Lawn Cemetery, Halifax on 8th May 1912 in *Titanic* Grave No. 227. His body was identified from the National Sailors and Firemen's Union card (Number 35638) he had on him when the ship plunged to her final resting place. His close friend, John Priest, survived the disaster. James Cameron commented that he was not aware of Joseph Dawson's existence until after he completed his screenplay for the movie. However, this did not stop love struck fans of the movie making their way to Joseph's grave where they left cinema stubs, flowers, hotel room keys, personal photos and pictures of Leonardo DiCaprio.

Did You Know That?

There are some resemblances between Joseph Dawson and Cameron's character. Both were Irish, both were poor and both worked with 'coal': Joseph shovelled it and Jack drew with it (as charcoal).

Captain Edward John Smith, RD, RNR

Edward John Smith as born on 27th January 1850 in Hanley, Stoke-on-Trent, England. His father was a potter and married his mother, Catherine Hancock (*née* Marsh), on 2nd August 1841. When he was a young boy his parents owned a small shop and he attended the Etruria British School until he was 13 years old. In 1863 the teenage Smith moved to Liverpool to commence a career at sea and became an apprentice on the clipper ship, the *Senator Weber*, an American-built sailing vessel which was owned by A. Gibson & Co., Liverpool. On 18th October 1870, he

THE LATE
CAPTAIN E. J. SMITH, R.N.R.
OF THE ILLFATED LINER "TITANIC".
"GREATER LOVE HATH NO MAN THAN THIS,
THAT A MAN LAY DOWN HIS LIFE FOR HIS FRIENDS."

Published by Tom Harvey, Redruth.

Captain Edward Smith photographed aboard the *Titanic* at Southampton on the morning of 10 April 1912 (Jonathan Smith postcard collection)

joined the *Amoy* as an able-bodied seaman and a year later he moved to Liverpool and served as a seaman on the *Madge Wildfire* (March–July 1871); was second mate on the *Record* (August 1871–January 1872); second mate on the *Agra* (February–July 1872); second mate on the *N. Mosher* (September 1872–March 1873); and then had three different spells aboard the *Arzilla* (July 1873–May 1875).

Having obtained his Master's Certificate in 1874, he was able to take charge of his first command, the *Lizzie Fennell* (May 1876–January 1880). When he was 30 years old Smith joined the White Star Line (March 1880) as the Fourth Officer (and later as Third Officer) of SS *Celtic* and quickly impressed his new employers on voyages to Australia and New York. He served as Second Officer on SS *Coptic* for two years (March 1882–March 1884) to gain valuable experience of the route from England to Australia. Between March 1884 and July 1885, Smith served aboard SS *Britannic* and after serving as First Officer aboard SS *Republic* from July 1885–April 1887, he was given temporary command of the *Republic* (April–August 1887). On 13th January 1887, Smith married Sarah Eleanor Pennington at St. Oswald's Church, Winwick. Following a second period aboard the *Britannic*, this time as her First Officer (August 1887–February 1888), he was given command of SS *Baltic* (April–May 1888) and command of the *Britannic* (June–September 1888). In December 1888, he was given the command of SS *Cufic*, a cattle transporter, for her maiden voyage and in the same year awarded his Extra Master's Certificate and joined the Royal Navy Reserve as a Lieutenant.

In January 1889, Smith took command of the *Republic* for a second time before moving over to SS *Celtic* as her captain (April–July 1889). Further commands followed: SS *Coptic* in the Australian service (December 1889–February 1890); SS *Adriatic* (December 1890–February 1891); SS *Runic* (March–April 1891); the *Britannic* for a second time (May 1891–May 1893); the *Adriatic* for a second time (June 1893); the *Britannic* for a third time (July 1893–January 1895); the *Cufic* for a second time (January 1895); a fourth spell aboard the *Britannic* (January–April 1895) and SS *Germanic* (May–June 1895). The White Star Line moved Smith over to captain SS *Majestic* in 1895, a ship he commanded for eight years (July 1895–November 1902 and May 1903–June 1904) his longest period in charge of any vessel. Captain Smith's wife gave birth to a baby girl, Helen Melville Smith, in Waterloo, near Liverpool in 1898. When the Boer War started in 1899, Smith and the *Majestic* were called upon to transport troops to Cape Colony, South Africa (he made two trips). By the turn of the 20th century his stature among White Star Line captains had risen immensely and he was generally regarded as the company's 'Safe Captain'. Between December 1902 and May 1903, Smith commanded the *Germanic* for a second time whilst the *Majestic* was undergoing a refit. In May 1903 he resumed command of the *Majestic* and that same year King Edward VI presented him with the 'Transport Medal' showing the 'South Africa' clasp for his services during the Boer War. Many rich passengers would only sail across the Atlantic if they knew Captain Smith was in command of the vessel, and he soon became known as 'The Millionaire's Captain'.

In 1904, he took command of the White Star Line's new passenger liner, RMS *Baltic*, the largest ship in the world at the time, and negotiated her maiden voyage from Southampton to New York on 29th June 1904 without incident. Then in 1907, the White Star Line placed him in charge of the fourth of their quartet of ships dubbed 'The Big Four' measuring in excess of 20,000 gross registered tons, RMS *Adriatic*. The *Baltic* and Captain Smith would cross paths again: the *Baltic* sent warnings of icebergs to *Titanic* when the latter was making her doomed maiden voyage. Under his command the *Adriatic* safely made her maiden voyage from Liverpool to New York on 8th May 1907. It was during his command of the *Adriatic* that Captain Smith was awarded the Royal Naval Reserve's long service decoration, along with a promotion to Commander in the RNR. Captain Smith was well liked and very highly respected by his crew on all of his ships and was very often simply referred to as 'EJ' among them, such was his easy-going management style. He was awarded the Royal Distinction in 1910. Captain Smith was on a salary of approximately £1,200 per year with a £200 'crash bonus' payable if any new vessel under his command did not suffer any damage in its first twelve months.

It came as no surprise when J. Bruce Ismay, the Chairman of the White Star Line, asked Smith to captain the first of the White Star Line's new Olympic class passenger liners, RMS *Olympic*, in May 1911. When she set sail on her maiden voyage from Southampton to New York on 14th June 1911, this leviathan and older sister to SS *Titanic* was the largest vessel afloat. She arrived safely in New York seven days later but not without incident. As the *Olympic* was attempting to dock at Pier 59 under the command of a New York harbour pilot, one of the twelve tugs, which were assisting her into the pier, *O. L. Hallenbeck*, got caught in the backwash of the *Olympic's* starboard propeller. The swirling water spun the tug around, causing it to collide with the *Olympic* before the tug managed to move safely away from the giant liner. Then just five months later, on 20th September 1911, the *Olympic* once again under the command of Captain Smith collided with HMS *Hawke* leaving two gaping holes in the White Star Liner and the *Hawke* minus her prow. At the subsequent Royal Navy inquiry the *Olympic*, with Captain Smith on the bridge at the time of the collision, was held to blame for the incident.

In February 1912, bad luck befell the *Olympic* once more when she threw a propeller blade in the North Atlantic and yet again was forced to return to her place of birth for emergency repairs, again delaying work to her younger sister, *Titanic*. It was around this time in early 1912 that it was reported that the 62-year-old Smith was considering retirement after having spent almost half a century at sea. Indeed, it is claimed that Ismay had to persuade his most famous of captains to command his newest passenger liner, the *Titanic*, on her maiden voyage from Southampton to New York. However, an article in the *Halifax Morning Chronicle* on 9th April 1912, the day before *Titanic* was due to set sail, claiming that a White Star Line official had stated that Smith would remain in charge of the *Titanic* 'until the Company (White Star Line) completed a larger and finer steamer'. If it was true

that Smith was persuaded not to retire and to take command of his third transat-lantic maiden voyage on a White Star Liner then his decision cost him his life. Assuming Smith had no intention of retiring in 1912 then he would have most definitely wished to stay in command of the *Titanic* until the last of the three Olympic Class vessels ordered from Harland & Wolff by the White Star Line, the *Gigantic*, was launched in 1916, taking Smith up to his 65th birthday. Around 6.15 am on Wednesday 10th April 1912, Captain Smith said farewell to his wife at their home, 'Woodhead', on Winn Road, Highfield, Southampton for the last time, taking a taxi to the harbour where he boarded *Titanic* at 7.00am. Four days, 19 hours and 20 minutes after setting foot on the world's most famous ship, Captain Smith died, going down with her at 2.20am on Monday 15th April 1912 having struck an iceberg at 11.40 pm the night before. Some survivors said that they saw Captain Smith walk calmly to the bridge with the sole purpose of going down with his command. His body was never recovered.

Did You Know That?

As a result of his position as a Commander in the Royal Naval Reserve (RNR), Captain Edward John Smith had the distinction of being able to fly the 'Blue Ensign' of the RNR under Warrant No. 690. Most ships were only permitted to fly the 'Red Ensign' of the merchant marine.

Joseph Bruce Ismay – The Visionary Shipbuilder

Joseph Bruce Ismay was born on 12th December 1862 in Crosby, Liverpool, England. From the moment he was born shipping was in his blood and it would subsequently both consume and claim his life. His father was Thomas Henry Ismay, a Director of the '*National Line*' who purchased the bankrupt 'White Star Line' on 18th January 1868 for £1,000; founder of the 'Oceanic Steam Navigation Company' in 1870; and the senior partner in 'Ismay, Imrie & Company' (founded in 1870 with William Imrie). His mother was Margaret Bruce, the daughter of Luke Bruce, a ship owner. His grandfather, Joseph Ismay, was a builder of small boats at Maryport, Cumberland. Young Joseph was educated at Elstree School and Harrow as well as being tutored for a year in France. As a young boy he excelled at sport, winning numerous prizes in lawn-tennis tournaments and playing football to a reasonable standard. The young Ismay also enjoyed shooting and fishing and became a first class shot and an expert fisherman in his teenage years. Following his education he spent four years as an apprentice at Ismay, Imrie & Company before taking a sabbatical in which he toured the world. Upon his return from his world tour he went to New York, where he worked for his father's White Star Line (a subsidiary of the Oceanic Steam Navigation Company) before being appointed the company's USA agent. On 4th December 1888, he married Julia Florence

Schieffelin, a society belle and daughter of George Richard Schieffelin and Julia Matilda Delaplaine of New York (heiress to her father's pharmaceutical fortune) at the Church of the Heavenly Rest, Fifth Avenue, New York. The couple had four children (Margaret, Henry, Evelyn and George); a fifth died in infancy.

In 1891, he returned to England with his family to take up a partnership in Ismay, Imrie & Company. When his father died in 1899, J. Bruce Ismay took control of the company and in 1902 agreed to a merger with J. Pierpoint Morgan's influential International Mercantile Marine Company (IMMC) for the sum of £10 million. The White Star Line also formed part of the new company under the terms of the deal. At the time the IMMC was headed by C. A. Griscom, President of the American Line, but Ismay succeeded Griscom in 1904. Ismay and Morgan wanted to challenge the highly successful Cunard Line which dominated transatlantic passenger travel at the turn of the 20th century. In 1907, Ismay and his wife had dinner at the home of Lord William James Pirrie in Belgravia, London. After their meal Ismay and Pirrie, a senior partner in the Harland & Wolff Shipyard in Belfast, enjoyed a drink and shook hands on a deal for the Belfast yard to build two Olympic-class passenger liners for the White Star Line, the RMS Olympic and the RMS *Titanic* with the option to build a third vessel, the RMS *Gigantic*. Ismay wanted ships which would challenge the Cunard Line's RMS *Lusitania* and RMS *Mauretania*, both winners of the coveted blue riband for making the fastest Atlantic crossing. However, Ismay was not concerned with speed, opting instead to make his ships not only the biggest in the world but the most luxurious.

On 10th April 1912, Ismay boarded the *Titanic* along with his valet, Richard Fry, and his secretary, William Henry Harrison, for the ship's maiden voyage from Southampton to New York. He survived the sinking in Collapsible Lifeboat C and was rescued by the RMS *Carpathia* but his life was never the same. He was heavily criticised by both the British and American press for taking a place in a lifeboat when more than 1,500 other poor souls lost their lives. He was accused of cowardice and generally made the scapegoat for the disaster, having taken the decision to reduce the number of *Titanic*'s lifeboats from 48 down to 16 to make the vessel more pleasing to the eye. The American press was particularly scathing of Ismay, with many taking the view that he should have sacrificed his own life and gone down with the ship. After he gave evidence at the subsequent US Senate and British Board of Trade inquiries, he became a recluse, shunned and ostracised by the high and mighty of London society. He resigned from his position as Chairman and Managing Director of the White Star Line, after almost a quarter of a century at the helm, and President of International Mercantile Marine Company on 30th June 1913. However, despite resigning from the latter two posts he continued with many other business interests: he was the Chairman of the Asiatic Steam Navigation Company, Chairman of the Delta Insurance Company and Chairman of the Liverpool & London Steamship Protection & Indemnity Association Limited (a company founded in 1881 by his father and some of his father's business friends as a private insurance company for ship owners). Indeed, this insurance company handled many of the claims submitted by survivors and relatives who lost family members in the *Titanic* disaster. Ismay's other business interests included serving as a Director of the Liverpool, London and Globe Insurance Company, Director of the Sea Insurance Company, Director of the Birmingham Canal Navigation Company and Director of the London, Midland and Scottish Railway. He also served as Chairman of the 'War Risks Board' in World War I.

During the mid-1920s he retired from all business affairs and left London with his wife to live in a cottage in Costelloe, County Galway, Ireland. He was practically a recluse during his time on the west coast of Ireland. In the early 1930s his health began to deteriorate and he had a part of his right leg removed in 1936 after being diagnosed with diabetes. He moved back to England and lived in the Wirral near Liverpool. On 17th October 1937, he died aged 74 of cerebral thrombosis at his London home in Mayfair and was buried in Putney Vale Cemetery, London. He left an estate worth £693,305. His wife, who became an American citizen on 14th November 1949, died on 31st December 1963 in Kensington, London aged 92.

J. Bruce Ismay is often portrayed in movies about *Titanic* as being an arrogant businessman who forced Smith to push the ship to the limit in order that it would arrive in New York a full day ahead of its scheduled arrival. The press seized this story with one first-class passenger, Miss Elizabeth Lindsey Lines, stating in an interview that she overheard a conversation between Ismay and Smith in the first-class reception room on D Deck on the afternoon of 13th April 1912 in which she claimed Ismay told Smith that *Titanic* would beat Olympic's time and arrive early in New York. However, no witness at either inquiry into the disaster gave evidence to support such claims and as Commander Smith went down with the ship, Ms Lines's claim remains unsubstantiated.

In numerous letters between Ismay and the International Mercantile Marine Company (owners of the White Star Line) Ismay always made it clear that he was against *Titanic* making an early arrival in New York.

Ismay was also a very generous man: in 1908 he inaugurated a cadet ship named *Mersey* which was used to train mercantile marine officers; he donated £11,000 to the pension fund for widows of seamen on the *Titanic* shortly after the disaster; and in 1919 he made a generous donation of £25,000 to inaugurate the National Mercantile Marine Fund to recognise the contribution of merchant mariners during World War I. He also gave practical support to camp training for the auxiliary forces and to Mr Alfred Mosely's scheme of exchanging visits between British and American teachers.

Did You Know That?

Following his death, the obituary of J. Bruce Ismay published by *The Times* failed to even mention the *Titanic*.

Archibald Gracie IV – *Titanic's* Colonel

Archibald Gracie IV, was born on 17th January 1859 in Mobile, Alabama, USA. He was a graduate of West Point Military Academy and served as a Colonel in the Seventh Regiment, United States Army. In early 1912 he booked a trip to Europe on the *Oceanic* to take a holiday having just published a book, *The Truth About Chickamauga*. His wife and daughter remained at home. Fully rested Colonel Gracie booked his passage home on *Titanic's* maiden voyage to New York and boarded the ship at Southampton as a first-class passenger (Cabin C-51: Ticket No. 113780, £28 10s). On the evening of Sunday 15th April 1912, Gracie had dinner with Edward Kent and J. Clinch Smith. Shortly after 8.00pm the Colonel returned to his cabin for the evening with the intention of getting up early the next morning to play squash with the ship's racquet attendant, Frederick Wright, and then work out in the gymnasium with the ship's Physical Education Instructor, Mr McCawley. At 11.45 pm he was awakened by a sudden movement of the ship, just five minutes after *Titanic* had side-swiped an iceberg. When he opened his cabin door and heard the sound of escaping steam, he got dressed and went up to the boat deck. However, up on the deck he saw no other ships close by, and met only a couple walking arm-in-arm. A short while later he met J. Clinch Smith who told him that the ship had collided with an iceberg. When Captain Smith issued the order to load the lifeboats, Gracie escorted four unaccompanied ladies, whom he had promised to look after, to the boat deck. He helped Second Officer Charles Lightoller load Lifeboat No. 4 and assisted the pregnant wife of John Jacob Astor IV into the lifeboat. Just as the *Titanic* was about to disappear from sight, Gracie jumped into the water and managed to seize a wooden grating floating close by him. After resting for a while he noticed a large canvas and cork liferaft bobbing up and down in the water and swam towards it. It was the overturned Collapsible Lifeboat B and he was helped onto it. In the months following his rescue the terrible events of the *Titanic* disaster never left his mind and he decided to write his own account entitled *The Truth About The Titanic*. However, he never lived to see this published. He died on 4th December 1912 at his apartment at the Hotel St. Louis, East 32nd Street, New York and the book appeared in early 1913. His family claimed that he never really recovered from the shock that he experienced in the early hours of the morning of 15th April 1912.

Millvina Dean – The Darling Of The *Titanic*

Ask anyone to name someone who survived the *Titanic* disaster and 9 times out of 10 the name of Millvina Dean will be mentioned. Elizabeth Gladys 'Millvina' Dean was born on 2nd February 1912 and at just 67 days old was the youngest passenger when she boarded the *Titanic* at Southampton with her parents, Bertram Frank Dean and Georgette Eva Light Dean, and her 1-year old brother, Bertram. The family, from London, was supposed to have emigrated to Wichita, Kansas, USA on a different ship but because of a coal strike in progress they were transferred to the *Titanic* as third class passengers. Her father hoped to open a tobacconist shop. When the *Titanic* struck the iceberg Millvina, her mother and brother were lowered to safety in Lifeboat No.10 and later rescued by the *Carpathia*. Her father went down with the ship. Millvina returned to England with her mother and brother onboard the *Adriatic*. When she was on the *Adriatic* she was in huge demand from her fellow passengers who could hardly believe that the tiny baby survived the disaster. At the time *The Daily Mirror* reported that she 'was the pet of the liner during the voyage' with 'rivalry between women to nurse this lovable mite of humanity'. Millvina was 8-years old when she learned from her mother that she was on the *Titanic*.

It was not until the early 1980s when she was in her seventies and living in retirement in Southampton that Millvina became a *Titanic* celebrity, attending various conventions, dinners and appearing on the radio and television. In April 1996, Millvina visited Belfast for the first time as guest of honour for a Titanic Historical Society convention. Then in 1997 she was invited to travel aboard the QE2 to the US to finally complete her family's voyage to Wichita, Kansas. During the last few years of her life she was forced to sell several precious personal items to pay the £3,000 per month costs of her medical care after she suffered a broken hip. Among the items she was forced to sell was a compensation letter to her mother from the Titanic Relief Fund and a suitcase given to the family to place their few remaining belongings in when they returned to England. However, these prized possessions were returned to Millvina by the person who had bought them at auction. Speaking of the *Titanic* disaster Millvina once said: 'My Mum, brother and I were among the lucky ones. I put our survival down to the bravery of my father who was alert to the dangers and made sure we got off.' Millvina, the last living survivor from *Titanic*, died from pneumonia aged 98 on 31st May 2009 at her nursing home at Ashurst in the New Forest, a few miles from where she had boarded *Titanic* at Southampton docks.

Did You Know That?

Millvina died exactly 98 years after the *Titanic* was launched at the Harland & Wolff Shipyard in Belfast.

BIBLIOGRAPHY

Websites

http://www.keyflux.com/titanic
http://www2.sptimes.com/titanic/Titanic_trivia.html
http://www.belfasthistory.net/belfast_ship_building.html
http://www.titanicinbelfast.com/resourcecentre.aspx
http://www.encyclopedia-titanica.org/
http://atlantic-cable.com/CableCos/CCC-Teleg/index.htm#mackay
http://en.wikipedia.org/wiki/Thomas_Andrews_(shipbuilder)
http://www.libraryireland.com/Thomas-Andrews-Shipbuilder/Contents.php/
http://en.wikipedia.org/wiki/Edward_James_Harland
http://www.encyclopedia-titanica.org/harland-sir-edward-j.html
http://en.wikipedia.org/wiki/List_of_White_Star_Line_ships
http://en.wikipedia.org/wiki/Four_funnel_liner
http://www.titanicstory.com/interest.htm
http://en.wikipedia.org/wiki/Blue_Riband
http://en.wikipedia.org/wiki/RMS_Lusitania
http://en.wikipedia.org/wiki/RMS_Mauretania_(1906)
http://en.wikipedia.org/wiki/RMS_Adriatic_(1907)
http://www.mun.ca/
http://en.wikipedia.org/wiki/SS_Californian
http://www.encyclopedia-titanica.org/mount_temple_pv.html
http://en.wikipedia.org/wiki/SS_Mount_Temple
http://www.ssmounttemple.com/
http://www.nomadicpreservationsociety.co.uk
http://www.britishtitanicsociety.co.uk
http://www.starway.org/Titanic/Publications
http://www.titanicsite.kit.net
http://www.scandtitanic.com/
http://www.titanic-titanic.com/
http://www.whitestarmemories.co.uk
http://www.canadian-titanic-society.com/
http://www.titanic-nautical.com/
http://www.titanicverein.ch/

http://www.titanic-facts.com/
http://en.wikipedia.org/wiki/Benjamin_Guggenheim
http://en.wikipedia.org/wiki/John_Jacob_Astor_IV
http://www.titanicberg.com/Titanic_Trivia.html
http://www.webspawner.com/users/titanicbuffsweb/
http://webtech.kennesaw.edu/jcheek3/titanic.htm
http://ourworld.compuserve.com/homepages/Carpathia/
http://connections.smsd.org/titanic/index.htm
http://www.encyclopedia-titanica.org/ship/195/
http://www.catchpenny.org/titanic.html
http://www.anusha.com/cursed.htm
http://www.encyclopedia-titanica.org/titanic-biography/william-
    thompson-sloper.html
http://en.wikipedia.org/wiki/Michel_Marcel_Navratil
http://members.tripod.com/~DonaldsonA/index-45.html
http://www.henry-aldridge.co.uk/default.htm
http://codybateman.org/2008/09/07/the-titanics-last-hero/
http://titanic.pottsoft.com/
http://www.hf.ro/
http://www.encyclopedia-titanica.org/ship/183/
http://www.encyclopedia-titanica.org/news/nomadic-conservation-plan-
    released-1253274109.html
http://www.encyclopedia-titanica.org/news/7-million-restoration-of-titanic-
    ship-goes-ahead-1253133300.html
http://www.fast-rewind.com/raisetitanic.htm
http://www.guardian.co.uk/society/2009/jan/26/regeneration-titanic-
    quarter-property-development
http://en.wikipedia.org/wiki/Raise_the_Titanic!
http://en.wikipedia.org/wiki/Titanic_Memorial_(Washington,_D.C.)
http://209.85.229.132/search?q=cache:ZF0VZd4WklcJ:
    www.encyclopedia-titanica.org/president-taft
http://en.wikipedia.org/wiki/William_Howard_Taft
http://www.arlingtoncemetery.net/awbutt.htm
http://www.encyclopedia-titanica.org/titanic-victim/archibald-butt.html
http://news.bbc.co.uk/1/hi/england/london/3017955.stm
http://titanic.gov.ns.ca/index.html
http://www.titanicnewschannel.com/xfiles.html
http://fsmat.at/~bkabelka/titanic/part3/chapter3.htm
http://www.titanicandco.com/curse.html
http://www.encyclopedia-titanica.org/titanian-echo-titanic.html
www.historyonthenet.com
http://en.wikipedia.org/wiki/Helen_Churchill_Candee
http://www.addergoole-titanic.com/Titanic_Memorial_Mayo/Default.8.html

http://www.wilhelmgustloff.com/welcome.htm
http://news.bbc.co.uk/1/hi/scotland/2155617.stm
http://www.bbc.co.uk/archive/titanic/5047.shtml?all=2&id=5047
http://www.rmstitanic.net
http://www.manchestereveningnews.co.uk/news
http://www.bbc.co.uk/hampshire/content/articles/2006/01/04/
    titanic_tour_feature.shtml
http://www.pottsoft.com/titanic/titanic_chronology.html
http://www.sfmuseum.org/1906/background.html
http://www.ithaca.edu/staff/jhenderson/titanic.html
http://www.titanic-nautical.com/Contact.html
http://www.calvinsun.com/articles_written/A%20Name%20at%20Last.pdf
http://www.encyclopedia-titanica.org/titanic-connections-with-liverpool.html
http://www.archaeology.org/0101/etc/titanic2.html
http://www.encyclopedia-titanica.org/titanic_owners_settle.html
http://209.85.229.132/search?q=cache:uPA1GErSSOEJ:www.immigrantships.n
    et/v3/1900v3/cincinnati19131203.html+SS+CINCINNATI+AND+
    TITANIC&cd=1&hl=en&ct=clnk&gl=uk
http://www.greatships.net/distress.html
http://danielmacdonald.tblog.com/post/1969736948
http://www.therhondda.co.uk/facts/av_coal_prices_1875_1912.html
http://www.telegraph-office.com/pages/Titanic_Disaster_Radio_1929.html
http://www.avsia.com/djohnson/titanic.html
http://www.encyclopedia-titanica.org/wireless_operator.html
http://en.wikipedia.org/wiki/Arthur_Rostron
http://www.findagrave.com/cgi-bin/fg.cgi?page=gr&GRid=9550788
http://www.encyclopedia-titanica.org/titanic-biography/arthur-
    henry-rostron.html
http://www.encyclopedia-
    titanica.org/discus/messages/5921/5620.html?986394889
http://www.senate.gov/reference/reference_item/titanic.htm
http://209.85.229.132/search?q=cache:FQccAM7fbuwJ:www.bbc.co.uk/southa
    mpton/features/titanic/onboard1.shtml+tITANIC+AND+The+Atlantic+
    Daily+Bulletin&cd=9&hl=en&ct=clnk&gl=uk
http://history1900s.about.com/od/1910s/p/titanic.htm
http://www.fundinguniverse.com/company-histories/Harland-and-
    Wolff-Holdings-plc-Company-History.html
http://www.culturenorthernireland.org/article.aspx?art_id=797
http://books.google.co.uk/books?id=uipeP5pgb7AC&pg=PA27&lpg=PA27&dq
    =harland+%26+wolff's+rivals&source
http://www.encyclopedia.com/doc/1O245-WorkmanClarkCompany.html
http://www.chriscunard.com/samuel_cunard.htm

http://www.nmm.ac.uk/researchers/library/research-guides/rms-titanic/
    research-guide-d1-rms-titanic-fact-sheet
http://museum.gov.ns.ca/mma/titanic/victims.htm
http://www.gov.ns.ca/nsarm/virtual/titanic/deaths.asp
http://www.anesi.com/titanic.htm
http://maritime.elettra.co.uk/titanic/index.html
http://titanicgazette.blogspot.com/search/label/annie%20funk
http://www.encyclopedia-titanica.org/titanic-victim/annie-clemmer-funk.html
http://www.volgagermans.net/norka/
http://www.encyclopedia-titanica.org/the-real-jack-dawson.html
http://library.thinkquest.org/18626/BMap.html
http://www.nationalarchives.gov.uk/catalogue/RdLeaflet.asp?sLeafletID=96&j=1
http://en.wikipedia.org/wiki/Edward_Smith
http://www.titanic-titanic.com/titanic_memorial-edward_john_smith.shtml
http://www.euronet.nl/users/keesree/captain.htm#General
http://www.bbc.co.uk/stoke/content/articles/2006/04/10/local_heroes_
    captain_edward_john_smith_feature.shtml
http://www.titanic-model.com
http://www.titanic-
    model.com/articles/flags/FLAG_REFERENCE_MultiPage_ver2.pdf
http://www.rms-republic.com/index1.html
http://www.titanic-museum-germany.de/
http://www.abratis.de/
http://en.wikipedia.org/wiki/Dragon's_blood
http://www.experiencefestival.com/a/RMS_Titanic_-
    _Comparable_maritime_disasters/id/4697046
http://en.wikipedia.org/wiki/RMS_Tayleur
http://en.wikipedia.org/wiki/MS_Hans_Hedtoft
http://marconigraph.com/titanic/faqs/faqs2.html
http://query.nytimes.com/mem/archive-
    free/pdf?_r=1&res=9803E2D91031E433A25756C0A9619C946195D6CF
http://www.encyclopedia-titanica.org/the-turn-of-a-card.html
http://www.encyclopedia-titanica.org/titanic-survivor/paul-chevre.html
http://www.titanicinquiry.org/
http://209.85.229.132/search?q=cache:zvXBzzPrsVIJ:www.titanicinquiry.org/
    USInq/AmInq08Gill01.php+ERNEST+GILL+TITANIC&cd=1&hl=
    en&ct=clnk&gl=uk
http://www.encyclopedia-titanica.org/rhoda-abbott.html
http://www.encyclopedia-titanica.org/titanic-survivor/theodoor-de-mulder.html
http://www.encyclopedia-titanica.org/titanic-victim/henry-sutehall.html
http://www.encyclopedia-titanica.org/titanic-survivor/john-edward-hart.html
http://www.encyclopedia-titanica.org/titanic-survivor/trevor-allison.html
http://www.encyclopedia-titanica.org/titanic-survivor/latifa-baclini.html

http://www.encyclopedia-titanica.org/ismay-left-ship-at-womens-plea.html
http://www.euronet.nl/users/keesree/cabins.htm
http://www.titanicinquiry.org/lol/claims/futrelle-c15.php
http://en.wikipedia.org/wiki/J._Bruce_Ismay
http://www.titanichistoricalsociety.org/articles/ismay.asp
http://www.encyclopedia-titanica.org/titanic-biography/j-bruce-ismay.html
http://titanicstation.blogspot.com/2007/08/j-bruce-ismay.html
http://www.vindicatrix.org/Bruce%20ismay%20obituary.pdf
http://www.blackcountrybugle.co.uk/blackcountrybugle-
    news/DisplayArticle.asp?ID=461320
http://www.hhs.gov/nvpo/who.htm
http://www.pbs.org/wgbh/nova/typhoid/quarantine.html
http://www.encyclopedia-titanica.org/titanic-survivor/colonel-
    archibald-gracie.html
http://www.lcc.ie/Library/Local_Studies/History/Aspects/Titanic2/John_
    Kennedy.htm
http://www.acmewhistles.co.uk/xcart/pages.php?pageid=10
http://www.encyclopedia-
    titanica.org/discus/messages/5914/98856.html?1156363310
http://web.mst.edu/~rogersda/american&military_history/TITANIC%
    20LECTURE%20NOTES.pdf
http://marconigraph.com/titanic/telegraphs/mgy_eotelegraphs1.html

Books

Archbold, R. *Last Dinner on the Titanic.* Madison, 1997.

Armstrong, Warren. *Last Voyage.* New York: John Day Company, first American edition, 1958.

Ballard, Robert D. *Adventures in Ocean Exploration: From the Discovery of the Titanic to the Search for Noah's Flood.* National Geographic Books, 2001.

Ballard, Robert D. *Exploring the Titanic.* New York: Madison Press, 1988.

Ballard, Robert D. *The Discovery of the Titanic.* Madison Publishing, 1987.

Bardon, Jonathan. *Belfast: An Illustrated History,* 1983.

Behe, George & Goss, Michael. *Lost at Sea,* Prometheus Books, 1994.

Beveridge, Bruce; Andrews, Scott; Hall, Steve and Klistorner, Daniel. *TITANIC: The Ship Magnificent,* volumes I and II. The History Press Ltd., 2008.

Booth, J & Coughlan, S. *Titanic – Signals of Disaster.* White Star Publications, 1993.

Bracken Robert L. *Irish Titanic Passengers,* Titanic Historical Society, 2000.

Bristow, Diana E. *Titanic: Sinking the Myths.* Katco Literary Group. 1995.

Bryceson, Dave (compiler). *The Titanic Disaster: As Reported in the British National Press April–July 1912.* 1st American edition, W. W. Norton & Co, 1997.

Chirnside, Mark: *The Olympic Class Ships: Olympic – Titanic – Britannic.* Tempus Publishing, 2004.

Clary, Jim. *The Last True Story of Titanic.* Brooklyn, NY: Domhan Books, 1998.

Contract Ticket List, White Star Line 1912 (National Archives, New York; NRAN-21-SDNYCIVCAS-55[279])

Cronin, Anthony. *R.M.S. Titanic.* Dublin, Ireland: Raven Arts Press, 1981.

Davie, Michael. *Titanic: The Death and Life of a Legend.* New York: Holt: Distributed by Random House, 1987.

Davie, Michael. *The Titanic – The Full Story of a Tragedy.* Bodley Head, 1986.

Everett, Marshall. *Wreck and Sinking of the Titanic.* New York: L.H. Walter, 1912.

Gardiner, Robin. & Van der Vat, Dan. *The Titanic conspiracy: cover-ups and mysteries of the world's most famous sea disaster.* New York: Carol Pub. Group, 1996.

Garrison, Webb B. *A Treasury of Titanic Tales.* Rutledge Hill Press, 1998.

Gracie, Archibald, 1858-1912. *The Truth About the Titanic.* Kenerley, 1913

Harland & Wolff. *Steel Ships and Iron Men: Shipbuilding in Belfast, 1894–1912,* 1989.

Heyer, Paul, 1946- *Titanic Legacy: Disaster As Media Event and Myth.* Westport, CT: Praeger, 1995.

Howe Colt, George, 'The Tragedy of the Titanic', Life magazine, June 1997.

Hutchings, D *RMS Titanic: A modern legend.* Waterfront Publications, 1993.

Lightoller, Charles H. *Titanic and Other Ships.* Ivor, Nicholson & Watson, 1935.

List or Manifest of Alien Passengers for the United States Immigration Officer At Port Of Arrival (Date: 18th-19th June 1912, Ship: *Carpathia*) – National Archives, NWCTB 85 T715 Vol 4183.

Lord, Walter, 1917- *A Night to Remember.* New York: Henry Holt and Company: New York, 1955.

Louden, Paul – *The White Star Line; An Illustrated History 1869–1934,* Titanic Historical Society, 2000.

Lynch, Don (with paintings by Ken Marschall), *Titanic: An Illustrated History,* Madison Press, 1992.

Lynch, John. *An Unlikely Success Story: the Belfast Shipbuilding Industry 1880–1935,* Belfast Society, 2001.

McCaughan, Michael, *Steel Ships and Iron Men: Shipbuilding in Belfast 1894–1912,* Belfast: Friar's Bush Press, 1989.

McCluskie, Tom. *Harland and Wolff: Designs from the Shipbuilding Empire,* Chartwell, 1998.

Marcus, Geoffrey Jules, 1906- *The Titanic Disaster: Complete and documented account of the maiden voyage.* New English Library, 1976.

Molony, Senan (1999) *The Irish Aboard Titanic.* Wolfhound Press, Dublin.

Moss, Michael S., and Hume, John R., *Shipbuilders to the World: 125 Years of Harland and Wolff, Belfast 1861–1986,* Belfast: Blackstaff Press, 1986.

Mowbray, Jay Henry. *Sinking of the Titanic*. New York: Geo. W. Bertron, 1912.

Names and Descriptions of British Passengers Embarked at the Port of Queenstown, 11 April 1912 (PRO London, BT 27/776/2).

Pickford, Nigel. *Lost Treasure Ships of the Twentieth Century.* National Geographic Books, 1999.

Pierson, J. Gordon, *Great Ship Builders; or the Rise of Harland and Wolff,* A.H. Stockwell Ltd.: London, 1935.

Ray, Noel (1999) *List of Passengers who Boarded RMS Titanic at Queenstown, April 11, 1912.* The Irish Titanic Historical Society.

Rivett, Norman C. *Some Aspects of R.M.S. Titanic (1912) and her sister ships.* Sydney: The Naval Historical Society of Australia, 1993.

Robertson, Patrick. *The Shell Book of Firsts.* Elbury Press & Michael Joseph Ltd. London.

Shapiro, Marc. *Total Titanic : The Most Up-To-Date Guide to the Disaster of the Century.* Byron Press Multimedia Books, 1998.

Smith, Marian L. – 'The RMS Titanic passenger manifest: Record of survivors – and revival of a record', in *Voyage* (Journal of the Titanic International Society, Inc.), Volume 29 (1999), pp. 4–9).

Spignesi, Stephen J. *The Complete Titanic: From the Ship's Earliest Blueprints to the Epic Film.* Birch Lane Press, 1998.

Thayer, J. B. *The Sinking of the Titanic.* Riverside, Connecticut, USA, 1984.

Thresh, Peter. *Titanic, the Truth Behind the Disaster.* New York: Crescent Books, 1992.

Walter, L.H. *Sinking of the Titanic: The World's Greatest Sea-Disaster.* 1912.

Woodroffe, D & MacDonald, F. *Titanic*, MacDonald, 1984.

Reports

Lord Mersey's Report (British Parliamentary Papers, *Shipping Casualties (Loss of the Steamship Titanic)*, 1912, cmd. 6352, *Report of a Formal Investigation into the circumstances attending the foundering on the 15th April, 1912, of the British Steamship Titanic, of Liverpool, after striking ice in or near Latitude 41° 46' N., Longitude 50° 14' W., North Atlantic Ocean, whereby loss of life ensued.* (London: His Majesty's Stationery Office, 1912).

The Report of the Inquiry into the Loss of the Titanic – published as Command Paper Cd.6352 in House of Commons Parliamentary Papers (1912–1913).

White Star Line (1912): Record of Bodies and Effects (Passengers and Crew S.S. *Titanic*) Recovered by Cable Steamer *MacKay Bennett* Including Bodies Buried at Sea and Bodies Delivered at Morgue in Halifax, N.S.

The 'Olympic' Class Ships: A Business Perspective – Mark Chirnside.

Journals

Ballard, Robert D. 'A Long Last Look at the Titanic'. *National Geographic* (December 1986), 698–727.

Ballard, Robert D., and Michel, Jean-Louis. 'How We Found Titanic'. *National Geographic* (December 1985), 696–719.

Kirkpatrick, Jennifer A. 'I survived the Titanic'. *National Geographic World* (July 1996), 24–9.

Lee, Erika. *Journal of American Ethnic History*. University of Illinois Press (June 1999).

MacInnis, Joseph B. 'Titanic: Tragedy in Three Dimensions'. *National Geographic* (August 1998), 120–7.

Mandel, Peter. 'What Really Sank the Titanic?' *National Geographic World* (April 2002), 26–8.

Newspapers

The Belfast Telegraph
The Chicago American
The Chicago Tribune
The Cork Examiner
The Daily Express
The Daily Graphic
The Daily Mail
The Daily Mirror
The Daily Sketch
The Daily Telegraph
The East Cork Journal
The East Galway Democrat
The Evening Standard
The Evening Star (Washington D.C.)

The Evening World (New York)
The Irish News
The New York Sun
The New York Times
The News Letter
The Portland Oregonian
The San Francisco Chronicle
The Southend Standard
The Southern Star (Cork)
The Sphere
The Syracuse Herald
The Times
The Washington Times

Television Programmes

James Cameron's Last Mysteries of the Titanic – Discovery Channel
Ships That Changed The World – Wednesday 6th, 13th & 20th February 2008, BBC1 NI at 10.40pm, presented by Colonel Tim Collins.
The Golden Age Of The Liners – BBC Four
The Last Days Of The Liners – BBC Four
The Men Who Built The Liners – BBC Four
Titanic Documentary – http://cheddarbay.com/0000Tea/Titanic/passengers/survivors/survivors3.html

Other Sources

All testimony quoted from the United States Senate Committee inquiry and the British Board of Trade inquiry into the *Titanic* disaster has been sourced from *The Titanic Inquiry Project* online at www.titanicinquiry.org